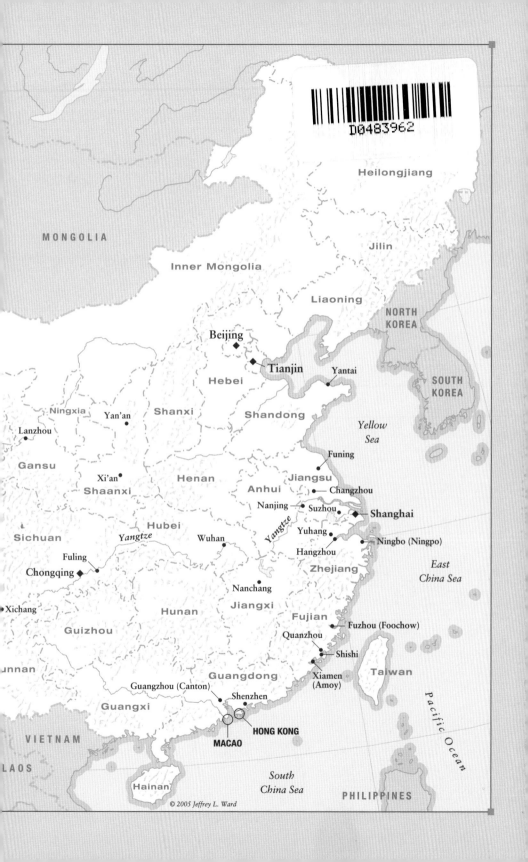

MONGOLIA

Heilongjiang

Inner Mongolia

Jilin

Liaoning

NORTH
KOREA

SOUTH
KOREA

Beijing

Tianjin

Hebei

Yantai

Shandong

Yellow
Sea

Ningxia

Yan'an

Shanxi

Lanzhou

Gansu

Funing

Xi'an

Henan

Jiangsu

Shaanxi

Anhui

Changzhou

Nanjing

Suzhou

Shanghai

Yangtze

Hubei

Yuhang

Sichuan

Yangtze

Wuhan

Ningbo (Ningpo)

Fuling

Hangzhou

Chongqing

Zhejiang

East
China
Sea

Nanchang

Xichang

Jiangxi

Hunan

Fujian

Guizhou

Fuzhou (Foochow)

Quanzhou

Shishi

Xiamen
(Amoy)

Taiwan

nnan

Guangdong

Pacific Ocean

Guangzhou (Canton)

Shenzhen

Guangxi

HONG KONG

VIETNAM

MACAO

LAOS

Hainan

South
China
Sea

PHILIPPINES

© 2005 Jeffrey L. Ward

WALL
STREET
JOURNAL
BOOKS

One Billion Customers

Lessons from the Front Lines of Doing Business in China

James McGregor

A Wall Street Journal Book

Published by Free Press

New York   London   Toronto   Sydney

A WALL STREET JOURNAL BOOK
Published by Free Press
Rockefeller Center
1230 Avenue of the Americas
New York, NY 10020

For information about special discounts for bulk purchases,
please contact Simon & Schuster Special Sales:
1-800-456-6798 or business@simonandschuster.com

Endpaper map © 2005 by Jeffrey L. Ward
Book design by Ellen R. Sasahara

Manufactured in the United States of America

10   9   8   7   6   5   4   3   2   1

Library of Congress Control Number: 2005044398

ISBN-13: 978-0-7432-5839-5
ISBN-10:   0-7432-5839-8

To my family
Cathy, Sally, and Grady
John, Sally, Armando, Bruce, Laura, Donald,
Douglas, Lisa, John, and Mary

Contents

Cast of Characters

Chinese Government Officials

Deng Xiaoping The leader of China from 1978 to 1989 who established market-oriented reforms and sparked the ongoing economic boom.

Ding Guangen China's "propaganda czar," director of the Communist party Propaganda Department who controlled the Chinese media throughout the 1990s.

Gao Xiqing A key founder of China's stock markets and longtime senior securities regulator who most recently was vice-chairman of the National Council for Social Security.

Hu Jintao President of China and Communist party boss starting in 2002.

Jiang Zemin President of China and Communist party boss who carried out Deng's reforms from 1989 to 2003.

Li Peng Premier of China from 1987 to 1998 who became the belligerent face of the government during the Tiananmen demonstrations. Despite his reputation as a conservative hardliner, he pushed government acceptance of a 1992 U.S.–China market access agreement that led to China's first significant commercial regulatory reforms.

Long Yongtu Senior Chinese trade official who handled China's negotiations for the country's 2001 entry into the World Trade Organization.

Mao Zedong Chinese Communist revolutionary leader who defeated Chiang Kai-shek in 1949 and led the People's Republic of China from triumph into tragedy. His rule ended with his death in 1976 after the country's economy and social system were destroyed by the Great Leap Forward and the Cultural Revolution.

Shi Guangsheng Minister of trade from 1998 to 2003.

C. H. Tung A shipping company executive who was Hong Kong chief executive after the handover of Hong Kong to China from Britain in 1997. He resigned in 2005 due to deep unpopularity in China and Hong Kong.

Wang Qishan Most recently the mayor of Beijing and formerly president of China Construction Bank from 1994 to 1998. He oversaw the Morgan Stanley joint-venture investment bank, China International Capital Corporation (CICC). The son-in-law of Yao Yilin, who was vice-premier in charge of finance and economics from 1979 to 1993, Wang is also the godfather of China's stock markets.

Wu Jichuan As the minister of the Ministry of Information Industry (and its predecessor, the Ministry of Posts and Telecommunications) from 1993 to 2003, he was known as China's "telecom czar" and architect of the world's largest telephone system.

Wu Yi Most recently vice-premier and health minister who served as trade minister from 1993 to 1997.

Zhao Weichen The first chairman of China Unicom and creator of the "Chinese-Chinese-Foreign" investment structure that gathered more than $1 billion in investment from international telecom companies without giving away any equity in China's telephone operating system.

Zhao Ziyang The premier of China who was ousted after the Tiananmen Massacre and held under house arrest until he died in 2005. He was the architect of Deng's first wave of reforms and mentor to a generation of Chinese reformers.

Zhou Enlai Mao's right-hand man and longtime premier of China who is credited with working to curb many of Mao's excesses. He died in 1976.

Zhou Xiaochuan Most recently governor of China's central bank, the People's Bank of China, he earlier served as China's top securities regulator and chairman of China Construction Bank.

Zhu Rongji Premier of China from 1998 to 2003 who is credited with designing and implementing the country's most significant financial and economic reforms.

Zou Jiahua The vice-premier of China in the 1990s who served as the key patron of Unicom and advocate for breaking the China Telecom monopoly of China's telephone system.

U.S. and British Government Officials

Charlene Barshefsky The U.S. trade representative from 1997 to 2001 who engineered the U.S.-China agreement that led to China's entry into the WTO.

George H. W. Bush The forty-first president of the United States, from 1989 to 1993, who had served as Nixon's representative in China in 1974–75 and later personally ran China policy from the oval office as president.

George W. Bush The forty-third president of the United States, assuming office in 2001, who initially considered China a second-priority country for the United States in Asia because of its lack of democracy, but befriended China after the September 11, 2001, Al Qaeda attack on the World Trade Center towers and Pentagon.

Bob Cassidy The U.S. trade representative's chief negotiator for China's accession to the WTO.

Warren Christopher The U.S. secretary of state from 1993 to 1997 who was strongly criticized by the American business community while carrying out Clinton's policy of threatening to cancel China's MFN status on human rights grounds.

Bill Clinton The forty-second president of the United States, from 1993 to 2001, who initially threatened to cancel China's "most favored nation" trading status on human rights grounds but soon capitulated and oversaw successful U.S. efforts to bring China into the WTO.

Christopher Cox Republican congressman from California who headed the congressional committee that issued the hyperbolic "Cox report" on China's systematic stealing of American nuclear and military technology, thereby igniting a frenzy of racism against Chinese in America.

Henry Kissinger Nixon's national security adviser and secretary of state who negotiated and engineered Nixon's rapprochement with China and later became a fixture in U.S.-China political and business relations.

Richard M. Nixon The thirty-seventh president of the United States, from 1969 to 1974, who led U.S.-China rapprochement by traveling to China in 1972.

Chris Patten A British Conservative party leader and the last British governor of Hong Kong who enraged China by pushing democratic reforms in the colony prior to the handover.

Robert Rubin The U.S. secretary of the treasury during the Clinton administration who advised Clinton to reject an agreement for U.S. approval of China's entry into the WTO brought to Washington by Chinese premier Zhu Rongji in April 1999.

Gene Sperling The national economic adviser to President Clinton and the head of the National Economic Council from 1996 to 2000 who also advised Clinton to reject Zhu's proposed WTO deal.

Chinese Businesspeople

Payson Cha Chairman of the Mingly Corporation Ltd. and one of the founders of China International Capital Corporation (CICC).

Fang Fenglei The vice-president of CICC from 1995 to 2000 who was the leader of the Chinese side of the joint venture and steered huge investment banking deals to Goldman Sachs because Morgan Stanley executives failed to take him seriously.

Pan Shiyi The chairman and co-CEO of SOHO China Ltd. who with his wife, Zhang Xin, established a new real-estate development model for China and struggled with blending Eastern and Western management systems in their company.

Tang Shisheng The powerful human resources director of CICC who rejected many of Morgan Stanley's proposed executives.

Wang Boming A founder of China's stock markets who turned to business and is now publisher of the investigative *Caijing* magazine that is setting new standards in Chinese journalism.

Wu Ying A founder of UTStarcom who successfully outmaneuvered China "telecom czar" Wu Jichuan to establish the "Little

Smart" mobile phone technology across China, despite Wu's disapproval.

Zhang Xin The co-CEO of SOHO China Ltd. who struggled to impose Western management systems in the company, but eventually acceded to her husband's Chinese management ways.

Levin Zhu The son of Zhu Rongji and most recently head of CICC who turned the enterprise into the equivalent of a well-run state enterprise once Morgan Stanley withdrew from management of the venture.

Zong Qinghou The founder and chairman of the Wahaha Group who built a beverage conglomerate that challenges Pepsi and Coke in China by combining astute politics, clever marketing, and strict Chinese management practices.

U.S. Businesspeople

John Bruns The McDonnell Douglas China hand and troubleshooter in China who handled the export licenses for the machine tools that later led to a federal indictment. He was not implicated in the charges.

Gareth Chang The president of McDonnell Douglas Asia/Pacific who put together the company's aircraft assembly facility in Shanghai and later headed Hughes Electronics International and oversaw its satellite launches in China.

Bob Hitt McDonnell Douglas production boss who oversaw the assembly of airliners in Shanghai and was indicted by federal prosecutors when Chinese partners diverted machine tools to a military factory. The politically motivated charges were later dropped.

Austin Koenen The third CEO of CICC who was making progress in soothing the company's culture clash when he died of a sudden heart attack in Beijing in 1998.

Elaine La Roche The fourth CEO of CICC and longtime deputy to Morgan Stanley CEO John Mack.

Edwin Lim The first CEO of CICC and former chief representative for the World Bank in China who produced the first foreign studies of the Chinese economy in the reform era.

Rupert Murdoch The head of News Corp. and media mogul who gained access to the China market and helped modernize China's propaganda machine only after convincing the Communist party that he was interested in making money, not trouble.

Jack Wadsworth The chairman of Morgan Stanley Asia in the 1990s and visionary creator of the joint-venture CICC investment bank with China Construction Bank.

Harrison Young The second CEO of CICC.

Chinese Media

Guo Chaoren The president of Xinhua when the state-controlled news agency attempted to take over the financial data business in China of Dow Jones and Reuters.

Hu Shuli Managing editor of *Caijing* magazine and crusading reporter who has set new standards for watchdog journalism in China.

Liu Changle Founder, chairman, and CEO of Phoenix Satellite Television and media entrepreneur who guided Rupert Murdoch into China.

Wang Wenlian The first director of Xinhua regulatory body, the Foreign Information Administration Center, that monitors foreign news and financial information coming into China.

Yun Yiqun Famous wartime reporter in China and founder and director of several journalism schools who as a political outcast taught Hu Shuli the importance of ethical and responsible journalism.

Historical Figures

Chiang Kai-shek (1887–1975) The Chinese Nationalist leader who fled to Taiwan in 1949 after losing the civil war to Mao Ze-dong.

Carl Crow (1883–1945) American journalist-turned-businessman and author of *400 Million Customers* published in 1937, who lived in Shanghai for twenty-six years and founded one of the first advertising agencies in China.

Charles George "Chinese" Gordon (1833–1885) A British mercenary and adventurer who led the "Ever Victorious Army" in crushing the Taiping Rebellion for the Qing dynasty.

Emperor Qianlong (1711–1799) The fourth emperor of the Qing dynasty who rebuffed British attempts to open China to foreign trade.

Empress Dowager (1835–1908) Also known as Cixi, a powerful and charismatic imperial concubine who was the de facto ruler of China at the end of the Qing dynasty in the late nineteenth and early twentieth century.

Hong Xiuquan (1814–1864) Leader of the Taiping Rebellion in 1851 who declared himself to be the "Younger Brother of Jesus Christ" and ruled much of southern China for a dozen years.

Li Hongzhang (1823–1901) Chinese official in the Qing dynasty who became the country's first and foremost barbarian handler.

Lin Zexu (1785–1850) The Chinese commissioner in Canton who was ordered to put an end to the illegal opium trade.

Lord George Macartney (1737–1806) An envoy sent by King George III in 1793 to open China to British trade who was rebuffed by the emperor.

Scholars

Justin Lin Academic entrepreneur who founded the first independent economic research institute in China, the China Center for Economic Research, and Beijing International MBA (BiMBA), one of the first MBA schools in China.

Lucian Pye MIT Sinologist and political psychologist who wrote *Chinese Negotiating Style*.

John Yang A mainland native and Fordham University management professor who is the U.S. dean for the BiMBA school and leading theorist on blending the East and West to build new business management systems in China.

Lai Changxing Case

Lai Changbiao Lai Changxing's brother, accused of running the cigarette smuggling business. He ended up a paraplegic after a bar fight.

Lai Changtu Lai Changxing's brother, who ran the automobile smuggling operation and is serving fifteen years in jail.

Lai Changxing Peasant entrepreneur who built the $6 billion Yuanhua smuggling empire in partnership with Chinese military and police organizations and went from respected tycoon to China's most-wanted criminal when Premier Zhu Rongji cracked down on smuggling by the Chinese military.

Lai Shuiqiang Lai Changxing's oldest brother who died in prison after convincing thirteen others involved in the case to return to China from overseas and face charges.

Lan Fu Vice-mayor of Xiamen and inveterate gambler who was sentenced to death for taking some $600,000 in bribes from Lai. His death sentence was commuted to an indeterminate prison term after he assisted prosecutors.

Li Jizhou Close friend to Lai and vice-minister of China's Public Security Bureau who headed China's antismuggling efforts and was sentenced to death after he, his wife, and his daughter received more than $600,000 from Lai. His death sentence was commuted to an indeterminate prison sentence after he assisted prosecutors.

Yang Qianxian Award-winning chief of Xiamen customs and Communist party secretary for the organization who was sentenced to death for taking $170,000 in bribes from Lai. His death sentence was commuted to an indeterminate prison term after he assisted prosecutors.

Zhuang Rushun One of Lai's closest friends and deputy chief of the Fujian province police who was sentenced to death for taking bribes from Lai. His death sentence was commuted to an indeterminate prison term after he assisted prosecutors.

Zhu Niuniu Lai's business partner who wrote a seventy-four-page report to authorities, detailing Lai's smuggling operation after Lai refused to help him pay off gambling debts.

Preface

I T SHOULD HAVE BEEN a routine flight from Beijing to the coastal city of Fuzhou. The government-owned airline was new and the airplane was fresh from a foreign factory. But I began to get a sense that this ride wouldn't be entirely routine when I saw how cheerfully untrained our crew was. The flight attendants sat giggling in the front row, eagerly putting together take-home bags of the best food from the extra meals. The cockpit door was open throughout the flight. The flight engineer came back to snooze in the front row.

Finally we began our descent. The lush green countryside, populated by farm huts and pigpens, loomed closer and closer. As the aircraft swung around to line up on the rapidly approaching runway, two of the flight attendants stood behind the pilot and copilot as if surfing the plane onto the runway. Then, with barely fifty feet between us and the rubber-scarred runway, the pilot suddenly jammed the throttles forward. Engines screaming, we began an abrupt climb. Amazingly, neither of the flight attendants toppled over, but they did stumble back to their seats with a look of fright. Up and around we went, once again lining up on the runway. Then I heard the distinctive *eerrrrrrrr* of the landing gear being lowered and felt the shuddering as the wheels entered the airstream. I hadn't noticed any of that on our first approach. So that's why we did the sudden go-around!

I was thinking about how sensible it was to travel by train as I walked into the terminal. Then I saw a propaganda poster on the wall that has since remained firmly in my mind as the perfect description of the transformation China is undergoing: STRIVE TO FLY NORMAL. That is the essence of what China is trying to do: become a normal country, one that is integrated into the world economy, a place where citizens can concentrate on their prosperity and happiness instead of suffering from political power struggles. Like our novice flight crew, China has spent that past twenty-five years alternately stumbling and soaring through a massive trial-and-error reform process, and so far most of the landings have been smooth.

It is difficult for anyone in the West to overestimate China's growing role in the global economy. With 1.3 billion mouths to feed, its consumer market has the potential to be larger than North America and Western Europe combined. Measured by purchasing power parity, China's current per-capita GDP is $5,000 and rising steadily each year. It has surpassed Britain as the world's fourth-largest economy. China consumes 25 percent of global steel, 30 percent of cement, and is the world's largest market for electrical appliances. Foreign companies are flocking here, both to sell and to buy. Contracted foreign investment in China now averages $420 million a day.

Since 1978, when Premier Deng Xiaoping launched a set of economic reforms that included using foreign companies and their capital, technology, and management skills, China has become a manufacturing powerhouse, combining technologically sophisticated factories with energetic, intelligent, and low-cost labor. But China has allowed foreigners in only on its own terms, and those terms are often opaque, contradictory, and bewildering. All too often, laws are only the law when they benefit China. Negotiations can take forever and the resulting agreements can be promptly ignored. Corruption is frequently the lubricant that greases the wheels of commerce. Business in China has always been conducted behind multiple curtains and amid much subterfuge, and that hasn't changed. Foreign companies rightly fear that Chinese partners, customers, or suppliers will steal their technology or trade secrets or simply pick their pockets. Testy relations between China's Communist leaders and the United States and other democracies requires that politics be an integral part of business plans. China's entry into the World Trade Organization in 2001 and the country's desire to transform local companies into global leaders is bringing more international practices into China by the day. But I still see foreign executives confidently breeze into China only to be run over by their Chinese competitors, the Chinese government, or their Chinese partners—or sink themselves through various combinations of unrealistic expectations, impatience, and lack of common sense. The more business in China changes, the more it stays the same. As a journalist, I have traveled the entire country and enjoyed a front-row seat for this historic drama. As a businessman, I've been involved in the power plays, the complex negotiations, and the political intrigues that are a routine part of doing business in the country.

This book is intended to show rather than tell what it is like to do business in China. There are no simple formulas or magic solutions. Only by showing the sometimes complex details of how certain deals came together or fell apart, how the people involved viewed and treated each other, how politics and prejudices tainted expectations and outcomes, will I be able to convey to you the nuances that have made China such a frustrating yet rewarding place for so many foreign businesses. Each chapter begins with a simple introduction of the characters and situation. Next, in an overview section, I put the characters and situation in their proper context. The story then unfolds as a straightforward narrative. At the end, in a section entitled "What This Means for You," I explain how what happened in this chapter can affect how you do business in China. Finally, I summarize—pithily, I hope—many of my own observations in a takeoff on Mao's Little Red Book.

Demographers may quibble with the title: China's current population is 1.3 billion. But it is the round "billion" that matters, that threshold number that symbolizes the vast and untapped continental-size market, the teeming Chinese masses waiting to be turned into customers, the dream of staggering profits for those who get here first, the hype and hope that has mesmerized foreign merchants and traders for centuries. The title is my tribute to another American journalist-turned-businessman, Carl Crow, who lived in Shanghai for twenty-six years and in 1937 wrote *400 Million Customers*, a rich trove of anecdotes and insights about the Chinese people and doing business in China, much of which still holds true today. I share Crow's deep respect and admiration for, as he put it, "the interesting, exasperating, puzzling, and, almost always, lovable Chinese people." My goal for this book is to also share Crow's ability to convey timeless insights and commonsense lessons about Chinese business practices, and the deeply ingrained thinking and behavior patterns of Chinese people, through a combination of scholarship, grassroots experience, lively narrative, and good humor that transports the reader deep into the China business world.

Please enjoy the journey.

James McGregor
Beijing, 2005

Introduction

A Startup and a Turnaround

With one foot firmly in the past, and the other stepping into the future, China is simultaneously the world's largest startup and turnaround.

I PRESUMED THAT WEARING a Peking Opera outfit in the land of pinstripes would get some attention.

There I was, in New York's World Financial Center, standing before nearly all of Dow Jones's top executives in a mahogany-paneled conference room, wearing a hat like a silver chandelier, a wispy beard that went to my knees, and a blue-and-gold embroidered silk robe that billowed like Cinderella's dress.

It was early 1994 and after years of reporting and writing about China for *The Wall Street Journal,* I had just been appointed chief business representative in China for Dow Jones, the paper's mother company. My mission was to build footholds for Dow Jones in a country that was closed to outside media companies. Since I hadn't had time to accomplish anything toward that goal, I didn't have much to report. So while my colleagues showed snappy PowerPoint presentations, I was empty-handed but clad in the costume of Bao Gong, a Song dynasty official known for his integrity and vision.

I was taking a page from the very effective marketing strategy that China so expertly employs to make the Western world salivate: with empty pockets but big ambitions, sell the China mystique and the dream of one billion customers. With its strange history—two thousand years of continuous imperial rule, followed by a crippling encounter with communism that left an impatient, hungry, and hardworking population determined to get rich and regain its rightful place in the world—China would present opportunities and challenges to the global business community of a scale and magnitude perhaps never seen before.

I said that it would be risky, difficult, and time-consuming for Dow Jones to build a media and information business in China where the Communist party was still obsessed with information control and propaganda. But I reminded them that while Chinese leaders still mouthed the slogans of Marx and Lenin, their actions focused on markets and leverage. When Deng launched reforms fifteen years earlier, I said, there was only one place in the world with a significant population of poor Chinese people—China. The several tens of millions of ethnic Chinese who lived outside the country were among the world's most ambitious and successful scientists, inventors, engineers, merchants, and business tycoons.

"What Deng is doing isn't brain surgery," I said. "He is letting the Chinese people move beyond their debilitating political struggles and do what comes naturally: focus on education for their children, focus on acquiring individual wealth, focus on building the nation and gaining international respect, and always remember that anyone who openly challenges the government's authority will be ruthlessly crushed in the name of national stability.

"And one more thing," I said. "As we have seen in Taiwan, Hong Kong, Macao, and Monaco, the Chinese people love nothing more than playing with money. Gambling and financial speculation are hardwired into their genes. So the question is when, not if, China will have the world's largest financial markets. That is something that Dow Jones must get out in front of."

My scheme worked. Even those in the room who figured I was half-insane became enchanted with and excited about China. I was soon flooded with visitors from our wire services, databases, stock indexes, television production, print publications, and other divisions. For Dow Jones, like corporations across the globe, China was an exciting new business frontier, as well as a fun and fascinating place for a business trip.

I didn't think of it this way at the time, but what I was describing was a China that is simultaneously the world's largest startup and the world's largest turnaround. The country can draw on a two-thousand-year tradition, but it also is inhaling Western business know-how and technology and doing everything at the same time and for the first time. That is why China has been able to progress so quickly.

If you think about the last decade of China's economic and social development in terms of comparable changes in the history of the United States, you can feel the wind on your face. China is undergoing the raw capitalism of the Robber Baron era of the late 1800s; the speculative financial mania of the 1920s; the rural-to-urban migration of the 1930s; the emergence of the first-car, first-home, first-fashionable clothes, first-college education, first-family vacation, middle-class consumer of the 1950s, and even aspects of social upheaval similar to the 1960s.

It almost seems as if Deng used Harvard Business School's turnaround guidelines as his blueprint. Consider just a few.

Establish a Sense of Urgency: This was easy after the Cultural Revolution. The Communist party had to change course or lose power.

Form a Powerful Guiding Coalition: Deng empowered practical reformers but also left Long March veterans with enough of a grip to apply the brakes.

Create a Vision: Deng challenged the country to quadruple per-capita GNP from 1980 to 2000, a goal achieved four years early.

Communicate the Vision: Day and night, the state-owned press celebrates progress and exhorts new goals.

Institutionalize New Approaches: All major reforms, from farming to housing to finance and privatization, were tested and refined as local experiments before being spread nationwide and surrounded with regulatory structures.

The startup side of the equation is where foreign businesses and governments come in. China needed capital, technology, manufacturing expertise, management know-how, and overseas markets for its products. Like all startups, the Chinese have progressed through frantic trial and error, making it up every day, copying and modifying practices and products of others, always sprinting to capture the market first, always aiming at the next pile of quick profits.

Journey to the East

I first came to China as Deng's turnaround was starting to get traction. My interest in Asia started at age eighteen when I served as an infantry soldier in Vietnam. I went from the army to journalism school, to a Los Angeles crime beat, to a correspondent's job in Washington, D.C., covering the U.S. Congress. All along, my ultimate goal was to return to Asia as a reporter. So in 1985 I hooked up with my sister Lisa, who was working in refugee camps in Thailand, and we set out on a six-week backpacking trip across China. We bounced around the country in filthy, jam-packed trains and buses. We spoke not a word of Chinese but found ourselves hounded by eager students desperate to practice the English they were learning in school. Physicians, professors, and even government officials volunteered to serve as our guides just for the opportunity to speak English and learn what they could about the outside world. I returned to the United States convinced that China's eventual emergence onto the world scene would be the economic event of my lifetime. After convincing my wife, Cathy, that Taiwan was "just like Hawaii" (I had never been there but knew that petrochemical plants were more prevalent than pineapple plantations), we sold everything we owned and in early 1987 flew to the island with two suitcases each and moved into a threadbare YWCA. The idea was, at our ripe old ages of thirty-three, to learn Mandarin and then head off to mainland China.

A few months after we landed in Taiwan, *The Asian Wall Street*

Journal hired me as its Taiwan bureau chief. It was the perfect time to be a journalist in Taiwan. Martial law was lifted. Fistfights in the legislature signaled the start of a democratic revolution. Gangsters built flimflam empires. The stock market soared by 1,800 percent, then tanked. Everybody bought cars, and then sat fuming in traffic jams. The government scrambled to pretend that it was in full control. The next three years were a preview of many things I would see again in China.

When *The Wall Street Journal* sent me to Beijing as bureau chief in 1990, the tears of the Tiananmen Massacre still streaked the face of China. The government was patching up its internal split and exercising white-knuckled repression. Rage was widespread, but only vented to close friends and family. I rode my bicycle around Beijing almost every night, trying to probe the thoughts of those puffing along in the smoky, polluted blackness beside me. Most people were afraid to talk to foreigners, but I turned our lovely one-year-old daughter, Sally, into an interview lure. Chinese love children and with her Shirley Temple blond curls, Sally could easily gather talkative crowds of several dozen, and sometimes several hundred, when I plopped her on the dusty counter of a state department store or strapped her onto the back of my bike and trolled for people to talk to.

I also traveled throughout the country. I witnessed firsthand the official efficiency and private practicality of the Communist party. Everywhere I went, from dust-blown Qinghai in the northwest, to sweaty and humid Guangdong in the southeast, party and government officials from the top to the bottom would mouth the latest party line. But once the official political regurgitations were over, the talk always turned to business. I found a country littered with wasted talent—bellboys with economic degrees carried my bags and highly trained engineers drove my taxis—and ravenous to resume progress.

Business Thoroughbreds

I found that despite forty years of Communism, the mainlanders were just as ferocious and thoroughbred economic animals as their cousins in Taiwan and Hong Kong. I met Cao Bing on my first reporting trip to Guangdong province, adjacent to Hong Kong. He sat next to me in the first-class section of the airplane from Beijing. A short man with a stubbly beard and disheveled hair, he was wearing blue jeans, a green sweater with holes in it, and a pair of tattered Nike sneakers. He hugged a black gym bag protectively as we took off. For most of the flight, he poked like a maniac on the keys of a tiny calculator and recorded his calculations on scraps of cardboard from a cigarette carton. I thought he was deranged until we started chatting. Cao lived in the Golden Hero massage parlor next to the Guangzhou city airport. He said that he flew around China twenty-five days a month. He also whispered that he had $20,000 U.S. dollars in the gym bag. China didn't yet have an official foreign exchange trading system, so Cao had established a nationwide foreign exchange business out of the massage parlor. Cao had street currency traders working for him in a dozen major cities, where they stood outside hotels and traded the Chinese currency, renminbi (RMB) for dollars with foreign tourists. His profits came from arbitraging the different street exchange rates in various cities. He and his partners flew around China selling dollars where they got the highest price or buying them where prices were cheap. This was a forty-five-year-old man with an eighth-grade education who had previously been a tobacco grower in the far west province of Yunnan.

A little later, in Shanghai, I met a man who called himself Millions Yang, a forty-year-old steel factory worker with a jumble of bad teeth and a bundle of big ideas. With a ninth-grade education he was making the then-unheard of sum of $100,000 a year from his base in a seedy coffee shop on the balcony of a dilapidated movie theater in the city's former French quarter. Millions got rich by buying government bonds from workers who were forced to accept them as part of their pay. He bought them for pennies from workers in remote towns who figured they were worthless paper, and brought them back to Shanghai and sold them for huge profits on the city's nascent bond market. While the business models that Cao and Millions had formulated were crude, they were pioneers in China business practices that prevail in much more sophisticated forms to this day: mining the cracks in half-reformed systems and arbitraging between the state and private economy.

Mad for Money

The speed at which China went from communism to embracing capitalism should be no surprise. This is a country where the traditional greeting for Chinese New Year, the equivalent of saying "Merry Christmas," is *Gongxi facai,* or "Congratulations on getting rich." Similarly, a central part of funerals in China is the burning of fake paper money to send assets for the departed in the afterlife. In southern China, papier-mâché mansions, luxury cars, and entertainment centers are burned to provide some extra comforts. At weddings, guests line up at a table outside the reception hall where their red gift envelopes of cash are ripped open, counted, and recorded as everybody in line watches.

Given the distrust of the political system resulting from the Cultural Revolution and the corruption and constant change of the reform era, many Chinese place their complete trust only in money. This was most bluntly put to me by a cynical and scruffy twenty-nine-year-old cigarette smuggler surnamed Yang whom I met one day while wandering the streets of the city of Wuhan between meetings. A week earlier, two policeman had been shot when they tried to extort money from a street vendor. When I told Yang that I was American, he told me of the shooting as if it were a positive event.

"America is great because guns make everybody equal," he said. "Freedom in China is a pocketful of money," he added, showing me a six-inch-thick wad of fifty-yuan notes. "In China, you either have money or you have to be obedient."

To Serve the People

Given their cultural proclivities, I'm not surprised that I have never met a real Communist in China, somebody who believes in the abolition of private property or the philosophy of "from each according to his ability, to each according to his need." "Mao Zedong Thought" is still a core part of China's official ideology, and the "Yan'an Spirit" of self-sacrifice and simple living are still the professed ideal for Chinese officials. The Chinese Communist Party has recently tweaked its liturgy to protect private property and to state that the party is the vanguard of all Chinese people, not just the workers and the peasants. But officials still endure endless speeches and propaganda study sessions where the words of Marx and Lenin are swirled into ever more creative combinations. Then they climb into their Audi or Mercedes sedans and check stock prices on their mobile phones as they head home to apartment buildings named Beverly Hills, Park Avenue, or Palm Springs, where their sons and daughters with Harvard or Wharton MBAs wait to discuss privatization deals.

For most party officials, life is guided by the proverb *Zhi Lu Wei Ma,* which means "Point at a deer and call it a horse." Saying one thing and doing another is a way of life because the party believes that to do anything else would risk destabilizing the system. The 1989 Tiananmen Massacre was a tragedy but also a turning point. It was caused by a deep split between conservatives and reformers in the party. Conservatives won the battle but lost the war. In the aftermath of Tiananmen, the Party accelerated privatization and market reforms because its credibility was shredded and could only be rebuilt by quickly improving people's lives. Throughout the 1990s, in fact, the Communist party has resembled trickle-down Republicans. Private enterprise was not only allowed but the newly rich became celebrated as the country's new model workers— except when they were being jailed for corruption. The nation's resources were turned away from social programs and into the construction of mind-boggling amounts of infrastructure aimed at supporting a market economy that can compete in the world. I was once told that an ideal Chinese government should be like a strong water-skier behind a boat. The raging entrepreneurial drive of the Chinese people is the boat. The government is the skier who drags along behind, every now and then yanking on the rope with sufficient force to alter the boat's direction a bit if it heads off course.

All of this isn't a cynical exercise. If the business community is the "old boys' network" in the West, the Communist Party is the "old boys' network" in China. While few, if any, officials believe in communism, they do believe in the system, that it should be protected and that it should and can be improved. The party today operates much like a corporation in the way it makes decisions and deals with people. Bright young officials are selected for ideological indoctrination and management training, and moved through increasingly responsible positions. Like a corporation, there is some democracy at the top of the party and almost none at the bottom.

This fairly modern system is grafted on ancient attitudes and practices, however. China is ruled by its deeply ingrained culture more than anything else. For the party, this is manifesting itself in the wealth that the political aristocracy is rapidly accumulating, wealth being a necessity to keep their families on top in a market economy. Nobody will ever admit this publicly, but it is quietly accepted that the families of senior Communist Party officials will use their status and connections to quietly build assets. This unspoken practice could be viewed as a permutation of the old Inner Court and Outer Court system that dates back to the Han dynasty two thousand years ago. In those days, the Inner Court was the extended imperial family and its trusted retainers. They had a right to the nation's wealth and controlled the military and the entities responsible for policing the government bureaucracy, or Outer Court. In China today, the Inner Court is the top several hundred Communist party leadership families that emerged from the revolution and its aftermath. The Chinese military and government watchdog organizations today report to the party, not to the government bureaucracy, the equivalent of the old Outer Court.

Rough Justice

The Chinese government is obsessed with social order and for good reason. With the demise of socialism and the rise of capitalism creating a society of haves and have-nots, China is a social powder keg. I looked Chinese justice in the eye at a death rally in Mangshi, a city of one hundred thousand near China's southwestern border with Burma. When I was there in the early 1990s, eastern Burma was one huge poppy field and heroin factory, and much of the production was smuggled through China on its way to the United States and Europe. Chinese addiction was rising fast as the contraband spilled across China on its way to the coast. The government's solution: shoot every drug dealer it finds.

At daybreak, people began streaming into the city's main sports stadium. A little later a file of police jeeps and motorcycles with screaming sirens escorted a convoy of thirteen army cargo trucks into the stadium. In the back of each truck were two or three prisoners, leaning over the railings with placards detailing their crimes hanging from their necks. The prisoners were lined up, guarded by machine guns atop each truck. The air crackled with the sounds of walkie-talkies.

I stood face-to-face with the prisoners, astonished at how well behaved they were. A woman prisoner arrived alone. She was brought into the middle of the line. A male prisoner tried to say something to her and then I could see why they were all so quiet. The prisoners all had fishing line tied in individual slipknots around their necks. When the man tried to talk, a policeman holding the line quickly choked him. I later learned that the two prisoners were husband and wife. Then the stadium loudspeakers began to boom out the individual death sentences amid cheers from the crowd. Shortly afterward, the prisoners were taken to the edge of town, forced to kneel next to one another, and shot in the back of the head.

Firm control from the top has always been considered the only path to peace and prosperity in China. One reason is that China is a shame-based society, very different from the guilt-based West. In the West, with society's religious orientation, many controls are internalized. Guilt, which is ultimately the fear of sin and eternal damnation, puts a check on bad behavior. In China, it is the fear of exposure and the accompanying shame that tarnishes the entire extended family. As a result, the Chinese can feel pretty good about doing almost anything as long as they don't get caught. In that atmosphere, the only efficient form of law and order is a strong and omnipresent government that increases the likelihood of getting caught if you do something wrong.

Global trade, foreign investment, and the commercialization of China's economy have brought in an extensive body of laws and a constantly improving legal system. But the core philosophy is rule by law, not the rule of law. The blindfolded goddess of justice isn't part of Chinese culture. In China, the law is a set of handcuffs to rule society in the interests of the rulers. In drafting laws and building a court system in the past two decades, China has adopted the civil law philosophy of Japan and Germany, rather than the common law philosophy of England and the United States. As a result, judges are not impartial referees but inquisitors. The judges, in turn, are supervised by an organization called the *zhengfawei,* or political-legal committee, a Communist party organization that extends from the party's security chief in Beijing all the way down to the lowest court. Justice in China is ultimately a political decision.

It isn't surprising that throughout China's history people have chosen to settle disputes themselves instead of seeking government intervention. In imperial times, justice was dispensed by local mandarins who lived in fortified compounds and had little contact with the general public. Their brand of justice discouraged people from seeking government arbitration. If one was involved in a dispute, or accused of a crime, you were never considered completely innocent. The assumption was that you must have done something wrong just to be in that position. Even today, Chinese people instinctively try to settle things among themselves.

Sweet and Sour Success

When I arrived in Beijing in 1990, the foreign business community was shell-shocked from Tiananmen. Nobody would take my phone calls, including the country bosses of IBM, Motorola, and other major American corporations. China had become an international human rights pariah and these Western executives didn't want to bring any attention to the fact that they were continuing to do business in the country. It would be very difficult to write *The Wall Street Journal* business stories without access to those people, so I applied to join the American Chamber of Commerce in China, popularly known as AmCham, then still a very small group. I figured that if I could attend their luncheons and receptions I could get to know the businesspeople in a social setting and they would become more comfortable later accepting my interviews. Several people threatened to resign if they allowed a journalist to join. But I was finally accepted after agreeing to stay away from their regular meeting with the ambassador. To me it made sense that they could discuss their China business issues with the ambassador outside the earshot of a reporter.

Before long, AmCham members began complaining to me that the press was transfixed on writing negative stories, ignoring the fact that China was recovering from the tragedy and business was improving. I said, "Great, I would be glad to write about your business." Then they would scurry away. I spent several months researching a story about American business success in China. You would have thought I was probing their sex lives. Nobody would talk to me, even the global CEO of Procter & Gamble, a company that was very successfully spreading its shampoos and other personal care products across the country. Once I became a businessman myself, I understood their reticence.

While the intensity ebbs and flows, foreign businesses are trapped between profits and politics. From the Chinese side, they fear that trumpeting success will bring platoons of bureaucratic pickpockets to their doors. While Deng welcomed foreign investment in China, nobody in the Chinese government has endorsed foreign companies making large profits. Even today, there is a lingering attitude that foreign profits in China carry the taint of exploiting the Chinese people.

The foreign companies themselves—especially American companies—are squeezed between investors and activists. With China's rocketing growth, companies often must publicize their aggressive China initiatives and profitable China businesses to boost their stock price. On the other hand, the contentious politics of China relations also forces them to duck for cover when Western politicians are criticizing China for its weakness in human rights, for stealing American manufacturing jobs, and a litany of other issues.

As a result, foreign businesspeople must be politically active in China and at home. Politics in China is a feudal and brutal contact sport. This is true within China's leadership circles and ministries, but it is sometimes most evident when China deals with foreigners who have the temerity to challenge the Middle Kingdom. Just ask Chris Patten.

The Uncomfortable Monk

The onetime chairman of Britain's Conservative party, Chris Patten was the last British governor of Hong Kong before the colony was handed back to Chinese rule in 1997. Soon after his appointment, Patten proposed stretching the Sino-British handover agreement and dramatically expanding the democratically elected seats in the final prehandover Hong Kong legislative council elections. The Chinese government reacted with explosive personal invective, labeling Patten an "eternally unpardonable criminal" and "jade-faced whore," and describing his actions as "a monument to chastity erected by a prostitute." China rallied Hong Kong's pliant business community to attack Patten. Chinese diplomats stirred up British China hands who assailed the proposal as a publicity stunt to revive Patten's political career at home.

Several months after the pummeling began, Patten summoned

me to Government House for cocktails. He wanted to talk to me because he was looking for viewpoints outside his foreign office advisers. Sitting in the sunroom of the white-columned governor's mansion overlooking Hong Kong harbor, the witty and articulate Patten was jovial but his slumped shoulders and the dark circles around his eyes bespoke weariness.

Cool drink in hand, he leaned toward me. "I want to have a civilized and reasonable discussion with the Chinese," he said. "How can I do that when they talk like we are engaged in a fistfight?"

I told him the fistfight would end only if he threw in the towel. Patten said he believed that increased democracy in Hong Kong would help protect the island's citizens against the machinations of their new authoritarian masters. I said that China viewed his proposal as a cynical attempt by Britain to destabilize Hong Kong as Britain walked out the door. My advice to Patten was to act like an elected official himself, engage the citizens in a serious dialogue, wander the markets, kiss the babies, and set a standard that China's appointed Hong Kong leader would have to follow.

When I returned home to Beijing a couple of days later, a Chinese tourism magazine featuring super-strength stunts by the famous Shaolin Temple kung-fu monks was sitting on my desk. One full-page photograph was of a monk crouching naked atop two granite blocks, rear to the camera, with a third granite block the size of two car batteries dangling by a thick rope tied around his testicles.

I mailed the photo to Patten with a note that read: "I have found a guy in a worse position than you."

To make sure that they didn't end up like Patten and the Uncomfortable Monk, Hong Kong's elite abandoned Patten and engaged in traditional Chinese politics: shamelessly sucking up to the powers in Beijing. China appointed a decent but hopelessly indecisive shipping tycoon, C. H. Tung, to lead Hong Kong after the handover. Surrounding himself with other tycoons as advisers, Tung shaped a government that was of, for, and by the billionaires. The place ran like a country club. When government reforms were being considered, or some government entity or function was being privatized, the policies were generated by committees made up of the sons and daughters of billionaires, which ensured any opportunities that arose would be theirs. Governing Hong Kong under the thumb of Beijing is, of course, a difficult task. But instead of advocating artful policies that accomplish China's goals while as much as possible preserving Hong Kong's interests, Tung and the tycoons practiced what I call "preemptive capitulation": making kowtowing policies based on what they assume China is thinking. Deeply unpopular both in Beijing and Hong Kong, Tung resigned "for health reasons" in March 2005 and was replaced by lifetime Hong Kong civil servant Donald Tsang, who promised his government would pay attention to the common people.

Hong Kong today is the only Chinese city whose best days are behind it, but it is still the best place in the world to live as a millionaire. Taxes are low, housing and recreation are first class, lots of cops ensure social order, there is good flight access to the entire world, household help is cheap, and sophisticated financial managers are a local specialty. But Hong Kong is no longer a suitable place to headquarter a China business. Mainland Chinese today are generally better educated and have better English language skills than their counterparts in Hong Kong. Indeed, the Hong Kong government and elite seem intent on proving true the Chinese proverb, *Fu Bu Guo San Dai,* which means, "Wealth can't last more than three generations."

The Nation Family

Patten was put in his awkward position not only by his democracy proposal but by the burden of history. China was very emotional and nationalistic about recovering Hong Kong—and Macao from Portugal two years later. Regaining control of those two regions would finally erase the deep humiliation that began in the mid-1800s when Western powers forced the country to open for trade and business by carving out foreign enclaves called treaty ports.

Patten's other transgression was to put himself between the Chinese government and the Chinese people. To the Chinese government, even the descendants of Chinese who emigrated to America, Europe, Hong Kong, Singapore, or elsewhere centuries ago still have responsibilities to the motherland. The overseas Chinese are not considered insiders, nor are they necessarily trusted, but they are deemed to be part of the tribe. In Chinese, the word "nation" is *guojia,* two characters that mean "nation" and "family."

Overseas Chinese have been key to the startup side of China's economic and business development. Hong Kong and Taiwan factory owners and managers have brought in the manufacturing expertise and modern management that has provided the base for China to become the world's workshop over the past two decades. Hong Kong property developers built the first five-star hotels and modern housing necessary to attract foreign business, and in doing so provided local developers with a model they quickly followed and have improved upon. Overseas Chinese managers at the foreign multinationals have also often been instrumental in building huge and profitable operations in China while mentoring and training new generations of local Chinese managers. That's the good side.

Overseas Chinese have also been largely responsible for reviving a China business culture that is at least as corrupt as that of the 1930s, which helped bring the Communist Party to power in the first place. Many of the first Hong Kong businessmen who came into China with their own companies, or as foreign multinational bosses, had no instincts for China because they grew up under a British colonial government. Many of them made blatant bribery their primary business tool. In the mid-1990s, I met a Hong Kong fishing rod manufacturer in Shandong province whose business model embodied this. He would go into a small town and give bribes to local officials to allow him to set up a fishing rod factory under the government's umbrella. He would take them overseas a couple of times a year for shopping excursions and tourism junkets disguised as board meetings.

"I teach them how to enjoy and spend money," he said. "But after about three years, they want to interfere in the business and take the profits for themselves." That's when he would pick up and move his operations to another town.

The Taiwanese often have been just as corrupt, albeit more subtle because they have better instincts for China as the result of growing up under a corrupt authoritarian Chinese government themselves. The most hopeless group has been the Singaporeans, who grew up in a nanny state and have the equivalent of a learning disability when it comes to China. Many of them simply can't grasp the lack of order and rules. They haven't been unduly corrupt, just incompetent to deal with the messiness and vulgarity of China. Overseas Chinese coming from America or Europe have often been in similar straits.

All of this is changing today. Young people from Hong Kong, Taiwan, and Singapore are flooding into China because they see it as the land of opportunity. These people are often as humble as those in the earlier waves were arrogant. They are often starting at the bottom, working their way up through companies, or establishing their own companies. The Singaporeans have made the most dramatic turnaround. Recognizing that its business executives weren't equipped for the rough-and-tumble of China, Singapore instead has focused on importing the best brains from China and packaging this talent with government venture capital money to create cutting-edge research facilities and business startups at home.

Satisfied but Unsettled

As I sit in my apartment in Beijing in mid-2005, I find myself constantly amazed at how normal business in China has become, both in terms of international practices and the traditional Chinese way of doing things. The startup and the turnaround aspects of China's economic rebirth are blending together.

When I arrived in Beijing fifteen years ago, the coming of winter was signaled by the piles of cabbage on every street corner. Cabbage was the only vegetable available until spring. People would shove it under stairwells, windowsills, and beds in their chilly cement-floored flats, and eat it throughout the winter, cutting away more and more rotten leaves to find palatable bits as winter progressed. Today street corners in Beijing are littered with department stores, mobile phone shops, foot massage parlors, Starbucks kiosks, and fashionable pedestrians who must sprint when crossing the street. The millions of new Chinese auto owners seem to feel that a gas pedal and steering wheel are tools for unleashing their inner aggression and creativity that is otherwise so squelched by political and parental controls.

I live in a new but nondescript apartment building on the city's east side. My Chinese neighbors are entrepreneurs or executives for multinationals who often buy one apartment to live in and one to rent. On weekends we all converge on the dozen or so pirated DVD shops in the neighborhood where any Hollywood movie or American television series of note is available with Chinese subtitles for one dollar per disc. Our building, like nearly all residential apartments in major Chinese cities, has broadband access to the Internet, where porn is plentiful but nonsanitized news and political sites are usually blocked. In the winter, my neighbors store away their fake Callaway golf clubs, bundle up in their fake North Face parkas, grab their fake Prada purses, lace up their fake Nikes, and speed away in their China-made Buicks and Audis to meet friends at first-rate restaurants serving Italian, Thai, Japanese, Indian, California-fusion, or French cuisine, unless they are seeking comfort food and opt for a Chinese bistro and a warm plate of sea slugs, chicken feet, or peppered pork intestines.

A couple of decades of averaging 9 percent annual growth has transformed China in terms of material goods. It has created a society of haves and have-nots, with significant poverty remaining in many rural areas and rust-belt cities and tremendous wealth evident in cities large and small across China. The vast majority of the population is much better off. Government social programs are weak, but fast economic growth and the country's strong family system have so far provided a safety net. In poor villages I have visited in western China, most people have televisions and other conveniences because they have children who have gone off to the cities to work in factories or on construction projects who send much of their income home.

A country that was until recently poor but safe has become one that is unsettled and insecure. There is nothing to believe in but making money. Personal introspection is not a strong suit in Chinese culture. Discipline is the first thing people learn in life, not happiness. In traditional Chinese philosophy, emotions damage your body. Anger hurts your liver, too much happiness hurts your spleen, worry hurts your lungs. Kids are taught not to cry. Adults are supposed to suppress, suppress, suppress. The saving grace of China and the allowable release valve is that the people have a fabulous sense of humor. When I was a reporter visiting different cities, I would sometimes seek out and drink beer with migrant worker peasants. They typically lived ten or more to a room in plywood hovels as they worked twelve-hour days building luxury high-rises. Instead of complaining to me about the unfairness of their lives, they would tell me jokes and tease one another. One of the first expressions a foreigner will learn in China is *chi ku,* or "eat bitterness," because the Chinese take great pride in their ability to endure hardship. Many hardships are endured today because rapid economic improvements of the past twenty-five years have made Chinese people optimistic that life will continue to get better.

Great Atmosphere

Some foreign businesspeople in China are very deeply integrated into the Chinese business scene. Foreign businesses are no longer an oddity, but a part of the fabric of Chinese commercial life, though the foreigners themselves are still outsiders in the eyes of Chinese society. A young man I met a few years ago from my hometown of Duluth, Minnesota, learned this at a wedding. In the mid-1990s, Mark was an English teacher at a Chinese school in the coastal city of Quanzhou in Fujian province, across from Taiwan. One day a student invited Mark to attend his brother's wedding, to be held in a village in the mountainous interior of Fujian, about an eight-hour bus ride from Quanzhou.

On the day of the wedding, Mark was a little nonplused when he arrived at the banquet hall to find the bride, groom, and entire wedding party waiting at the curb to greet him. When he was escorted into the banquet hall, Mark was even more surprised when everyone in the room rose and applauded. He was seated at the head table, then invited to accompany the bride and groom as they made the rounds toasting each table. By the end of the banquet, Mark was more than a bit drunk and reveling in his inexplicable celebrity status. As they walked out of the banquet hall, Mark's student put his arm around Mark's shoulder and said into his ear: "Thanks for coming, you really added great atmosphere." Now Mark understood: he was nothing more than an exotic decoration. As foreigners living and doing business in China, we really should remember that in the eyes of many Chinese, we are here only to add a bit of atmosphere— and some technology, know-how, and money, of course.

In viewing China as the world's biggest startup and turnaround, and considering the role of foreign business and Chinese tradition in the process, it is helpful to remember a slogan from the Qing Dynasty that was often quoted by Mao: *Gu Wei Jin Yong, Yang Wei Zhong Yong,* which means, "Make the past serve the present, make foreign things serve China."

1

The Grand Bargain

Two hundred years of foreign domination and duplicity have left a residue of suspicion and distrust. Understanding that history is essential to doing business with the Chinese.

T HE NEGOTIATIONS THAT BROUGHT China into the World Trade Organization in 2001 began in 1793 when Lord George Macartney landed his fleet of British ships on the north China coast. One of King George III's most experienced diplomats, Macartney was intent on opening China's vast market to British business. It was a simple matter of fairness. China exported such exotica as silk, tea, furniture and porcelain, yet bought little or nothing from outside its own shores. Money flowed into China— some twenty million ounces of silver each year—but none flowed out. So Macartney brought along the best that Britain produced. It took ninety horses and three thousand coolies to transport Macartney's gifts for the emperor. There were rifles, cannons, telescopes, horse carriages, a twenty-five-foot-tall clock, mountains of the finest woolens, and a hot air balloon complete with pilot.

But Macartney failed to grasp China's profound indifference to the rest of the world. China was the world's most prosperous and populous nation. Although he was old and his reign was nearing its end, Emperor Qianlong had during his years on the Dragon Throne effectively doubled China's landmass. Chinese maps of the day covered five scrolls hung side-by-side displaying a huge landmass labeled the "Middle Kingdom," surrounded by tiny islands labeled "England," "Germany," "France," "America," "Russia," and "Africa." China was the center of the world and everyone else was a barbarian, the degree of barbarity determined by the distance from China.

The negotiations between Macartney and the mandarins representing the emperor became a prolonged dance. At one banquet after another Macartney demanded to see the emperor to present his gifts and to request greater access to China's markets. The mandarins praised the gifts and explained that it would take time to set up a meeting with the emperor. Diaries and letters from both sides reveal startlingly different perceptions of what happened at these banquets. Macartney and his subordinates would congratulate themselves on having won the mandarins' confidence and prepare to depart for Beijing. The mandarins would send reports to the emperor explaining how they had massaged the barbarians' egos while placing more barriers in their way. They predicted the foreigners would soon tire and sail away.

Macartney persisted and finally won an informal courtesy call with the emperor, but only after an intense struggle over protocol. Anyone meeting the emperor was required to kowtow by dropping to their knees and touching their forehead to the ground three times, a gesture that was to be repeated eight more times. But a proper Englishman kowtowed to no one, and only went down on both knees for God. The Chinese suggested a face-saving solution. When Macartney entered the emperor's presence, there would be a curtain hanging behind the emperor, and behind that curtain would be a portrait of King George III. Macartney could make his kowtow to the king's unseen portrait. Macartney refused, and he was finally granted an informal courtesy call with the emperor just so they could finally be rid of him and his vexing entourage.

The meeting was amicable and Macartney headed home confident that Qianlong would satisfy some of Britain's modest requests. The Chinese once again saw things differently. Macartney was sent on his way with a letter to King George that said China had no need for British goods. The letter cautioned: "You, O King, should simply act in conformity with our wishes by strengthening your loyalty and swearing perpetual obedience so as to ensure that your country may share the blessings of peace." That was the beginning. The end—China's full-fledged admission to the global trading community—would come 206 years later.

Overview

I suspect that most Westerners doubt that the two hundred years between Lord Macartney's trip to China and China's eventual admission into the world trading community have much bearing on how you do business in China. Ancient history, you might call it. But foreigners doing business in China must understand that there's nothing ancient about the last two hundred years and the humiliations they have held for the Chinese. The belief that foreigners strong-armed their way into China in the past two hundred years in order to plunder the country's wealth is deeply ingrained in the Chinese psyche. They are taught from childhood that China was the world's mightiest empire, the best at everything, until the foreigners came knocking at the end of the eighteenth century to ruthlessly exploit a people who had done them no harm. So even today many Chinese are quick to anger when discussing the role of foreign powers in China. Indeed, it is impossible for anyone to put a positive spin on the opium trade and the disastrous epidemic of addiction that the British foisted on China or on Japan's occupation of much of China, and the accompanying ruthless slaughter of millions of Chinese, in the 1930s and early 1940s.

An examination of the interactions between China and various foreign nations that have wanted to do business there over the past two hundred years demonstrates why the Chinese today still harbor suspicions about foreigners. It also illustrates how the Chinese have adapted that suspicion to their advantage in negotiating tactics and strategies, both in government and industry. The Chinese genius for playing foreigners against each other is certainly present in modern business dealings, as is the Chinese art of brinksmanship and creative practicality of the sort that almost parked King George's portrait behind the emperor's curtain. As the story unfolds, China's commercial transformation increasingly depends upon what amounts to a rocky marriage of necessity between China and America. The political relationship is volatile due to ideological differences, domestic political proclivities, and the natural friction of a superpower bumping against a could-be superpower. But China has also placed an amazing reliance on the United States in the past three decades as an influential adviser and a model commercial system.

China today is a strange hybrid. In many ways it resembles the United States. It has a continental-size domestic market that sets businesspeople worldwide salivating, a population of ambitious, risk-taking entrepreneurs who can use the country's massive domestic market to build world-class products and businesses, and, by virtue of its size and stature, can force others to deal with it on terms it dictates. But, unlike the United States and almost all other nations that have become successful global commercial powers, China has an authoritarian and often paranoid political system that crushes dissent, controls information, and injects itself into every facet of business. There is constant experimenting with new political slogans, but the country really has no leading ideology other than enriching itself. The relentless drive of international trade and commerce that has shaken China out of its imperial stupor has now become an end unto itself. As a result, commercial negotiations in China often carry the weight of national aspirations, focused government planning, and, often just below the surface, the belief that you as a barbarian owe China something for past transgressions.

Commerce in China is all about making money, just as anywhere in the world, but business is also intertwined with China's struggle to change and adopt the ways of the West while retaining its Chinese "essence," as reformers in the final dynasty termed it. Foreigners have always sought not just commerce with China, but to change China, as well. Richard Nixon explained that desire in a

1967 *Foreign Affairs* article in which he said, "the world cannot be safe until China changes. Thus, our aim, to the extent we can influence events, should be to induce change."

Those who do business in China need to remember that this struggle sets a backdrop for the business environment.

The Barbarian Handler

A nation that eschews relationships with other nations doesn't need a foreign minister and China had none when Lord Macartney so rudely imposed himself on China. Macartney left China empty-handed, but his trade mission to China set the stage for many more. As the West industrialized, it sought new markets and raw materials. The Portuguese, Germans, French, Japanese, Dutch, and Americans were as eager as the British to open China for trade. The increasing presence of foreigners demanded that someone try to control them. For years the task of "barbarian handler" fell to Li Hongzhang, a commercially minded Confucian Renaissance man. To foreigners, Li cut an odd figure. A small man with a wispy beard, he was always clad in traditional gowns. Li hobnobbed with the foreign merchants and diplomats, attending their Christmas parties and other celebrations, but he was more respected than liked. Western diplomatic wives were thoroughly disgusted by Li's oft-used pocket spittoon and his habit of blowing his nose into a teacup.

But from 1860 until the turn of the century, Li was the most important man in China's dealings with the outside world. While accepting that China had fallen behind in science and commerce, Li believed that China's governing system based on morality and the Confucian "superior man" was the best in the world. China could survive by learning science and technology from the West and grafting those elements onto Chinese culture and the country's Confucian governing systems: modernizing while retaining the "essence" of China.

Li was a child when China underwent its first military humiliation. Eager to recoup some of the massive amounts of silver its traders were paying for Chinese tea, silk, and porcelain, the British began shipping opium from India to China. The drug found instant appeal. So strong was the taste among Chinese for the "foreign mud" that by 1830, opium amounted to half the total trade that Britain did with China. Britain's success prompted other nations to jump into the opium trade, as well, including Americans who brought opium from Turkey. Although repeated imperial edicts banned opium smuggling and imposed death by strangulation for violators, foreign traders found Chinese officials more than eager to facilitate the illegal trade in exchange for generous bribes.

In 1839, the Qing court sent Commissioner Lin Zexu to Canton to eradicate the opium trade. He burned twenty thousand chests of opium and threatened to behead anyone who smuggled the drug. The British government demanded compensation for the destroyed opium and deployed warships along China's southern coast. The First Opium War started when armed Chinese junks skirmished with the warships, giving British commanders an excuse to shell coastal cities. When British ships sailed up the Yangtze River into the heart of China, the Qing court realized that the Western barbarians with their superior weaponry were positioned to take over the country's most prosperous southern provinces.

Chinese efforts to preserve its isolation formally ended in August 1842 when China signed the first of what became known in China as the "unequal treaties." The Treaty of Nanjing allowed Western traders to begin carving out their first pieces of China. Hong Kong was ceded to Britain. Five Chinese ports—Canton (now Guangzhou), Amoy (Xiamen), Foochow (Fuzhou), Ningpo (Ningbo), and Shanghai—were opened to foreign residents and trade. A year later, Britain forced China to sign another treaty promising "most favored nation" status so that if any other country got better trade concessions from China, Britain would automatically receive the same treatment. A year after that, the Americans forced China to grant American residents (and eventually all foreigners) extraterritoriality, giving them immunity from prosecution in Chinese courts.

Tensions in the treaty ports, the murder of a French missionary, and more attempts to stop the opium trade led to the Second Opium War. It ended when twenty-thousand French and British troops captured Beijing and then torched and looted the emperor's opulent two hundred-building Summer Palace. Treaties to end the Second Opium War, signed in Tianjin in 1858 and Beijing in 1860, granted further concessions. The opium trade was legalized and foreign embassies were established in Beijing.

Along with the merchants who invaded the coastal cities came missionaries who headed into the countryside to bring salvation. While the missionaries built churches, hospitals, schools, and orphanages, they also brought close behind terrifying technology and machinery that the peasants blamed for upsetting the rhythm of life and causing widespread drought and famine. Railroads steamed along like angry dragons, telegraph lines whistled in the wind like spirits, and deep mines dug into the earth upset the buried bones of their ancestors from which the Chinese peasant's fate and fortune had always emanated. The Empress Dowager herself stoked peasant hatred of foreigners with stories of how Chinese orphans taken in by the missionaries had their eyes plucked out for medicines and their bodies eaten.

Li Hongzhang carefully noted how the West's weapons and methods decimated the Chinese military. As he rose in stature among the bureaucrats and mandarins in the imperial court, he was constantly asked to negotiate settlements when Chinese peasants killed missionaries or ripped up train tracks and telegraph lines. The foreigners always wanted new trading or territorial rights in compensation. In the negotiations, Li was usually playing with an empty hand. Foreign military power was simply too powerful for China to resist. Li's strategy was to offer expanded business opportunities instead of ceding territorial control to foreigners. When foreign powers did carve out land, Li directed local officials to make their life miserable in myriad bureaucratic ways.

Rebellion

Not everyone resented the missionaries. A failed imperial scholar named Hong Xiuquan was so smitten with the message of Protestant missionaries that he founded the Society of Godworshippers and titled himself the "Younger Brother of Jesus Christ." Widespread poverty and the obvious corruption of the imperial court allowed Hong to recruit some five hundred thousand peasants to stage a revolt in 1851, known as the Taiping Rebellion. For a dozen years, he ruled much of southern China from his capital in Nanjing. Hong's *Taiping Tianguo,* or Heavenly Kingdom of Great Peace, attracted the dispossessed and disgruntled from all over China. Land and private property were taken from landlords and distributed to peasants, foreshadowing the policies of Mao a century later.

Hong's constant hostile presence in southern China threatened both the Empress Dowager and the Western merchants. To end that threat, Li helped organize an army of imperial troops and mercenaries under the leadership of British Major Charles George "Chinese" Gordon to end the Taiping Rebellion. In 1864 Gordon led his "Ever Victorious Army" out to crush Hong's kingdom. On the way to Nanjing, Gordon was brought into negotiations between the Taiping officials ruling the city of Suzhou and the commander of imperial troops, General Ching. Through General Ching, Li had told the Taiping rebels that their lives would be spared if they surrendered without fighting. Gordon spoke almost no Chinese and didn't understand what was being said during the negotiations, but he left the talks confident that his presence guaranteed that Li would abide by his promise to spare the rebels' lives.

When Li himself met with the princes, their swaggering insolence enraged him. Li immediately ordered them beheaded and their heads hung on the city gates.

Gordon was astounded that a promise could so easily be broken. His word of honor had been violated. He grabbed a pistol and went into the city to kill Li. When he couldn't find Li, a disconsolate Gordon took the head of one rebel from the city gate to his home where he talked to it, asking forgiveness. Gordon then ordered the Ever Victorious Army to retreat.

Gordon was persuaded to rejoin the Taiping campaign after Li declared publicly that Gordon had nothing to do with the broken promise. The Qing troops soon conquered Nanjing. Hong Xiuquan died from eating wild herbs to ward off starvation, and imperial Chinese troops slaughtered the remaining one hundred thousand Taiping followers who didn't commit suicide.

Barbarian Rule

Li handled the barbarians as skillfully as anyone could have expected, yet he was often blamed for China's problems at the hands of foreigners. Indeed, he was labeled a traitor after a Japanese army in 1895 decimated Chinese troops in a five-month conflict. Li ended the war when he signed the Treaty of Shimonoseki that forced China to cede influence over Korea and Taiwan to Japan and to open more of China to Japanese trade. Li was vilified at least in part because Japan's victory so stunned China. Here was an island nation that had adopted its culture and civilization from China. The difference was that when Westerners came calling on Japan, in the form of Commodore Matthew Perry's expedition in 1854, Japan's Meiji government had rapidly adopted Western technology and methods instead of resisting as China had.

The Japanese victory was the last gasp of the Qing dynasty. As the century ended, Britain, Russia, Japan, Germany, and France all had pieces of China. The country was becoming another Africa, with separate colonies carved out by the West, when U.S. Secretary of State John Hay proposed an "open door" agreement among the countries that had "spheres of influence" in China. The agreement secured equal commercial opportunity for all throughout China. While the open door agreement kept the West from colonizing China, it also served the self-interest of the United States, which had fallen behind the other nations in China while preoccupied with developing the American West.

The foreign encroachments helped spawn a secret sect called the Society of Righteous and Harmonious Fists. The Boxers, as they were known to the West, combined martial arts, animistic rituals, and superstitions into a messianic movement aimed at toppling the government and chasing all foreigners out of China. As the movement grew in numbers, it became increasingly violent. Thousands of Boxers roamed China killing foreign missionaries, merchants, and their children. They also killed tens of thousands of Chinese Christian converts (many of them "rice Christians," who prayed because they got free food) by skinning them alive or hacking them to pieces. Fearful for her life, the Empress Dowager co-opted the Boxers, urging them to rid China of the "foreign devils." Soon some fifteen hundred foreign diplomats and businesspeople and their families were barricaded in the foreign legation districts in Beijing and Tianjin. The rebellion and siege generated global headlines and cemented an international image of the Chinese as fanatical savages.

Li counseled the Empress Dowager against aligning with the Boxers. He distrusted and disliked the foreigners in China as much as anyone, but he also respected their firepower. When she ignored his advice, Li knew that it was only a matter of time before foreign soldiers would come to Beijing to crush both the Boxers and the imperial army. It took an eight-power army two months to break the siege and then occupy and loot Beijing. Li once again assumed his role of de facto foreign minister, despite an illness that prevented him from attending many negotiation sessions aimed at settling the Boxer Rebellion.

The Boxer Protocol that Li negotiated and signed just weeks before his death was a simple document that required China to pay $335 million in reparations to the foreign powers (about $4.3 billion in year 2000 dollars), punish the Boxer leaders, and allow the foreigners to permanently station troops in Beijing. Few other details were needed. The ambassadors and ministers for Britain, America, Japan, and the other major foreign powers in Beijing formed a council that became a guiding hand for the Qing court. China was in the hands of the barbarians.

The Pro-Business Warlord

In 1911, the Qing dynasty finally fell, ending more than two thousand years of imperial dynastic rule in China and ushering in a period of unprecedented access for Western business. Sun Yat-sen, a Guangdong-born medical-doctor-turned-revolutionary, had brought together several anti-Manchu groups while in exile in Japan in 1905. His Nationalist party (the Kuomintang, or KMT) created and nurtured the new Republic of China using Soviet advisers and Soviet aid money. He formed a cooperative relationship with China's budding Communist movement and the Communist party was formally established in 1921. But Sun died of cancer in 1925. His successor, Chiang Kai-shek, hated the Communists.

Generalissimo Chiang, who had been Sun's military aide, drove out the Soviets and purged the Communists from KMT ranks, triggering the start of a twenty-five-year civil war. The generalissimo built a base of support among wealthy Chinese landlords and merchants, as well as foreign businesses in China and their governments back home. From 1911 until Japan's occupation of much of China in 1937, Western commerce and private business blossomed in China. All the big players piled into China. Standard Oil provided fuel for lamps, Bethlehem Steel built ships for the Chinese navy, British American Tobacco built hundreds of warehouses across China, while Siemens connected the treaty ports by telegraph and IBM installed its business machines in Beijing. Modern Chinese companies emerged, as well, obtaining loans from Japanese banks, employing European and American engineers and accountants, and creating technical schools to train Chinese industrialists.

Life was grand for the foreign businessmen. Their mansions were well staffed with servants and they spent weekends playing golf, betting at the horse races, or relaxing on houseboats pulled by teams of coolies along rural canals. Young Western men recruited through newspaper advertisements to work in China had the services of some seventy thousand prostitutes in Shanghai's foreign concession to help fill their idle hours. As Harold Sheridan, a young

American working in Shanghai, wrote to his mother in 1913: "I tell you, I can easily understand the fascination of the Far East where living is cheap, and a white man need never lift his little finger unless he cares to."

Chiang Kai-shek allowed businesses to flourish as long as they supported his government financially. Gangsters allied with the KMT collected tolls from small merchants. Tycoons were taught lessons through high-profile arrests. It wasn't difficult for the Communists to make capitalism a dirty word in China as relatives of the generalissimo's American-educated wife, Soong Mei-ling, turned the Chinese economy into a family business. While business boomed in the big cities, the Communists were organizing the country's peasants and dodging KMT military assaults. Antiforeign movements and worker strikes also spread across China. When Japan occupied Manchuria in 1931, some Western businessmen began to leave China. The early trickle turned into a flood as Japan continued to take more Chinese territory. As Beijing, Shanghai, and much of China's east coast fell to the Japanese in 1937, Chiang's KMT government fled to new wartime headquarters in the far west city of Chongqing.

The Triumph and Failure of Communism

When World War II ended, China's economy was in tatters. American military and diplomatic advisers tried to act as mediators between the KMT and the Communists, but when their efforts failed the United States sided with the KMT. American money and munitions had funded the KMT opposition to Japan's occupation. Chiang now turned those weapons on the Communists. But the Communist message to China's millions excoriating the corruption and poverty under Chiang was too powerful. In 1949, the KMT government fled to Taiwan. U.S. and European sanctions against doing business with China isolated the otherwise triumphant Communist government. China's tycoons fled and reestablished their businesses in Hong Kong, Taiwan, the United States, Europe, and Southeast Asia.

While Mao and his compatriots had obtained funds and equipment from the Soviet Union to fight their battle against the KMT, Mao had always been wary of Stalin. He had no desire to become a Soviet satellite like Eastern Europe. He thwarted a Soviet attempt for joint control of China's military but did sign a mutual defense treaty. China needed money and technical assistance to build its industrial base and the Soviet Union was the only place to turn. With the February 1950 Treaty of Friendship, Alliance, and Mutual Assistance, Mao signed onto the Soviet industrial model, getting $430 million in Soviet loans, ten thousand Soviet technical experts, and various forms of assistance to rearm and reorganize the People's Liberation Army (PLA). By the time that China was ready to talk business again with the West two decades later, the country's economy was flat on its back. The rapid Soviet-backed industrialization of China for most of the 1950s dissolved into the political madness of the Great Leap Forward in 1958 and the decade-long Cultural Revolution that began in 1966. In preserving his own political position, Mao destroyed the country's economy and tore apart the fabric of Chinese society.

The Door Opens Again

War, peace, and a presidential election rekindled relations between the United States and China in December 1970. President Richard Nixon secretly signaled Beijing that he wanted to open serious talks with China. Nixon wanted the Chinese to influence North Vietnam to cooperate in a dignified U.S. exit from South Vietnam. He also wanted a cooperative alliance with China to entice the Soviet Union into détente with the United States. Prominent Democrats, including Hubert Humphrey and Edward Kennedy, were becoming increasingly vocal about opening trade and political relations with China and giving up the fiction that the KMT government on Taiwan was the government of all of China. Nixon's offer to talk met a willing reception. China faced forty-five hostile Russian army divisions along the 4,800-mile border with Russia. Brutal skirmishes in the spring and summer of 1969 between Chinese and Russian troops had left China feeling vulnerable. The country was in dire need of investment capital, technology, know-how, and overseas markets to rebuild its shattered economy.

As the two sides exchanged notes aimed at bringing Nixon to China, Zhou Enlai demonstrated that China hadn't lost its knack for playing one barbarian off against another. He sent a message that China might invite the three Democrats then lining up to challenge Nixon—Senators Kennedy, Muskie, and McGovern—to visit China, as well. Aghast, National Security Adviser Henry Kissinger cautioned that no other American "political visitors" should be allowed into China before Nixon. Nixon's arrival and well-staged excursions in Beijing, Shanghai, and Hangzhou were broadcast around the world in what amounted to a huge campaign commercial. The resulting Shanghai communiqué provided for the United States to recognize that Taiwan was part of China and indicated that the United States wanted a peaceful settlement of the issue "by the Chinese themselves." Nixon vowed to progressively reduce the eight thousand-person American military contingent on Taiwan and establish channels for Sino-U.S. cultural exchanges and business development. Nixon's resignation because of the Watergate scandal and internal politics on both sides delayed formal diplomatic recognition until 1979. Then Deng toured and charmed America, opening the way for a decade-long honeymoon between the United States and China. U.S. recognition not only sent a flood of U.S. businesses into China, it also made Europe and Japan more comfortable and aggressive in pursuing China trade and investment. New York bankers and German engineers found themselves sleeping on cots in the hallways of the overcrowded Beijing Hotel. The Chinese established a special Negotiations Building in Beijing with a warren of rooms to which they would invite foreign companies competing for government investment and purchasing contracts. Chinese negotiators would move back and forth among supplicants, extracting more and more concessions. In the end, many foreign companies struck money-losing deals as their entry fee into the China market. Later, when new deals were offered, many of these pioneering firms weren't even invited to bid. Foreign businessmen spent much of their time "walling and ducking," a term for the inevitable excursions to the Great Wall and the seemingly endless Beijing duck banquets that gave English-speaking Chinese a chance to pump the foreigners for information about their businesses and sniff out divisions among the foreign negotiators.

An Unstoppable Power

The flood of business into China was spurred by the creation of an updated version of the "treaty ports." The new bases for foreign business—special economic zones—offered tax breaks and simplified permit and licensing regulations. But this time the "unequal treaties" were purposely and proudly all on the Chinese side. Just how unequal soon became apparent. The foreign companies wanted to establish factories in China to tap into that immense market. But China wanted investment that would then be turned toward export production to earn foreign exchange for China and provide jobs for Chinese. Deng wanted to follow the examples of Taiwan, Singapore, Hong Kong, and the other Asian Tigers that had built prosperity on export-driven economies. The special economic zones would serve as study centers for Chinese companies to learn from the foreigners so that they could supply China's industrial needs and create the country's own brands and consumer products.

The members of the foreign business community soon began to complain to their governments about ignored contracts and blocked access to Chinese markets. American businesses especially found the U.S. government was far more interested in the strategic relationship created by the American presence in China than business concerns. When Reagan's new secretary of state George Shultz visited Beijing in February 1983, he was showered with complaints from American business executives. One irate businessman pointed out that the governments of Japan and Europe were much more responsive to the needs of their businesses in China than was the American government.

"Why don't you move to Japan or Western Europe?" Shultz snapped.

Then came June 4, 1989, and the Tiananmen Square Massacre, followed by a brutal crackdown on the Chinese citizenry. Executives and employees of foreign companies jammed flights out of China, fleeing the danger and disorder. The few passengers on incoming flights were overseas Chinese business executives from Taiwan, Hong Kong, and Southeast Asia. They, too, were outraged, but they also sensed an opportunity. They figured that the Communist party would soon have things under control and would be offering good deals, since China desperately needed a few friends. A few Western companies took the same approach. Motorola got permission for a wholly owned telecom equipment facility in Tianjin, just southeast of Beijing.

Other foreigners soon returned, spurred by the relatively gentle treatment China received at the hands of President George H. W. Bush. Bush had run the U.S.-China liaison office in 1974–75, and he now ran China policy out of the Oval Office. While he froze the U.S. military relationship with China and imposed some economic sanctions on all weapons and many technology products, his priority was to keep the relationship with China stable. Bush believed it was delusional to try to "contain" China. China was an unstoppable growing power that needed to be befriended and steered in the right direction. His focus was to keep the governments talking and to promote increased business ties.

Congress, however, wasn't nearly as inclined to let Tiananmen slide by. China's most favored nation (MFN) status required annual congressional renewal. Thus the June deadline for renewal became an annual China frustration festival involving intense lobbying by the U.S. business community to fend off legislative maneuvers to try to kill MFN or add conditions. Presidential aspirant Bill Clinton was squarely in the camp of legislators who wanted to punish

China. During his winning campaign he berated Bush for "coddling dictators" in Beijing. The former Arkansas governor came into office with a domestic focus and a constituency of labor and human rights groups that wanted to use U.S. clout to force political and legal changes in China.

Clinton's "foreign policy" toward China consisted of a mish-mash of demands gathered from various U.S. advocacy groups. Bush had successfully deflected legislation that would have imposed conditions on China's MFN renewal, but Clinton, pressed by advocacy groups, signed an executive order that gave the Chinese leadership one year to improve its human rights policies or face losing MFN status.

Suddenly China's leaders saw history repeating itself. Once again the diplomats and merchants had opened the way for the missionaries, those who wanted to change the core of China's system, who wanted to remove the "essence" of China. Yet had Clinton looked more closely at what was actually happening in China, his attitude may have been different. The international furor that Tiananmen created had stunned President Jiang Zemin and Premier Li Peng. They seemed shell-shocked, uncertain what to do next. Then retired Paramount Leader Deng in 1992 took his family on a southern tour to Shenzhen on the Hong Kong border. He gave speeches and told officials that China's only way forward was economic reform and fast growth.

Deng's southern tour and proclamations triggered the fastest and most ferocious gold rush that China had ever seen. In 1993, China signed nearly eighty-five thousand contracts with foreign investors representing $111 billion in investment. The chief executives of hundreds of the world's largest companies rushed to Beijing, Shanghai, and Hong Kong. The Hong Kong property tycoons awoke from their slumber and began scribbling blueprints for billions of investment in Mainland China hotels, office buildings, shopping centers, and Western-style luxury suburban estates.

When Secretary of State Warren Christopher went to Beijing in

March 1994 to determine if China had made "overall, significant progress" on the issues in Clinton's executive order, Chinese authorities greeted him by arresting more than a dozen Chinese dissidents. Premier Li Peng, who loved to snarl and swagger when meeting with American officials, taunted Christopher with reports from the Chinese embassy in Washington that said Congress and the U.S. business community would prevent Clinton from canceling China's MFN. "China will never accept America's concept of human rights," Li said.

Christopher got another blunt warning about threatening China's MFN status at a Beijing breakfast meeting with the American Chamber of Commerce in China. The executives told him that the United States was essentially holding a gun to its own head. If China's MFN status were revoked, U.S. duties for Chinese products would soar, pricing Chinese exports out of the U.S. market. China's economic clout, the business executives warned, was now sufficient that the retaliation against U.S. businesses in China could threaten the global competitiveness of many. AT&T couldn't be blocked from a market that was building the equivalent of one Bell South system each year and GM couldn't hand Volkswagen and Toyota a market of a billion people that was just beginning to own cars. If the administration wanted to improve human rights in China, they said, let Chinese students flood into U.S. universities and allow U.S. business to penetrate deep into China's business and social culture.

Christopher realized that China's position in global commerce had shifted dramatically in the decade since Shultz had told the American businessmen in Beijing to move to Europe or Japan if they didn't like U.S. policy. Less than three months after Christopher's visit, Clinton executed an abrupt about-face and canceled the linkage between MFN and human rights. "We have reached the end of the usefulness of that policy, and it is time to take a new path," he said.

Pushing for Change

With business booming, China had applied in July 1986 to join the General Agreement on Tariffs and Trade, or GATT, which later became the World Trade Organization. The United States and other nations that traded extensively with China badly wanted to integrate China into global commercial law and regulation. Foreign businesses continually found access to China blocked by Chinese bureaucrats citing *neibu* ("internal") regulations that the foreigners weren't allowed to see. At the same time, Chinese companies were becoming increasingly bold in stealing foreign intellectual property and churning out fake, foreign, brand-name products. It was becoming common for a foreign company to send a prototype to a Chinese factory for production only to find that the Chinese company had registered the Chinese product patent and design rights for itself.

By early 1989, a basic GATT accession agreement for China was nearing completion. Since China's economy was still very undeveloped by world standards, China was set to enter GATT on the cheap, without having to open its markets widely or offer stringent protections for intellectual property rights (IPR). The Tiananmen Square massacre torpedoed that effort, but by 1991 the U.S. and Chinese negotiators were back at the table talking about opening China's markets and protecting intellectual property. The negotiations marked a turning point for China. For the first time Chinese officials seemed to realize that to do business with the rest of the world, they would have to reform their own commercial system and open their markets to foreigners. But the real power of the Chinese economy still was in the hands of the industrial ministries and state trading companies, which opposed making concessions to the United States or other trading nations. The talks genuinely rekindled memories of gunboat diplomacy and the treaty ports. Everything was viewed as political rather than commercial. To make matters worse in the eyes of Chinese bureaucrats, the United States began to employ serious threats using Section 301 of a 1974 trade law, under which the United States could impose trade sanctions against countries treating U.S. goods unfairly.

Chinese negotiators were in a bind. Entrenched bureaucrats had no desire to relinquish their power to please foreigners, but the negotiators also knew that China's economic growth was critically dependent on the one-third of Chinese exports that the United States purchased each year. Ultimately, it came down to personal power. Chinese negotiators were only able to beat back tremendous resistance from powerful ministries and state enterprises because Premier Li Peng actively pushed for the agreements. Premier Li, the belligerent face of the government during the Tiananmen Massacre, was widely despised both inside and outside of China. Many in the West considered him little more than a conservative troglodyte. They did not realize that Li played a vital role in pushing the agreement, motivated by a deep desire to be seen by history as a reformer.

The U.S. threat of sanctions, coupled with Li Peng's power, won the day. In 1992, China signed market access and intellectual property protection agreements. For conservative Chinese officials who lived by the mantra of keeping foreigners out of China's internal affairs, these new agreements were very frightening. Under its Soviet-inspired command economy, China had no need for commercial law. Central planners decided the allocation of raw materials and the volume and variety of products that factories would produce. The new agreements with the United States required China to enact new laws and build legal enforcement structures. China had five years to eliminate all the tariffs, quotas, import controls, and standards it had been using to block imports. All trade and commercial laws would be published openly. China would create a copyright law and would meet specific deadlines to join international agreements and organizations governing intellectual property protection. A timetable would be established for China's legislature to modify the country's laws to be compatible with these international conventions.

The "Win-Win" Iron Lady

That China signed open market and intellectual property agreements with the United States in 1992 was a step forward, but getting the Chinese to live up to the letter of their agreements was another matter. Charlene Barshefsky, a tough-talking lawyer, was just the person for the job. When U.S. Trade Representative Mickey Kantor was interviewing her for a post as a deputy in his department, she confided to him her ambitious goal: "I want to get China and Russia into the GATT."

Barshefsky knew China wasn't living up to the 1992 agreements. Chinese entrepreneurs were blatantly copying American software, movies, and music and making counterfeit U.S.-branded consumer products. Increasingly the illegal products were entering world commerce, threatening to undermine U.S. business support for China. In 1995, Barshefsky threatened to file a Section 301 action against China that would cost it $1 billion for failing to live up to its 1992 promises. At first, the Chinese resisted, threatening countersanctions and canceling several large pending U.S. contracts. But under continuing pressure, they agreed in February 1995 to an "action plan" that focused on specific intellectual property rules and their enforcement by specific dates. When China failed to reach important milestones in that agreement, Barshefsky in May 1996 applied more muscle. She asked the American movie, software, and music industries for specific names and locations of factories that were churning out illegal compact discs. She demanded China close the CD factories.

As a result of its 1992 agreement, China had set in place at the national level means of enforcing intellectual property rights. But now officials complained to Barshefsky that they had difficulties controlling what happened in the provinces, where local officials often were involved in factories producing illegal merchandise.

Okay, Barshefsky decided, if the problem is in the provinces, I'll take my case there. She set out for Guangdong province, adjacent to Hong Kong, where the military and local officials were involved in many of the CD factories. Barshefsky threatened sanctions on China's textile exports, by far the nation's largest export industry, if the CD factories weren't closed. She gave Guangdong officials a choice: "If the [CD] factories are not closed, your textile industry will bear the burden. Period."

Savvy lawyer that she is, she also refused to be lured into the theatrics of a high-level meeting. Like the emperors who came before them, top Communist party leaders want foreigners to feel grateful when they are granted an audience. Even Mao kept Nixon on tenterhooks, giving only one-hour notice before their meeting in 1972. As Barshefsky pressed the case against the offending CD factories, President Jiang Zemin invited her to meet with him. Barshefsky refused, shocking both the Chinese and her U.S. colleagues. Her crafty refusal put even more pressure on Chinese negotiators. She told Chinese officials that she didn't want to embarrass Jiang. If she met with him and then went ahead to impose sanctions on Chinese textiles, Jiang would lose face. Shortly after she spurned Jiang's invitation, the CD factories were closed.

Despite that success, Barshefsky decided that threatening China to force change wasn't a winning formula. Instead, she figured the only way forward would be to convince Chinese decision makers that Chinese reforms constituted a "win-win" situation for both sides. The prevailing mentality in China is that of the "zero-sum" game. China is all about "I live, you die," "you win, I lose," a vicious cycle of conquest and revenge. But Barshefsky convinced China that if it didn't institute laws and structures protecting intellectual property, then Chinese companies would be hampered in their own development of software, entertainment, and technology products. The result was a stronger structure for intellectual property protection, although enforcement won't be effective until China's own industries have built sufficient intellectual property to be worth protecting.

Barshefsky was struck during the intellectual property negotiations by how incompatible China's economy was with WTO rules.

She had the USTR office construct a detailed "roadmap" for China, showing how to transform its system to meet WTO standards. She marketed her road map to senior officials as another part of her "win-win" strategy, explaining how the changes would make China a global competitor and not just throw open the country's doors to foreign companies and products. Among the Chinese who bought wholeheartedly into the "win-win" principle was China's chief trade negotiator, Long Yongtu. Long, a graduate of the London School of Economics, was one of the emerging generation of Chinese officials who understood how the world worked.

The Endgame

The beginning of the end of China's long trade travails happened in April 1999 when Chinese Premier Zhu Rongji arrived at the White House carrying with him a deal that he had negotiated with Barshefsky. Zhu was confident that the agreement would pave the way for China to become a member of the World Trade Organization. Yet he was uneasy. The agreement would open China's agriculture, banking, telecommunications, and retail industries to a greater degree than the United States had been able to wrest from Japan, its biggest trading partner. The U.S. Congress and business community would love that. But the concessions he was going to make would infuriate his opponents in China, who knew little or nothing of the details when Zhu left Beijing for Washington. He needed to sign the deal now, before his opponents at home could rally support against it. He was gratified that on the day of his arrival President Bill Clinton signaled in a speech that if China were willing to play by WTO rules, "it would be an inexplicable mistake for the United States to say no."

When Clinton invited Zhu to the White House residence that evening for an informal discussion before the final negotiations were to begin, Zhu assumed that for all practical purposes he and Clinton would seal the deal in this intimate setting. He hadn't reck-

oned with the crisis atmosphere that hung over the Clinton administration. It had been only two months since the U.S. Senate had
rejected the embarrassing House-approved articles of impeachment
against the president. A congressional committee had just completed its severely flawed but politically charged report declaring
that China was systematically stealing American nuclear and military technology. Indictments were being prepared against Chinese-
American hustlers who raised money for the Clinton campaign
from donors alleged to be connected to the Chinese government.
Treasury Secretary Robert Rubin had warned Clinton that the U.S.
financial industry wasn't wholly satisfied with the China WTO deal
and Gene Sperling, Clinton's top domestic economic adviser, was
urging the president to delay because of strong opposition in Congress and from organized labor. The last thing Clinton needed now
was another fight with Congress, especially over China. To make
matters worse, Barshefsky hadn't had the opportunity to explain to
Clinton about Zhu's difficult political position in China.

Clinton greeted Zhu warmly, putting his arm around the Chinese
premier, whose blunt style, fluent English, and self-deprecating sense
of humor had made him a favorite of foreign leaders. Clinton leveled
with Zhu. We have two options, he told him. If Zhu really needed a
deal, they could do one right now. But then he said, "Let me tell you
about the politics on our side and then you decide how to handle
this." Clinton explained that he was worried that the poisonous
atmosphere in the Republican Congress could kill the agreement
amid charges that Clinton had given away the store to the Chinese.
Perhaps, he said, the two could announce they had made significant
progress tonight and finish the deal later in Beijing.

"You have to let me know," Clinton told Zhu. "Do you really
need a deal now?"

Zhu was both flustered and flattered by Clinton's physical famil-
iarity, but he knew what his answer had to be. The premier of the
great country of China, the upright official who was building a
commercial system using many aspects of the American system as a
model, a man steeled by years of Communist party discipline, could

not tell an American president that he needed a political favor. Zhu looked at Clinton and said: "We will take option two."

Clinton left the meeting relieved that he could avoid another immediate fight with Congress, and gratified that he and Zhu could be so honest and straightforward with each other. Zhu walked away angry and worried. Clinton was smart; how could he walk away from a deal that would have given the United States unprecedented access to Chinese markets? He must not be in touch with his constituents.

Trying Again

Then hell broke loose. To drum up support for the agreement from the U.S. business community, as well as to prevent China from backtracking on what had already been agreed to, the details of the agreement were posted on the Internet. When Beijing's industrial bureaucrats saw the posting, they were apoplectic. Chinese officials accompanying Zhu spent a sleepless night answering furious telephone calls from Beijing.

When the U.S. business community saw the details of the proposed agreement, they, too, went berserk. They had never expected such broad concessions and somehow Clinton had let the deal slip away. American CEOs lit up the switchboards in Congress and the White House. Realizing how badly he had screwed up, Clinton ordered his assistants to track down Zhu by phone as he toured America. When the American president finally got through to Zhu at the Waldorf-Astoria Hotel in New York, he told the premier that they could still strike a deal before he left North America. Zhu declined. Negotiations could resume in Beijing when China was ready.

Getting negotiations started again wasn't easy. When Zhu and Long returned to Beijing, Communist party conservatives accused them of selling out China's interests. On May 7th, exactly one month after Clinton rejected Zhu's deal, the situation worsened when U.S. jets bombed the Chinese embassy in Belgrade. The

United States called it a tragic mistake, the result of an outdated map, but nobody in China believed that. U.S.-China relations hit their lowest point since the Tiananmen Massacre.

Leaders of both countries still wanted the WTO deal. Both Clinton and Jiang Zemin saw China's entrance into the WTO as a legacy issue for their leadership. Zhu and Clinton had learned a lesson from the April debacle. Zhu knew he needed to drum up support for the WTO agreement among those who would benefit in China: the Chinese business community and local officials who constantly had their economic initiatives knocked down by Beijing bureaucrats. Zhu dispatched his former trade minister, Wu Yi, to travel around the country explaining to local officials the "win-win" of the WTO deal. After talking by phone to Clinton and meeting the president's emissaries in person, Jiang Zemin made a political decision to reopen negotiations to begin healing the deep political rift between the United States and China.

Barshefsky returned to Beijing in November, prepared to strike a deal. She argued loudly and long with Zhu over myriad details, often to the embarrassment of her USTR officials who thought perhaps the premier should be shown a little more deference. Zhu pushed to discover the U.S. bottom line. Barshefsky told him in no uncertain terms that it was the failed agreement that had been published on the Internet. After an initial round of talks with Zhu, Barshefsky found herself across the table from Trade Minister Shi Guangsheng, a sixty-year-old risk-averse Jiang Zemin loyalist who wasn't familiar with the details in the WTO agreement. Unbeknownst to Barshefsky, he served as little more than a mailbox for the leadership, taking messages from the negotiations back to the National Economic Work Conference, the annual meeting at which government officials reviewed the past year and set goals for the next. Zhu had shrewdly organized the confab to coincide with the WTO talks so that the entire Communist party hierarchy could be hectored and cajoled by Zhu and Jiang to support an agreement with the United States that would pave the way for WTO membership. Shi spent a lot of time telling old stories and wasting time.

Long Yongtu, seated next to Shi, would frequently look at the ceiling and roll his eyes in boredom.

Barshefsky's patience ran out on November 14. She announced that she was leaving for Washington the next morning; she had booked her flight. The announcement set off a busy night. Long Yongtu knew that China had a historic deal in its hands, so he committed a grievous political sin: He went over the head of his boss and called Zhu Rongji at home in the middle of the night. Long acted because he feared that Shi was scuttling the deal by reporting only the atmospherics of the talks, not the details, which he clearly didn't understand. Long bet that Zhu believed the talks were much less successful than was the case. He also was worried if they didn't come to agreement now, the pending U.S. election could set back any agreement for years.

Fortunately for Long, Zhu understood and appreciated what Long told him. Zhu ordered Long to reopen discussions immediately and said he himself would become involved. At about 3:00 A.M., Chinese negotiators called U.S. negotiator Bob Cassidy at his hotel and asked him to bring his team to the foreign trade ministry at 5:00 A.M. for more discussions. Cassidy called Barshefsky at 6:30 A.M. and said that it looked like China wanted a deal. Barshefsky came over and resumed discussions with Shi, although she was fully prepared to leave if there wasn't immediate progress. Her bags already had been sent to the airport.

While Barshefsky and Shi were talking, Zhu Rongji caused a huge stir at the National Economic Work Conference when he rose and walked out just as Jiang Zemin was beginning his keynote speech. The audience immediately began whispering among themselves. Was Zhu walking out to show his disapproval? Were the two leaders at odds? The truth was that Zhu was leaving the conference to meet with Barshefsky to settle the final deal. He had just obtained approval from the party's central standing committee to do the deed. Most remarkable was that Zhu was willing to cede protocol and travel to the foreign trade ministry rather than summon the negotiators to his own reception hall.

Barshefsky was on the verge of heading for the airport when Zhu arrived. He wasted little time with small talk. With a sheaf of typed and handwritten notes in front of him, Zhu plowed through the sticking points of the talks. I will give you this, you give me that. I will give one here, you give one there. The master was at work. Everybody else in the room was a spectator. Zhu had complete command of the brief. He knew exactly where his political limits were. A few hours later Barshefsky thought she had the best deal she could get. She took her lieutenants with her to the only private room she could find, the women's restroom, so they could call Clinton for the final approval. Her dialogue with Clinton, who was aboard Air Force One, was interrupted when a toilet flushed and a shocked female Australian journalist emerged from a stall.

In the end, the agreement mollified two of the biggest critics in the Chinese government, telecom and insurance officials. From the April pacts, China now would allow foreigners to own only 49 percent instead of 50 percent of insurance companies, and foreign ownership of telecom value-added services was reduced to 50 percent from 51 percent. In exchange, Zhu sped up the timetable to open various cities for these businesses. Otherwise, it was the same basic agreement that had been offered in April: There were significant openings in telecom, insurance, banking, professional services, the right of foreigners to directly import, export, and distribute products and quotas for farm product imports. After Zhu and Barshefsky reached agreement, their underlings huddled to fix the final language for an afternoon press conference. When foreign ministry officials showed up and tried to insert a boilerplate about Taiwan, the trade ministry officials, their position now endorsed by China's leaders, tossed the foreign ministry minions out of the room. That afternoon Jiang Zemin met with Barshefsky in front of the TV cameras to praise the agreement as a milestone for China's integration into the world of international business. They met in an imperial audience hall overlooking the island pavilion where the Guangxu Emperor had been imprisoned in 1898 after attempting Western-style reforms.

After negotiations with the European Union and others that improved on some of the U.S. terms, China joined the WTO on December 11, 2001—some 208 years after Lord Macartney opened the negotiations. Zhu Rongji retired in 2003, after more than a decade of driving reforms of state industry, legitimatizing private business, building stock markets, reorganizing Chinese banks, and building a regulatory system modeled on the U.S. Federal Reserve. As he left office, China had $400 billion in foreign exchange reserves, $850 billion in annual foreign trade, and foreign investment averaging about $150 million per day. China's general tariff levels fell to 10.4 percent from 42.7 percent. Through the WTO and other trade negotiations during Zhu's term as premier, China also established for the first time a system of interministry consultation. Zhu had learned his lesson in Washington. China's top-down command system was changing when it came to business and economics. Leaders would now have to seek consensus and ministries would now have to consult with each other, draft laws would be circulated and sometimes made public to solicit opinions, and the attitude and concerns of the Chinese business community would have an increasing voice in government policy making.

What This Means for You

The two hundred years of interaction that have humiliated, infuriated, and ultimately brought China into the world community were almost entirely government-to-government negotiations. Business was often a pawn, sometimes a driver of the negotiations, but always a hostage to the strategic realities of relations with China. Nevertheless, there are valuable business lessons to be learned from the two centuries of negotiations. To a great extent, both the Chinese businessperson and the bureaucrats who can make his or her life miserable share the same prejudices, fears, and misconceptions that have been created by China's experiences at the hands of foreigners.

Within China today much has changed, while much remains the

same. What has changed most is China's position in the world. When Macartney arrived, China was beginning to stagnate. It was an inward-facing, feudal society that had failed to understand and keep pace with global technological and economic changes. Today, China is a thriving economic powerhouse with nuclear weapons and its own space program, destined to become one of the most powerful nations the world has ever seen. But the country is still struggling with the dilemma it faced in the last days of imperial rule when foreign traders began forcing their way into China: how to adopt and adapt to the ways of the West and global commerce while maintaining the Chinese "essence."

What can you as an executive trying to do business with China take away from the history of China's encounters with the West? I'll explain my observations of what it means to you by looking at two central ideas: the context in which negotiations take place, and some of the techniques that the Chinese employ.

The negotiating environment, whether government or business, is all about China's perception of itself and foreigners. The humiliations visited on the Chinese are fresh in their memory, but so is the superiority complex that preceded the foreigners. Thus you will find yourself facing the yin and yang of Chinese suspicion and arrogance. Chinese expect to be treated differently. They want you to show deference, to recognize them as important and powerful players on the world scene. But they won't hesitate to try to make you feel guilty for the past two hundred years if it can give them an advantage in negotiations. Not all Chinese are consumed by this history, but I have yet to meet a Chinese person who is not extremely thin-skinned if even a hint is given that you aren't treating them as your equal or, for many, as your superior.

While proud of their ancient culture, the Chinese will pander their poverty. They love to convince you that you owe them something. They are poor, you are rich, and their poverty is your fault. They want you to help remedy this inequity with a gift, usually knowledge. The larger and more successful your company, the more they want to be given. The American WTO negotiators had a running joke that each of their negotiations opened with an "it's-all-your-fault" preamble about how foreign intervention had made China poor. This was regularly followed by a regular "you-don't-understand-China" refrain when negotiators wanted to reject U.S. proposals.

The Chinese are adept and subtle readers of foreign attitudes. The issue of basic respect is extremely important. It is okay to be tough and steadfast, but disastrous to be insulting.

Humor can lighten up stressful times in negotiations. The Chinese have a very good sense of humor, especially if you are poking fun at yourself, not them. But notions of equality, mutual benefit, and respect are one-sided in China. You are expected to be very sensitive to Chinese feelings, but don't expect the same in return. You are, after all, a barbarian on their turf.

A natural outgrowth of this is that Chinese have no problem pushing lopsided proposals and engaging in angry theatrics. The Chinese have a "no blush" gene when it comes to negotiations. No matter how egregious the demand, the Chinese can say it with a straight face. They will ask you for anything because you just may be stupid enough to agree to it. Many do. Western attorneys in China make a good living unraveling these contracts.

Chinese negotiators are masters at pushing the impression that you need them far more than they need you. It's all about gaining the psychological upper hand. Many foreign businesspeople who negotiate in China bring along too much goodwill and trust. Chinese negotiators have no qualms about exploiting that by outright lying. That ability is a tremendous advantage for them. For the Chinese, outcomes are more important than truth. That's why Li Hongzhang could promise not to kill the Taiping revolutionaries, then turn right around and have them beheaded. You may be told that some obscure regulation prohibits your counterpart from granting you something when no such regulation exists. That is why the devil will always be in the details. You will need expertise to verify virtually everything your Chinese counterpart tells you.

It is almost to the status of Olympic sport in China to seek advantage by pitting foreigners against each other. The tactics employed in Beijing's Negotiating Building in the early days of modern commerce still endure in government and private deals. On multibillion-dollar infrastructure projects, such as the Three Gorges Dam, Siemens, GE, Mitsubishi, and other giants were expertly pitted against one another, with contracts going to not only the companies with the best price and product, but to those who transferred the most technology and financed the deal themselves. Even so, when subsequent rounds of bidding occurred, it wasn't unusual for the company that secured the first contracts to not even be invited to participate.

How do you deal with this? One way is to adopt Barshefsky's notion of a roadmap. She assuaged the insecurities of Chinese trade negotiators, and provided them with arguments to work through their system, by providing a roadmap that framed China's WTO obligations in terms of a "win-win" for China. This helped inoculate Chinese proponents of WTO against critics who would predictably accuse them of selling out their country to foreign interests. Lay out for your Chinese counterpart a step-by-step technology transfer and domestic manufacturing plan that provides what China is seeking but keeps you in the game for the long term. If that isn't possible, make your money on the first deal and move on.

Many foreign executives set themselves up for China's divide-and-conquer tactics. Company CEOs love to come charging into China insisting on meeting with the country's top leaders, or at least the senior ministers responsible for their industry. They go into these meetings with little more than vague ideas and a determination to do business in China. The Chinese love these people. In many cases, the foreign CEOs will end meetings with an unfocused commitment to some sort of business deal. They then fly home, leaving their underlings to fill out the details. The Chinese know the boss wants the deal, so they squeeze the underlings for very favorable terms. If they don't get concessions, they might send messages to your headquarters complaining that your man on the ground in China doesn't understand China and is getting in the way of a good deal. The better approach is for the chief executive officer or other senior negotiator from your company to wait until the negotiations are almost over, then come in to seal the deal. If they insist on coming in the exploratory stage, make sure they ask questions and then shut up, listen and, above all, don't say a word that might even vaguely be construed as a commitment.

If you aren't careful, your CEO may become accepted as a "friend" of China. That is both good and bad. China categorizes foreigners as "friends" or "unfriendly." If your CEO is considered a "friend" of China, you will certainly have better access to officials and they will speak more frankly with you. As a "friend," you will be considered an enlightened foreigner who understands the complexities of China. But friendship in China carries heavy obligations. In China, it is considered almost immoral to turn down the request of a true friend. George H. W. Bush became a "friend" of China when he ran the U.S.-China liaison office in 1974 and 1975. When he became president the Chinese leadership called on his friendship obligation to help them emerge from the international condemnation that resulted from the Tiananmen Massacre, and Bush obliged.

If you don't give them what they want, the Chinese will quickly label you "unfriendly" to China. Your goal is to be friendly but not foolish. Don't be afraid to tell your Chinese counterparts that this is business, not friendship, but that you can do friendly business if both sides get a fair deal.

Just below the omnipotent exterior often projected by Chinese bureaucrats and businesspeople, there often lies a reservoir of insecurity and fear of making mistakes that results from a social system ruled by shame. Chinese politics and the country's commercial system are brutal and Chinese negotiators go to great lengths to protect themselves from criticism that could result in their dismissal or disgrace. Government officials especially try to avoid making decisions for which they can later be held accountable. Thus they like to diffuse decision making through many layers so that no one person can be blamed. In negotiations, this Chinese preoccupation with "face" can be crippling for them. Foreigners who are not fixated with "face" have a tremendous advantage. If the talks meet an impasse caused by the Chinese side, it is easy for the foreigner to accept blame and move discussions ahead. You also lose nothing by treating even the most obnoxious Chinese negotiator with exaggerated respect. Treat them with the inflated importance they expect, but look out for your own bottom line. Engage in the theatrics, but don't let it slide over into substance.

Barshefsky's "win-win" formula, while still rare, is living on beyond the WTO talks. Chinese WTO negotiator Long Yongtu became secretary general of the Boao Forum for Asia, an annual conference organized by the Chinese government that is modeled on the World Economic Forum. He gives speeches throughout Asia advising governments that they shouldn't look at trade negotiations as giving things away, but rather as gaining access to trading and business systems that will bring prosperity. His motto for the Boao Forum: "Asians Seeking a Win-Win."

After slogging through so much history, it is only prudent to question how much of this stuff is relevant today, and how much will remain relevant tomorrow.

I have asked this question of many friends who are veteran China business hands. Their general consensus answer is that negotiating your way through the China business landscape is increasingly similar to the rest of the world, but core Chinese business behaviors and ways of thinking are encoded by history and culture, almost into the genes. It is those elements that I have focused on in this chapter.

Foreigners are now mostly comfortably accepted as residents in China, and foreign business has become part of the fabric of daily life. Chinese businesspeople can be globe-trotters who carry MBAs and PhDs from the world's best universities. Products from Chinese factories fill the world's retail stores, and the Chinese consumer market is the most competitive in the world.

The country is a shifting plate of sand. When it comes to negotiating business deals, you will find government entities more steeped in cultural proclivities than today's more practical private entrepreneurs. Nonetheless, that Chinese Wharton-grad MBA seeking a software partnership with your company will be as wily as Zhou Enlai was in pitting foreign competitors against one another. The state-industry boss with a multibillion-dollar state-of-the-art manufacturing juggernaut will stretch the truth to obtain a desired outcome, just as much as Li Hongzhang did with the Taiping rebels.

One thing that hasn't changed at all is Chinese sensibilities. If you are shrewd, you can even use this to your advantage. Charlene Barshefsky got it right. She showed proper respect and deference to the Chinese, but she didn't get caught up in the shtick. She went toe-to-toe with Zhu Rongji in negotiations, but he respected her because she knew her stuff and she constantly demonstrated that what she was doing was good for China.

Finally, corporate executives should learn from Clinton's mistake. In tying China's MFN renewal to human rights issues, he cobbled together what he needed at home politically and then applied it to China. The result was a disaster. Many corporations make a similar mistake. They look at their company's internal needs and then apply that to their Chinese plans. That is only step one. Just as a foreign businessperson needs to understand the thinking and motivations of their Chinese counterparts, a company must understand what China as a country needs and wants. Only by blending that into your business model will you be successful.

There's more than a little history behind this.

The Little Red Book of Business

- Fatigue, food, and drink are negotiating tools. If your Chinese counterpart wants to finalize a deal after a *mao-tai*-soaked banquet, it is better to throw up on the contract than sign it.

- The Chinese government uses competition from foreign businesses to reform its own system and companies.

- To be truly powerful in China is to be able to avoid responsibility for your decisions.

- The Chinese now understand the outside world much better than the outside world understands them.

- China is seriously schizophrenic: It is confident, reasonable, and eager to become a world-class competitor while also paranoid and insecure about the outside world.

- China is modernizing, not Westernizing. The country's goal is to modernize but retain the Chinese "essence," which it is still struggling to define.

- China has lots of slogans but no leading ideology, other than to make itself rich and powerful by relentlessly pursuing international trade and commerce.

- Chinese negotiators are masters of making you feel you need them more than they need you.

- The Chinese often try to extract a payment, in the form of a lopsided deal, for the opportunity to do business in China.

- The Chinese will ask you for anything because you just may be stupid enough to agree to it. Many are.

- You will never be successful walking into a meeting cold. Know who you are dealing with and what they really want and need.

- The Chinese always need to get concessions from you.

- Don't take what your Chinese counterpart tells you to be the truth. They will often cite regulations or rules or practices that are nonexistent just to put you in a box in working out the deal.

- The Chinese try to play you as being "unfriendly" to China if you don't give them what they need. Don't be afraid to tell them that friendly business is based on a fair deal for all.

- Foreign businesspeople who come to China often have too much goodwill, too much trust, and too little patience.

- Pay attention to political trends and the priorities of the Chinese government so that you can fit your business within those when it works to your advantage.

- Mutual respect and equality are extremely important. It is useful in negotiations to wrap your position in these principles.

- Contracts are not a guarantee of anything. It is the relationship built in negotiating the contract that will give your business some hope.

- Frame your China strategy as a roadmap. This will help keep your own company on track through the inevitable difficulties, and show your Chinese counterparts the value of maintaining a long-term partnership.

- China has a survival culture with a "zero-sum" mentality. For somebody to win, somebody has to lose. The concept of "win-win" is new and not widespread, and will have to be constantly reiterated to be successful.

2

Same Bed, Different Dreams

Avoid joint ventures with Chinese government partners. The clash of civilizations in Morgan Stanley's
joint-venture investment bank shows why and offers
hard-learned lessons on how to cope.

IF ANY TWO PEOPLE could be expected to work together to
create China's first true investment bank it was Jack Wadsworth
and Wang Qishan. Wadsworth had parlayed his uncanny ability to
spot the next big thing into an illustrious career with Morgan Stanley, one of the world's most powerful and prestigious investment
houses. Wang Qishan was the politically adept and influential
adviser to China's top leaders and president of the huge China Construction Bank. Yet here they were in the Construction Bank's
boardroom in Beijing in March 1997, raising their voices, arguing
over who was really in charge of their two-year-old joint venture,
China International Capital Corporation, or CICC.

"We have the expertise," Wadsworth said, his voice steely. "We
have the network. You can't do this without me." He was irritated
that the translator might not convey his determination to Wang.

"Don't give me that American big-power bully attitude," Wang
retorted. "You can do the technology, but for direction and strategy, you should listen to me."

Frustrated, Wadsworth once again stated what he thought

should be obvious: "We're the experts and we know the business."

"So does Goldman Sachs," snapped Wang. "And I have the market."

Overview

Like most marriages, joint ventures, even among companies that share a common language and heritage, have their tensions. When the partners come from vastly different cultures, the tensions can be exacerbated. China has always been mysterious to westerners. The language, the customs, the bizarre shifts in politics can be powerful barriers to feeling comfortable about doing business in China. Yet behind those barriers lies a market of more than one billion people, many of them ambitious and energetic, eager to seize opportunity, to learn, and to get ahead.

It's only logical that many Western businesspeople look for a Chinese partner to help crack that huge market. They figure a joint venture with someone who knows the language and customs, who has contacts and customers, will ease the way. I'll supply the technology or capital or products, they figure, while my Chinese partner maneuvers through the government red tape, acquires factory or office space, advises on marketing and distribution strategies, and engages Chinese suppliers. It will, they assume, be the perfect "win-win" situation for both players.

I've been watching and participating in the development of the Chinese economy and Western efforts to tap into the market for many years and I've followed the course of many joint ventures. Most early attempts to form joint ventures in the 1980s failed. Foreign companies were hooked up with government-assigned partners, and their partnerships almost always fell victim to the leftovers of rigid Communist thinking and the country's lack of modern business practices. The business atmosphere in China changed significantly in the 1990s. China was still ruled by the Communist Party, but party leaders were determined to overcome decades of economic stagnation and to join the world economy, not as some bit player but as a major power. To get where it wanted to go, China imported technology and knowledge through joint ventures. Foreign companies were so eager to get into the Chinese market that they were willing to abide by Chinese government regulations that gave them some leeway in choosing their Chinese partners, but in many industries relegated them to a minority position under Chinese state-owned firms.

Atop China's agenda has been attracting foreign capital and financial know-how. This is the story of how some of the most powerful and influential people in China's nascent finance industry joined forces with one of America's most sophisticated investment firms to provide that much-needed capital and financial industry knowledge. I have been acquainted with Jack Wadsworth and Wang Qishan for years. When I heard that they were behind China's first joint-venture investment bank I pegged it as a certain winner. Within their own cultures, the two men are very much alike: forceful leaders with loyal followers, impatient visionaries who get things done. They would make a great team. I was wrong. This isn't a story of bad people and good people. It is a tale of two business cultures that came together in a clash of civilizations, an all-too-frequent problem for joint ventures in China. The only groups that seem to like joint ventures are the government, and the law firms that rack up endless billable hours putting the ventures together and then taking them apart a few years later.

Today, foreign companies in China avoid joint ventures whenever possible and this story shows why. But in many industries, a joint venture is still the only ticket into China. The story of CICC will show you what Morgan Stanley and China Construction Bank learned the hard way, but it also illustrates the pathways toward making joint ventures a success.

The Next Big Thing

Jack Wadsworth was looking for the next big thing. That was how he had built his stellar career among the smart, aggressive, and competitive bankers at First Boston and then at Morgan Stanley. His entrepreneurial bent enabled Wadsworth to see and take advantage of opportunities before his competitors, both within Morgan Stanley and at other big investment banks. If leveraged buyouts were hot, Jack Wadsworth was there at the head of Morgan Stanley's first LBO fund. When computers and memory chips drew attention, Jack Wadsworth was there at the head of Morgan Stanley's fledgling Silicon Valley venture capital group. And when Japan's stock market took off in the 1980s, Jack Wadsworth was there, representing one of only six foreign investment banks with seats on the Tokyo Stock Exchange.

From his vantage point in Tokyo, Wadsworth thought he saw the next big thing and it was *really* big: China! A government thoroughly worried about China's sagging fortunes had been trying for years to put in place economic reforms that would end decades of stagnation. Given the slightest encouragement, the entrepreneurial Chinese were frantically seizing any opportunity to do business. If they weren't setting up their own business, they were investing in somebody else's. Hundreds of state-owned companies seeking to break free of their bureaucratic masters were issuing shares in an unregulated and informal stock market, and the government was clumsily trying to figure out how to prevent the worst scams. Foreign investment banks accustomed to operating in regulated markets with some semblance of law and order were skeptical but intrigued by China. While others looked, Jack Wadsworth acted. If Morgan Stanley could get in on the ground floor of the immense economic boom that was building in China, it would trump all its competitors. To make Morgan Stanley the leader in China would be a triumphal capstone to Wadsworth's career.

The first step was to get out of Tokyo and go southwest to Hong Kong. In 1991, China's business systems were still primitive. Much of the business between China and the rest of the world was done in Hong Kong. It wasn't hard for Wadsworth to persuade his bosses in New York to let him take over Morgan Stanley's office there. "If

Morgan Stanley doesn't get China right, we will have failed in Asia," he told them.

If Wadsworth said so, then the bosses agreed.

The African Connection

If Jack Wadsworth could see the opportunities in China for investment banking, it was much easier for economically savvy Chinese to see them. To Edwin Lim, China's lack of financial infrastructure was glaringly obvious. From his World Bank office in Beijing in the late 1980s, the tall, stately Lim had exhaustively examined China's economy, suggested economic reforms, and tried to forecast where the country was headed. He knew how primitive and shaky China's finances were. He had also seen how desperate the entrepreneurial Chinese were to lay their hands on capital, to seize any opportunity to make money. In 1990, Lim left China for the World Bank headquarters in Washington, where he went stir-crazy heading the Nigeria desk. As the pace of change in China accelerated, Lim became increasingly impatient to return. Many of the reforms that were being put in place were ones he had recommended. He wanted to be a part of the action. Investment banking, he knew, was the key to China's emergence onto the world scene.

Under cover of a speaking engagement in China in July 1993, Lim paid a visit to an old acquaintance in Beijing. When Lim headed the World Bank's Beijing mission he became a well-known figure among Chinese officials. During the winter his toasty office was a gathering place for even high-level ministers, who would abandon their poorly heated offices and bike over to the World Bank to discuss economics. The Chinese respected Lim because of his knowledge and humble beginnings. His grandfather had migrated from China to the Philippines to work as a coconut plantation coolie, and Lim had earned scholarships that led to a Harvard PhD in economics. Among the visitors to Lim's office had been an economic planner named Zhu Rongji. Zhu, now a vice-premier and China's de facto economic czar, could be helpful.

As Lim was checking into the New World Hotel in Beijing, some-one tapped his shoulder. He turned and found himself facing Payson Cha, his long-ago tennis partner in Lagos, Nigeria. Lagos had been one of Lim's first assignments with the World Bank and he had been delighted to meet a fellow Chinese in such a remote out-post. Cha, the son of a Hong Kong textile tycoon, had been in Nigeria building his family business, Mingly Corporation, into the largest textile producer in Africa. The two men were regular tennis partners at the Ikoyi Club, a British colonial relic, where they would relax on the veranda overlooking lush gardens and talk about events in China and the future of their ancestral homeland.

Now, sipping tea in the hotel's lobby lounge, the two renewed their friendship. Cha had returned to Hong Kong to become a real-estate developer and had created the stunningly successful Discov-ery Bay development, an enclave of California-style homes for ten thousand residents on Lantau Island. Lim confided to Cha that he was going to suggest to Vice-Premier Zhu that China team up with a foreign investment firm to form a joint-venture investment bank to help Chinese companies raise capital.

Cha burst out laughing and began rooting through his briefcase. He pulled out a sheaf of paper. "Here you go," he said, thrusting the package into Lim's hand. "A little slow, aren't you?"

As do many wealthy overseas Chinese, Cha had been looking for a way to help the motherland and had hit on the idea of preparing a report that explained modern finance methods and advocated the establishment of a state investment bank. That was the plan that Lim was holding.

"Why don't you take over this project?" Cha told Lim. "I'm not out for personal glory. I'm too busy."

Lim was astounded. Here on paper was a plan very similar to what he had been thinking about. The report even suggested a joint venture between one of China's big state-owned banks and Britain's venerable Barings Bank, long a recognized player in Asian finance. That was one of the few things Lim changed in the plan. Rather than Barings, a second-tier factor in global finance that later collapsed in scandal, he thought it better to ally with one of the two biggest and most powerful investment banks in the world: Goldman Sachs or Morgan Stanley.

Lim's meeting with Zhu was friendly. It started with discussions about how China's financial sector could be further reformed, a topic that led naturally to Lim's idea of a joint-venture investment bank. Zhu liked it. He had long encouraged joint ventures among Chinese and foreign manufacturers as a way to transfer technology. The same could be true of financial knowledge, Lim told him. The Chinese could use a joint venture as sort of an apprenticeship to learn how sophisticated finance works. Zhu promised his support.

A Meeting of Minds

Jack Wadsworth had thought he understood Asia. In Japan, answers to questions weren't the straightforward "yes" or "no" that Western businesspeople expect. Everything was nuanced and understanding the nuances was the key to dealing with the Japanese. But as Wadsworth flew from his Hong Kong headquarters to Beijing and Shanghai to meet with executives of the various government banks that were emerging from China's reforms, he was shocked. There was no nuance here. Many of the officials clearly had no clue about sophisticated finance. Others were either intimidated by Wadsworth or tried to bully him. More than a few were so smarmily evasive and focused only on their personal gain that Wadsworth felt an urge to take a shower after such meetings. But amid those disappointments Wadsworth kept hearing the same name: Wang Qishan. Wang was reputedly the financial fix-it man for China's leadership and a straight shooter.

Wang Qishan was a forty-four-year-old vice-president of the China Construction Bank, a huge state-owned bank whose main role was funding the development of China's infrastructure. The son of university professors, Wang became part of the Communist Party aristocracy when he married the daughter of Yao Yilin, the vice-premier in charge of finance and economics. In the early 1980s,

Wang was one of a group of young policy advisers known as "the Four Gentlemen," who served as consultants to reformist Premier Zhao Ziyang. Eventually the other three fell by the wayside, the result of impatience or impertinence. But not Wang. He even survived the downfall of Premier Zhao after the 1989 Tiananmen Massacre. He knew when to push for changes, when to lay low, and how to frame step-by-step reforms in terms that made party leaders comfortable. He taught party leaders that capital markets and stocks were tools for getting money from foreigners without giving up control.

In the spring of 1992, Wadsworth drafted a letter to Wang Qishan. In it he outlined his idea for a joint venture between Morgan Stanley and the China Construction Bank. It called for a fifty-fifty partnership that would give Morgan a shot at financing many of the gigantic infrastructure projects that China was undertaking while showing the Chinese how modern financial methods could tap capital from around the globe.

Wang Qishan responded quickly, inviting Wadsworth to meet with him. Wadsworth liked Wang from the outset. He was indeed a straight shooter, willing to talk openly about China's many financial problems and to listen to Wadsworth's ideas about how those problems could be overcome. But before negotiations could become serious, one of those very problems ended the discussions. China's central bank, the People's Bank of China, needed to clean up the country's foreign exchange trading system. Government bankers across the country were playing foreign exchange markets like a casino and losing a bundle. Wang Qishan was called to the central bank to untangle the mess.

Wadsworth was disappointed. If he had done a deal with the China Construction Bank, Morgan Stanley could have generated millions in fees by raising capital for dams, airports, and highways. The firm would also have a ringside seat to watch the development of China's fledgling stock markets and perhaps help underwrite and sell Chinese shares around the world. Certainly with its 24,000 branches, China Construction Bank would have had a nearly endless supply of customers seeking Morgan's help in obtaining financing.

Wadsworth resumed his search for a possible banking partner while continuing to oversee Morgan's Asian business from Hong Kong. It was over dinner with a Hong Kong friend that Wadsworth learned about Edwin Lim's plan for a joint-venture investment bank. Within days Wadsworth was winging his way to Washington to have lunch with Lim. After forty-five minutes of cautious parrying, Wadsworth pulled out the letter he had sent to Wang. Lim himself might have drafted that letter, so close was it to what he had proposed to Zhu. Lim didn't tell Wadsworth that he had already approached Goldman Sachs. Goldman's Hong Kong office feared an alliance between Goldman and a Chinese government bank. Now here was Morgan Stanley coming to him. This time it might work.

Early in 1994 the last piece of the puzzle fell into place. Wang Qishan returned to China Construction Bank, this time as president. He carried a mandate from China's leaders to make a joint-venture investment bank his top priority. Not only would such an undertaking be a bold next step in China's financial reforms, it was necessary to prop up the country's four huge state-owned banks. The banks had long served as the fuel tanks for China's extensive welfare system. The banks were stuffed with the savings of China's thrifty citizens, who on average socked away 40 percent of their income. The banks, in turn, doled out that money in government-directed loans to state enterprises. Many of those loans went to unprofitable enterprises that existed only to provide jobs and paychecks to keep workers off the streets. A Chinese investment bank that could help Chinese state companies gather foreign capital was crucial to China's continued economic growth.

The Rules of the Game

Wadsworth was accustomed to getting what he wanted, and he wanted Morgan Stanley to have a 50 percent interest in a joint-venture investment bank with China Construction Bank holding the other 50 percent. Morgan's 50 percent stake simply wasn't negotiable, he said.

But Edwin Lim knew better. The Chinese thought the joint venture was too important to have only one foreign investor and Wadsworth would simply have to accept that. But to save Wadsworth some face, the Chinese did agree that there would be a fifty-fifty split between Chinese and foreign investors. Lim used his many contacts to bring together a disparate but accomplished group of investors, including his old friend Payson Cha. In the end China Construction Bank had a 42.5 percent interest in the venture, Morgan Stanley held 35 percent, and the rest was distributed among various investors. The initial capitalization was set at $100 million, with each partner contributing an amount equivalent to its stake.

The partners in what would become China International Capital Corporation, or CICC, went out of their way to show sincerity and goodwill at their first planning meeting in April 1994 on the Sentosa resort island in Singapore. The major question was how to organize and operate the joint venture. Wang Qishan explained that the Chinese preferred to develop mutual trust with their partners before working out such business details. Lim countered that in the West business discussions started with principles and details. The personal trust flowed naturally from those detailed discussions.

Then Wadsworth spoke up. "I agree one hundred percent with my friend Wang Qishan," he said. "If you can't become friends, then you can't do business. It doesn't matter if you're in the West or the East. You have to respect people and then you will be respected."

One of the biggest issues was who would run the enterprise. As president of China Construction Bank, which held the largest stake in CICC, it was logical that Wang Qishan would be the majordomo and would name the venture's chief executive officer. But Lim patiently explained to him that if China were going to get the maximum benefit from the joint venture, Morgan Stanley should lead the enterprise. Wadsworth was stunned when Wang yielded to his request that Morgan appoint the CEO. In exchange Wadsworth agreed to Wang's request that all other key positions would be filled after interviews and consensus by both sides.

Another major question was the relationship between CICC and Morgan Stanley's other Asian operations, including Hong Kong. Wadsworth planned to integrate the China investment banking operations in his Hong Kong office into CICC, and he expected CICC to include Morgan Stanley in many, if not all, of the deals it would do with Chinese companies. But Wang was reluctant. He envisioned CICC as an independent entity that should be able to partner with any firm it wished on specific deals and not be Morgan Stanley's stepchild. Competition among foreign investment banks to partner with CICC on deals would be good for CICC, he said. Wadsworth relented, but still expected that Morgan Stanley would be in on the lion's share of CICC's deals.

Then there was the matter of compensation. As the CEO of China Construction Bank, Wang Qishan had an annual salary of about $20,000. Even the lowliest of the Morgan Stanley executives that might be expected to join CICC would be paid at least ten times that amount and the senior executives would be earning one million dollars or more. Wang wasn't worried about the differential between his salary and what the Americans who would work for him would be paid. After all, there were many perks besides money for a senior government executive like himself and he had long known about the ridiculous sums paid to American financiers.

Even as he was negotiating the basic operating structure of CICC with Wang Qishan, Jack Wadsworth found himself in the unaccustomed position of having to simultaneously negotiate with Morgan Stanley's powerful partners back in New York. Big things were happening in the United States. Inflation was falling and corporate earnings were rising. Investors were throwing money at the stock market and technology stocks were rapidly becoming the belles of the Wall Street ball. Real-estate prices in New York, Boston, and San Francisco were soaring. The great American bull market of the 1990s was just beginning to run. Morgan Stanley's focus was on America and Wadsworth was having an unusually difficult time convincing the senior partners that he was on to something really big. Nobody was thinking much about China except for Morgan Stanley CEO John Mack. Mack had long admired and respected Wadsworth's abilities. He shared Jack's vision of China becoming a bonanza for Morgan Stanley. Together the two lobbied the firm's senior management to support the joint venture.

Wadsworth's basic argument was simple: If the joint venture failed, Morgan Stanley would lose the $35 million it had invested for its 35 percent stake. But if it was successful, the fee income would be enormous and, once China opened up to the world at large, Morgan Stanley could either buy the venture from its partner or sell its stake. The risk was paltry, he argued, compared to the potential rewards.

Part of the difficulty Wadsworth faced in New York came directly from his Hong Kong colleagues' sabotage efforts. Like most international banks, Morgan Stanley has regional managers like Wadsworth in major financial capitals. But the people who work in those capitals trading stocks and bonds, making loans, and underwriting stock and bond offerings report directly to whoever is in charge of their respective specialties back in global headquarters. The regional manager's job is to build client and government relations, help land the big deals, keep the offices in his region running smoothly, and be the eyes and ears in the area for headquarters.

When China was all but closed, many foreigners had concluded that Hong Kong was the ideal observation post from which to monitor and do what little business there was to be done with China. Executives and officials in Hong Kong made no effort to disabuse them of that notion. The Chinese working in Hong Kong for foreign governments and companies set themselves out as having special wisdom about China and were paid well for their expertise. But as many of those foreign governments and companies were to discover, Hong Kong Chinese for most of the first two decades of China's opening were often clueless about, and culturally incompatible in, most of China. Hong Kong managers did well in neighboring Guangdong province because they share the Cantonese language and distinctive Cantonese cultural behaviors, which come across as crude, loud, and arrogant to many Chinese. And despite setting themselves up as experts, Hong Kong Chinese generally had few instincts for China because they grew up under a British colonial system.

As Wadsworth negotiated with Wang, Morgan Stanley's Hong Kong–based staffers grew increasingly worried about their very comfortable and highly lucrative jobs. They launched a frenzied whispering campaign to undercut him and the deal. Their bosses back in New York regularly were told how risky the deal was and how it would jeopardize the company's business in China. Why risk missing our numbers, they were told—and, not coincidentally, our huge bonuses—by getting in bed with a Chinese bank? Everybody knows how corrupt and unscrupulous they are. The whispering campaign wasn't enough to stop the deal. Ultimately the senior partners, pressed hard by Mack, gave Wadsworth the go-ahead. But Morgan Stanley's Hong Kong office wouldn't be part of the CICC venture.

Rules and Reality

Setting up China International Capital Corporation took much longer than Wadsworth had ever anticipated. But when it finally won the approval of China's government and opened its doors for business on June 25, 1995, it still seemed to Wadsworth that China was the next big thing and that Morgan Stanley had one-upped all its competitors. Cash-hungry state businesses were continually pressing the Chinese government for more capital. More than three hundred companies were listed on China's two approved stock markets, in Shenzhen and Shanghai. After tentative first steps in the early 1990s to make shares of government-owned companies available to foreign investors through listings on the Hong Kong market, the government was stepping up the pace of approvals for companies to issue shares to foreigners. Morgan Stanley's competitors in Hong Kong were throwing around million-dollar salaries to hire "princelings," the sons and daughters of China's Communist party aristocracy, in the hopes that they could win some of the underwritings. But they didn't have what Wadsworth had: a partnership with one of China's major banks.

The first inkling that the laboriously drawn contract between China Construction Bank and Morgan Stanley wouldn't be rigidly enforced came early on as the joint venture hired staff. Wadsworth wanted the best talent he could find, a mix of experienced Morgan Stanley bankers and younger Western-educated Mainland Chinese who sported degrees from Harvard and Wharton, who spoke perfect English, and who had an understanding of Western finance and polished personal manners. But Morgan Stanley bankers making millions of dollars in New York weren't about to leave for a risky undertaking in a developing country run by Communists. Only eight Morgan Stanley employees joined the CICC staff. Edwin Lim, whom Wadsworth had named as the venture's first CEO, had much more success assembling a group of impressive mainlanders who were World Bank veterans.

But even as Wadsworth was vetting potential hires, he began noticing new Chinese faces turning up in CICC's offices. He knew he hadn't been introduced to them, hadn't seen their résumés, and in fact didn't even know their names or what they were doing there. They just appeared and began working. Tang Shisheng, the director of human resources who approved all new hires, was brought over from Construction Bank by Wang Qishan without consulting Morgan Stanley. Edwin Lim himself had taken Wadsworth over to the China World Hotel to meet the man that Wang Qishan had tapped as the top Chinese deal maker, Fang Fenglei. As Lim was introducing him to this fireplug of a man with a bad comb-over, Wadsworth thought that Fang Fenglei looked more like somebody's driver than a bank executive. How could this guy who looks like he just arrived from the countryside possibly be capable of bringing in billion-dollar deals to CICC? He can't even speak English, Wadsworth thought to himself. No one will ever take him seriously. The cavalier attitude the Chinese showed toward the personnel provisions of the contract really began to grate on Wadsworth's nerves when Tang, the HR director, began rejecting Wadsworth's nominees. A pattern seemed to be emerging. If Wadsworth's candidate knew Western finance and spoke fluent Chinese—exactly the kind of person Wadsworth thought CICC needed—Tang rejected him. It was pretty clear to Wadsworth that the China Construction side of the joint venture didn't want anybody representing Morgan Stanley who could speak Chinese. It was better from the Chinese viewpoint to be able to talk about the Americans without somebody overhearing and reporting back to them.

Yet had Wadsworth been able to have a man-to-man talk about all this with Wang Qishan he would have heard a very different interpretation. For Wang and his colleagues from the China Construction Bank, the establishment of China's first true investment bank was a critical step in China's efforts to rejoin the world economy. They couldn't fail. They needed the best people they could find, both Chinese and American. Yet Wadsworth couldn't convince the best and brightest at Morgan Stanley that CICC was an important undertaking, and the Chinese he was hiring were all overseas Chinese who knew nothing about how business worked in China. Wang felt strongly that he was getting second-rate, perhaps third-rate, players from his American partner.

Wadsworth suspected that Tang was behind the griping and grumbling that occasionally reached Wadsworth about compensation policies. Three distinct salary levels had emerged at CICC. At the top were the Morgan Stanley people with their huge salaries, cars, drivers, and luxury housing. Far below, at salaries ranging between $80,000 and $150,000, were the Western-trained Chinese executives recruited by Wadsworth and Lim. At the bottom were the China Construction Bank officials assigned to CICC, most of whom were paid less than $10,000 a year. Wadsworth had assumed that information about compensation would be held in close confidence. But Tang had access to all that information and now, apparently, so did everyone else in CICC.

The first casualty was Edwin Lim. Lim knew finance, but he

wasn't an experienced investment banker and he didn't know management. He was in over his head running an investment bank and both he and Wadsworth knew it. What's more, Wadsworth was unhappy that Lim didn't assert Morgan Stanley's interests more firmly in the early days of the joint venture. Only three months after CICC opened its doors, Lim resigned to return to the World Bank.

Wadsworth promoted Lim's deputy, Harrison Young, to the CEO's post. Young had worked with Wadsworth at Morgan Stanley in the early 1980s before leaving for senior positions at the Resolution Trust Corporation and then the Federal Deposit Insurance Corporation. Wadsworth recruited him to China in the belief that Young's background as a mediator would be useful in dealing with the Chinese government, as well as in soothing over any misunderstandings that could erupt between the partners.

Wind and Thunder

Even as Harrison Young was settling into his new job as CEO, it was beginning to dawn on Wadsworth that he had overestimated the role the CEO would play in the joint venture. Tang Shisheng, for example, seemed to have an amazing amount of power for an HR executive. In the United States, the CEO of a company was a virtual dictator and the HR director was several levels down on the organization chart. But here in Beijing, virtually all the Chinese working at CICC owed their jobs to Tang and he let them know it every day. Only if Tang approved something would it happen.

Then there was Fang Fenglei, the rough-hewn wheeler-dealer that Wang had insisted on bringing into the joint venture. Harrison Young may have been the CEO of the company, but it was pretty clear to most people working at CICC that Fang was the de facto boss. Fang's father had been a farmer before World War II, but after attending school in a cave during the war, he eventually became a senior administrator of the Chinese army's optics industry. When the Cultural Revolution closed China's schools in 1968, Fang Fenglei was sent to the countryside to live with the peasants. In 1971, he joined the Chinese army. When the universities reopened in 1978, Fang left the army and studied Chinese language and international economics. He was assigned to the foreign trade ministry, which sent him to Henan province in 1982 to advise on system reforms. Fang worked his way up in the trade bureaucracy in Henan, eventually cobbling together his first deal in 1988, the merger of the province's four biggest companies into one entity, in which Fang was second-in-command.

Fang met Wang Qishan when Wang came to Henan on a fact-finding mission for a rural reform policy development institute that he headed in Beijing. Fang eventually went to work for Wang as a troubleshooter at companies owned by China Construction Bank. Fang also began building a circle of friends among economic policy makers whom he met through his wife, whose father was a leading Chinese economist named Liu Guoguang. Wang sent Fang to the United States to learn how its financial system worked. While in the United States, Fang's father-in-law introduced him to Edwin Lim. The two men got along well and spent hours discussing finance and economics. During a visit to Washington's National Zoo they stood in front of the pandas and talked about the prospect of China building an investment bank that could do basic financing for state industries. When he returned to China, Fang suggested to Wang that his boss champion a joint-venture Chinese investment bank that would focus on restructuring Chinese state industry. He also persuaded his influential father-in-law to write a letter to Zhu Rongji and other top leaders suggesting that they study the U.S. investment banks as models for further Chinese financial reform.

At CICC, Fang, whose given name means "wind and thunder," lived up to that moniker. He was in constant motion, working in the office by day and working the banquet circuit and karaoke bars at night. He was Wang Qishan's eyes and ears. But Fang's entrepreneurial energy and creativity also made him the bank's key business driver, just as Wang had predicted. Much to their dismay, CICC's Western-trained Chinese investment bankers were put under Fang's tutelage. Many of them initially dismissed him as a rube who knew nothing about financial deals and capital markets. They quickly learned that he was a master of Chinese business style, a style that wasn't the least bit familiar to them. The young bankers had been trained in the straightforward approach that characterizes Western business. But they found themselves sitting with Fang and potential clients at smoky dives, eating and drinking late into the night as Fang and his clients told stories about the Cultural Revolution and complained how rotten the government was in those days. Fang knew how to get potential clients to open up, to tell him what worried them and what made them happy. He knew that at different stages of their careers they had to do different things. Clients identified with Fang and trusted him.

He also kept a keen eye out for what was happening within CICC, asking questions, listening to gossip, feeling for the pulse of the operation. Even more so than Tang, the China Construction Bank employees at CICC knew to fear and respect Fang. He was the typical Chinese entrepreneur boss. Everybody had to listen to him and he had every detail under his control. As one of CICC's founders put it, "he wanted everybody's balls in his hands."

Distrust worsened between the China Construction Bank faction and the CICC employees who felt beholden to Morgan Stanley. The Morgan Stanley group had envisioned CICC as a foot in the door of China's burgeoning financial market. While they tried to follow the systems and methods that had been so successful for Morgan Stanley over the years, the China Construction employees were doing business the Chinese way. The few deals that CICC won were small potatoes. Meanwhile, it was clear that the CICC employees feared that Morgan Stanley bankers would try to muscle in on their turf. And as CICC's Western-trained investment bankers went around knocking on the doors of potential corporate clients, they kept running into Morgan Stanley bankers from Hong Kong seeking the same business. Other investment banks were sending bankers into China to pursue clients unburdened by the bureaucracy and tensions dragging down CICC.

Mutual Distrust

The distrust became painfully evident in relations between Wadsworth and Wang. That surprised some employees, who had initially thought that the two powerful executives were so much alike. But they were alike only in the context of their own cultures. Both seemed to possess an unshakable self-confidence and they each had a powerful presence. Neither suffered fools well. Neither would take no for an answer. And both of them were generous and steadfast mentors for bright people they recruited to work for them. The problem was that Jack Wadsworth was "too" American, and Wang Qishan was "too" Chinese.

Their communications problems were typical. Neither man could pick up the phone and have a private chat with the other to solve problems. All their conversations necessarily included translators. The information about the joint venture that each man received was filtered through subordinates who had their own agendas. The infighting and problems were magnified and distorted by the time they reached the two bosses.

The leaders also became ensnared by cross-cultural differences. Wadsworth didn't mince his words. He always said what he thought, negative or positive. He was a stickler for rules, ethics, and good corporate governance. He was accustomed to getting his way and being respected by his subordinates and colleagues. Some of the CICC employees privately called him General Patton. Wang, on the other hand, exhibited the tough exterior characteristic of his generation of Chinese and, given his exalted position in Chinese society, he projected a strong sense of superiority. Yet he, like many leading Chinese government officials, also carried nagging feelings of inferiority, the result of how badly the Chinese had fallen behind the West in the past two centuries, after thousands of years of glorious history. Wang knew that while his bank was a giant, his commercial banking knowledge and skills were those of a beginner. Wang also had the Chinese politician's affinity for avoiding conflict or commitment by speaking in vague Chinese parables so that listeners can hear what they want to hear. That drove Wadsworth crazy.

"In American business, you can argue, pound the table, and then be drinking buddies," said a colleague of the two men. "But with the Chinese inferiority complex, every argument was more salt in the wounds for Wang Qishan." It wasn't long before the two men simply stopped talking to each other and began using Payson Cha, a board member, as an intermediary.

None of this helped Harrison Young. As CEO of the joint venture he quickly found himself squeezed between the two partners. The China Construction group wanted one thing, the Morgan Stanley group wanted something different. Young was deferential toward Wang Qishan, an attitude that marginally improved relations between the two sides. But Young had little clout with Morgan Stanley's senior partners back in New York, and the Morgan Stanley bankers in Hong Kong took advantage of that to continue to bad-mouth the CICC venture. As time passed, Young began to spend more and more time in his office with the door closed.

A Missed Opportunity

CICC was clearly floundering only a few months after the bank opened its doors. Fang Fenglei headed off to the United States and Europe to see how the investment banking business was done there. In Britain, he learned about the proposed merger between British Telecom and Cable & Wireless, which owned a majority stake in Hong Kong Telecom. With the July 1997 handover of Hong Kong to China looming large, Fang knew that Chinese leaders would soon be seeking a strategy for dealing with the fact that British interests would control Hong Kong's telephone system after it became Chinese territory.

At that time China was about halfway through the largest and fastest telecom buildout the world had ever seen. In the 1990s, China went from a phone system that would have been right at home in many impoverished African nations to a state-of-the art mobile and fixed-line network that was the envy of both the United States and Europe. From 1990 through 1995, the government invested about $30 billion in the network, mostly financed by foreign vendors and their governments. But that game was running out. Wu Jichuan, the powerful chief of China's Ministry of Posts and Telecommunications, needed a new source of capital.

Back in Beijing, Fang drafted a proposal for China to buy Hong Kong Telecom. It was an audacious scheme, one that typically conservative Chinese officials would reject out of hand. But Wang Qishan liked the idea. He passed it along to Wu Jichuan at the Ministry of Posts and Telecommunications. After reading the proposal Wu called Fang at home. "What I really want most is that company," he said, referring to Hong Kong Telecom.

All this time Morgan Stanley was among the leading investment banks financing a similar telecommunications boom in the United States. Fang figured it made sense to bring in Morgan Stanley to advise and market the creation of what would become China Telecom. Yet Morgan Stanley's telecom bankers in New York firmly rebuffed Fang. With the trademark hubris of New York investment bankers, they told him that China couldn't do a deal big enough to draw them away from their booming U.S. business.

"They treated him like a dumbshit," said a former Morgan Stanley executive familiar with the encounter. "The Morgan Stanley culture was that if you aren't one of us, you are a dumbshit."

But Fang had other options. As his relations with CICC's Morgan Stanley people worsened, Fang found himself being courted by John Thornton, the chairman of Goldman Sachs Asia. Goldman Sachs might not have wanted to do a partnership with China Construction Bank, but it badly wanted to do business with CICC. When Thornton learned of Fang's ambitious plans to launch overseas listings of China's telecom assets, he immediately summoned Mike Evans, head of Goldman's Equity Capital Markets, to China to encourage Fang to ally with Goldman. In January 1997, in a secret planning meeting at a resort on Hainan Island, Fang, Thornton, and a handful of Goldman Sachs bankers and MPT officials, worked out a plan to create China Telecom (Hong Kong) Ltd. The company would hold the assets of China's two largest mobile phone operations, Guangdong and Zhejiang provinces, which made up nearly 30 percent of the nation's mobile subscribers, and would later buy Hong Kong Telecom. Investors would also have the chance to own other provincial networks that would be injected into the company over time.

The bold plan would have to be approved at the very highest levels of the Chinese government, where the final decision on whether to go ahead and with which partners would be made. Wang Qishan, of course, had been kept fully informed by Fang as the outlines of the deal grew more detailed. Now, President Jiang Zemin and Vice-Premier Zhu asked Wang who would be the best partner for CICC to do the China Telecom deal. Wang recommended that Goldman Sachs get CICC's largest deal ever. Wang's recommendation reflected the deteriorating relationship within the CICC partnership. But China's leaders already had deep suspicions about Morgan Stanley's true intentions. The Chinese government had been promoting the Hong Kong market for Chinese listings and was trying to put the best possible face on the July handover of Hong Kong to China by the British. Then Morgan Stanley's oft-quoted stock market prognosticator, Barton Biggs, got worldwide press when he predicted that Asian stocks were a huge bubble just waiting to burst. Zhu wrongly assumed that Biggs's statement was clear evidence that Morgan Stanley was manipulating the markets, accumulating short positions before Biggs's comments helped trigger a sharp market downturn. There was no way the China Telecom deal was going to Morgan Stanley.

With Goldman Sachs as CICC's partner, China Telecom became the nation's first megadeal, one that for the first time gave foreign investors a shot at a nationwide Chinese industry. The company raised more than $4 billion when it was simultaneously listed on the New York Stock Exchange and the Hong Kong Stock Exchange on October 22 and 23, 1997.

The China Telecom deal was a disaster for Morgan Stanley and for Jack Wadsworth. Partners in New York who had been strong-armed by John Mack into backing the $35 million partnership were apoplectic. All they had heard from Beijing since CICC opened its doors in 1995 were problems. These were powerful people who went to the office every day intent on crushing Goldman Sachs. Now the biggest deal to ever come out of China—by a factor of ten—was going to Goldman, which had rejected the CICC partnership before Morgan Stanley bought in. Wadsworth's once invincible credibility at headquarters suddenly had a gaping wound.

The Openhearted CEO

Harrison Young took the fall. Austin Koenen, his deputy, became chief executive officer of CICC late in 1997. Koenen was a disci-plined and ambitious New Jersey farm boy who had graduated from the U.S. Naval Academy at Annapolis with four majors and served on attack submarines. He was one of the most level-headed and respected executives at Morgan Stanley in New York. Morgan Stanley CEO John Mack believed that Koenen had the strength of character to win over CICC's skeptical Chinese employees. Koenen didn't speak Chinese and he knew little about the history and cul-ture of China, but he went out of his way to show that he respected the Chinese and their country. He exuded leadership and confi-dence—on his desk was a sign that said NO WHINING—and he men-tored the Chinese employees like he was their father. He told them that his loyalty was to them and CICC, not to Morgan Stanley, because his mission was to build a first-class Chinese investment bank. Koenen kept communications with Morgan Stanley Hong Kong to a minimum. Instead, he talked to New York. He encour-aged Chinese employees to speak up at meetings and not be intimi-dated by the arrogant and tenacious foreign bankers. He told them to get on with their jobs and come to him when they needed advice. From the beginning of the CICC venture, the Chinese had stressed that Morgan Stanley was expected to bring investment banking "technology" to the venture. Once Koenen became CEO, the Chinese realized that Morgan's biggest contribution would be as a mentor to Chinese employees.

Chinese who worked with Koenen often used the same word to describe him: "openhearted." They meant they trusted his sincerity and believed that he genuinely cared about their careers and lives. Behavior imperatives in Chinese culture are extremely negative and fairness isn't a hallmark of the society. Parents motivate their children by focusing on their faults and inadequacies. The government rules through control, shame, and a ubiquitous presence. Worries about retribution for making mistakes guide the actions of most employees. Thus CICC's Chinese employees were extremely receptive to genuine kindness, sincerity, and coaching from their new boss, whose competence was without question. For many, it was the first time in their lives that somebody in authority had treated them kindly.

Koenen smoothed over much of the bickering between the two sides of the joint venture and it seemed as if CICC was finally gaining some traction. Then, in May 1998, six months after he replaced Harrison Young as CEO, Austin Koenen died of a heart attack in Beijing at age fifty-six. Fang and his Chinese colleagues were bereft. Years later, Fang would still be sending flowers to Koenen's grave, a mark of his respect. "It was in his heart, not his head," Fang said. "It wasn't his technical skills, it was his management style. He respected us."

The Rising Son

Elaine La Roche, a veteran Morgan Stanley executive in New York who had been a liaison between Koenen and Morgan's New York bosses, took over Koenen's job and quickly won the respect of CICC employees by working to mentor and empower the best among them. After so many years as an administrator at Morgan Stanley headquarters, she also focused on building the missing management systems. When setting up the joint venture, Wadsworth and the other Morgan Stanley executives had been so focused on the deal that they had given short shrift to the procedures and schedules for building the joint venture's corporate culture and values, overall organizational structure, risk management systems, training programs, internal controls, exit strategies, and all the other details of a normal business partnership. La Roche made up for lost time, pushing a culture of performance, merit, and integrity.

Yet no matter what La Roche did, the Chinese in CICC still considered Fang Fenglei the boss. He was increasingly bitter and dismissive of La Roche's sophisticated management systems. In turn, he became the focus of the joint venture's problems. After Fang took the China Telecom deal to Goldman Sachs, the Morgan Stanley side of CICC began to blame anything that went wrong on him. The dilemma was that Fang was CICC's only real rainmaker, but he had no desire to direct deals toward Morgan Stanley, not least because they were people who had treated him as an ignorant peasant. Goldman capitalized on its first success by continuing to relentlessly court Fang. For Goldman, CICC was a client to be wined and dined, mostly in the person of Fang. For Morgan Stanley, CICC was a troubled subsidiary with Fang the principal source of trouble. It seemed to some Morgan Stanley executives that Morgan Stanley was the wife with the responsibilities and headaches, while Goldman Sachs was the mistress with all the fancy jewelry. Fang continued to partner with Goldman whenever he could, including the firm's next megadeal, PetroChina's $2.9 billion IPO in April 2000.

In January 1998, Fang's mentor, Wang Qishan, was named deputy governor of Guangdong province, his first job to clean up a huge financial scandal there. Wang's successor as CICC chairman, Zhou Xiaochuan, who later became China's central bank governor, decided that Fang Fenglei had to go. Fang rejected Morgan Stanley's offer to send him to Harvard University to get an executive MBA because it contained a noncompete agreement. Instead, Fang joined Bank of China International in Hong Kong and set out to compete with CICC.

Even before Fang was ousted, though, there was an important

new development on the personnel front. Shortly before Austin Koenen died, he had told La Roche that the Chinese side of CICC was "preparing to bring in somebody big." A few months later that "somebody" turned out to be Levin Zhu, the son of China's new premier, Zhu Rongji.

The Communist party in China has an informal policy that the children of top leaders are expected to live in China and work for the government or Chinese companies. Levin Zhu had obtained a PhD in meteorology from the University of Wisconsin, and a master's degree in accounting from DePaul University in Chicago. After a stint as an accountant at Arthur Anderson in Chicago, he joined Credit Suisse First Boston in New York as a trainee. When his father became premier, Levin was called home. He was steered toward CICC as an appropriate place to build his career.

At CICC, Levin was the most junior executive in the investment banking department. At first he tried to be modest and low-key. He seemed happy putting together reports that went into excruciating detail on state company finances. But the Chinese bankers at CICC were quick to take advantage of Levin's presence. They dropped his name at every opportunity and dragged him along to meetings to solicit underwriting business. The presence among them of the premier's son soon pushed CICC's internal politics back into the ancient imperial dynasty style. The Chinese staff automatically kowtowed and deferred to Levin, as they would to the son of any Chinese emperor.

With Fang out, Levin became the de facto Chinese boss of CICC. La Roche tried to cultivate him, but it was like chasing a ghost. Levin was a quirky individual. He usually came to work in the late afternoon and stayed until the early morning hours. He didn't answer e-mails. He secluded himself in his office, communicating with others through his secretary. CICC bankers and analysts who wanted to see Levin stayed in the office at night, drinking coffee at their desks in hopes of a post-midnight audience. Nonetheless, Levin understood Western systems and recognized their value. He supported La Roche's strategic plan for systems and accountability.

To preserve his own privacy and privilege, of course, he had to be exempt.

When the frustrated La Roche resigned and returned to New York in June 2000, CICC was turned over to a management committee. The committee, of course, deferred to Levin for decisions. From the Chinese point of view, CICC had gone from being Fang Fenglei's company to Levin Zhu's company.

Despite the severely dysfunctional management, CICC had by then become wildly successful. The quality of management doesn't much matter when you're the only game in town. CICC had the charter as China's one and only investment bank. If an overseas listing was to be done, CICC was part of the deal. It turned out that Morgan Stanley's exasperating efforts to impose controls and systems on the company hadn't been in vain. The joint venture could handle domestic stock market listings and Fang and his team had been remarkably successful in generating business. More importantly, though, CICC could work well in tandem with international investment banks for overseas offerings. After basically breaking even each year from its inception, CICC brought in $170 million in gross revenue in 2000. The bank paid back the original investors their entire $100 million and surprised its Chinese bankers with million-dollar bonuses. Fang, forced out in January 2000, didn't get a bonus.

A Black Hole

After Elaine La Roche left CICC, management of CICC became a black hole from which no information flowed. Levin sometimes didn't show up at the office until 10:00 P.M. and when he did arrive, he would often be unshaven and wearing a rumpled sports coat. He had few friends. He lived in hotels. An emaciated chain-smoker, Levin was hospitalized for a period and ran the firm from his hospital bed. Levin had an accountant's obsession with numbers that drove the analysts and investment bankers at CICC to distraction. They were always forced to do more and more modeling and data input, even though they knew that the numbers at the state-owned enterprises were mostly meaningless. Underlings at CICC believed that Levin's obsession with tiny details was a way to mask his relative inexperience in investment banking.

Levin Zhu remains at the helm of CICC today. He makes decisions by himself, with little input from others. He has his father's stubborn self-confidence. People who disagree with Levin are frozen out. Decisions pile up at CICC because Levin is hard to find. But he also is a hard worker. He made CICC the equivalent of a better-managed state-owned enterprise. The venture positioned itself as the trusted hand-holder of Chinese companies that provides protection from the sharks at the foreign investment banks. Levin framed CICC's mission as the restructuring of Chinese state industry.

In 2002, Morgan Stanley threw in the towel, turning over complete control to the Chinese. CICC became a "portfolio investment" from which Morgan Stanley would collect annual dividends and perhaps realize a big gain in the event of a future CICC public listing. As one Morgan Stanley executive put it: "We capitulated to their vision." Since Morgan Stanley's surrender, Morgan Stanley had been appointed the co-underwriter of the most lucrative overseas listings of Chinese companies handled by CICC.

What This Means for You

We've just watched a promising marriage between Wall Street royalty and the Chinese Communist aristocracy turn into one of the most dysfunctional, troubled, and controversial joint ventures in the history of modern China. And, by dint of its monopoly, one of the most financially successful.

CICC's troubles were the result of clashing cultures. Neither side understood the other and neither side made much of an attempt to solve that problem. Had Austin Koenen lived, perhaps things would have turned out differently. But what happened to CICC is all too common among joint ventures between outsiders and the Chinese.

The partners made every textbook mistake. From the first day, they had dramatically different visions for CICC. Jack Wadsworth saw Morgan Stanley sitting in the catbird seat of a booming Chinese economy, capturing deals right and left and making millions of dollars in fees. He was firmly convinced that Morgan Stanley had a very good chance of making CICC a subsidiary. Wang Qishan dreamed of building CICC into a Chinese investment bank with global offices, one that could compete with the best in the business, including Morgan Stanley. Such ludicrously divergent visions are a common malady among joint ventures between the Chinese and foreigners. An ancient Chinese proverb captures it perfectly: *Tong Chuang Yi Meng*. It means, "Two people sleeping in the same bed but having different dreams."

As this story illustrates, the partners in joint ventures—especially when the Chinese partner is a government entity—all too often exhaust themselves in internal politics instead of focusing on the business. Jack Wadsworth confronted that when putting together CICC. He also felt huge competitive pressures as the world's major investment banks came sniffing around China looking for market entry. Wadsworth told me the contract that took so long to negotiate was put in a drawer almost as soon as it was signed and never referred to again. That is common, too. China is not the legalistic society that typifies the West. If the Chinese want to do something, they find a way to skirt rules or laws. Still, Morgan Stanley didn't pay enough attention to the day-to-day trivialities that could have smoothed the joint venture's way. Only when Elaine La Roche became CEO did she try to remedy the lack of such simple provisions as an organizational structure, risk management systems, internal controls, and training programs. Granted, it would have been a lot to ask of Wadsworth amid the fever to be the first investment bank into China, but anyone who doesn't pay attention to such seeming trivialities when negotiating a joint venture in China today may as well stay home and give the money to charity.

Working out those details can help create relationships and

establish a problem-solving mind-set among the partners. That is the purpose of contract negotiations in China. It is the relationships that develop between the negotiators that ultimately hold the venture together. Let your lawyers be the bad guys, raising the possibilities of what can go wrong and drafting legal protections in the contract. The exercise will raise points of contention, forcing both sides to work through methods to solve disagreements and problems. The resulting contract clause probably won't save your business in China, but the problem-solving practices and personal relationships that come out of the negotiations may give you a base on which to build your business relationship. Had Jack Wadsworth and Wang Qishan been the direct managers of the joint venture they might have worked out a better relationship.

Clearly there was a clash of personalities. Wadsworth is a typical high-powered American executive, confident, candid, and vocal. That works in boardrooms and executive suites throughout the United States, but it doesn't work in China, where elliptical parables and a polite veneer can mask the most deeply held animosities. Wang Qishan and Fang Fenglei resented Wadsworth's demeanor and took their revenge where they could.

Trying to negotiate and run a business through translators exacerbated an already bad situation. Both Wadsworth and Wang mostly relied on operating employees from CICC who spoke both English and Chinese. These people had their own agendas and reasons to filter the information received by their bosses. Don't repeat that mistake. Hire and use well-trained translators whose only job is to provide clear communications.

Jack Wadsworth retired from Morgan Stanley in 2001 and now lives in San Francisco. He views the CICC partnership as a valuable learning experience for Morgan Stanley, albeit a frustrating one. Morgan Stanley emerged with nearly a 50 percent market share for Chinese international IPO business. That made it all worthwhile.

"In hindsight, it's miraculous that we were able to tough it out and succeed," Wadsworth told me. "Going into this joint venture, our assessment was that it would be time-consuming and difficult, but we believed that the scale of the opportunity in the long-term would justify the commitment. And I think that judgment was absolutely spot-on. We thought China was unique at the time. The size of the market justified the commitment. The single most important factor for success is that both sides had a real interest in making it work. The Chinese wanted a template, and they wanted capital into their country. Morgan Stanley wanted access to China."

Wang Qishan is a leading candidate to be a future Chinese premier. When the SARS epidemic broke out in 2003, the Chinese government was caught lying to the world about it. Wang was appointed mayor of Beijing, which was hardest hit, and told to clean up the mess. Once that was done, he turned his attention to organizing the 2008 Beijing Olympics.

Creating CICC was a very important career milestone for Wang. Zhu Rongji and other senior leaders considered CICC to be a significant step in Chinese economic reforms. Morgan Stanley probably would have acted differently if it had viewed Wang more as a politician with political needs and less as an intransigent business partner. Morgan Stanley could have framed initiatives and operating plans for the joint venture in terms of what China needed for economic reform and what Wang needed to further his career.

Levin Zhu is a generation younger and Western-educated, but like Wang he illustrates the political fears that guide the behavior of Chinese officials and their families. In many ways, it is a curse to be the son or daughter of a senior Chinese leader. Levin was taught from childhood to be wary of others. Before Levin was in elementary school, his father was purged as a "rightist" in Mao's campaign to persecute liberal thinkers. The elder Zhu spent most of the next two decades in political disgrace. He didn't emerge until the end of the Cultural Revolution in the late 1970s. In the 1980s, as economic reforms took hold, and his father moved up fast, Levin seemed extremely wary of people befriending him in order to get favors from his father. Now that he is wealthy and successful, such fears still define Levin.

He and his colleagues in the senior management of CICC have the modern version of Levin's father's fears. They work as hard as any investment bankers in the West and they're well paid, but they constantly worry that if the political winds change in Beijing, they could be targeted in a political campaign that would characterize them as making millions of dollars from what is essentially privatizing state assets. "They worry about being exposed, ending up in jail for doing honest work, so they are all very secretive," said one CICC insider to explain why CICC rejected my requests to interview Levin and other current senior CICC executives.

Wang and Levin both display the typical Chinese government viewpoint of Sino-foreign joint ventures. The Chinese government often isn't really interested in forging genuine partnerships. It simply wants a vehicle to gain access to foreign technology, capital, and know-how while retaining Chinese control of the venture. This is why Chinese law requires joint ventures in key sectors like finance, insurance, auto production, and telecommunications.

If your industry requires joint ventures for access to China, proceed cautiously. Expect that you and your partner won't see eye to eye. Foreigners use joint ventures to learn how to do business in China and to access the China market. The Chinese will use the joint venture to learn the business. If you take those motivations as inevitable, then you can structure the business for peaceful coexistence. Get a clear majority ownership and management control, especially in personnel and finance. If you must settle on fifty-fifty or a minority stake, prepare for an adventure that will consume enormous amounts of management time and make your attorneys rich. There are some useful tricks. It is common for foreign companies to hold back crucial parts or technology from a joint venture in China. The company headquarters then acts as a third-party supplier to the joint venture and overcharges for the item. In this way, headquarters can book decent profits from its money-losing China operation. That is a nice Band-Aid, but hardly a business plan.

Companies that do joint ventures in which the government allows only a minority interest, such as Morgan Stanley, must have a larger agenda. If a joint venture is the only way a company can break into the China market, it may be worth doing as long as you realize it will be a learning experience. More often than not, these ventures blow up. Some companies sit back and wait for policy changes that will give them full control of their China joint venture. They enjoy watching those who got to China first digging themselves out of the hole.

Austin Koenen's success at CICC was short-lived but significant. In a perfect world, the manager of your China operations would speak and read Chinese, understand Chinese culture and history, enjoy strong support at headquarters, be steeped in the corporate culture and ethical standards, and have significant industry and management expertise. Such people are rare. The good news is that it is even more important for your China manager to be a true leader, a true expert, and a tough-minded mentor. Chinese people are eager to learn, and they learn very fast. They want to be led, but they will only follow and respect leaders who have the skills and intelligence to deserve it. Show Chinese employees that they have a path to top management. Build systems that put your Chinese and expatriate executives on equal footing. Too often, the Chinese side assigns its best and brightest to the joint venture while the foreign partner picks people based on their willingness to live in China, which often brings inexperienced foreign managers or deadwood pushed out of headquarters. Send in your most creative and driven entrepreneurs, not your risk-adverse corporate bureaucrats.

The real lesson to be drawn from Austin Koenen is that genuine sincerity goes a long way in China. One of his former Morgan Stanley colleagues put it this way: "Austin's approach was that the way to succeed in China is to submerge your ego, be secure in yourself and your position, be prepared to be a coach rather than a boss. The successful people in China are the ones who can attract, train, and retain senior Chinese employees. These people will walk through a wall for you if you help them. But if you fuck them, they will fuck you three times."

That colorful quote is the perfect lead-in to discuss Fang Fenglei's tenure at CICC. The distrust between the China Construction Bank contingent and the Morgan Stanley people in CICC started right at the top and trickled down through the entire organization. Once somebody became CEO of the joint venture, they were distrusted by both sides. The Chinese considered them a Morgan Stanley spy and Morgan Stanley's Hong Kong office considered them a competitor. It was easy for the Chinese to drive the CEO to the sidelines while Fang Fenglei or Levin Zhu exercised the real power. In a joint venture you will be bringing the Chinese business system and culture directly into your company. Many of the core characteristics of that system—dictatorial leadership, debilitating politics, personal reward over company gain, an obsession with avoiding risk and decisions, and almost inevitable corruption—will become the management riddles that keep you awake at night.

After leaving CICC, Fang held a few investment banking positions before creating his own investment bank and establishing a new securities firm to do a joint-venture deal with his old friends at Goldman Sachs. Goldman, which loaned $100 million to Fang to start his business, is said to have an option to buy his stake in the firm if rules change to allow foreign ownership. The arrangement is aimed at giving Goldman effective control of Goldman Sachs China without violating China's securities laws.

Fang has come a long way since Jack Wadsworth thought he looked like someone's driver. He wears designer labels and does much of his work on the golf course. He speaks highly of Jack Wadsworth and many other Morgan Stanley executives.

"Morgan Stanley never did understand me," Fang told me. "This was a learning experience for them. They didn't expect the Chinese to learn so fast. They expected it to take ten years for CICC to grow up."

The Little Red Book of Business

- Avoid joint ventures with government entities unless you have no choice. Then understand that this partnership is about China obtaining your technology, know-how, and capital while maintaining Chinese control.

- In a government joint venture, your partner's political power can easily trump even a significant majority equity share.

- If China requires that you joint venture, get a majority stake, control the board, and install your own CEO, CFO, and HR director.

- If you don't trust your CFO like your mother, give your mother the job.

- The position of HR chief in China is much more powerful than in the West because those who are hired often feel personally indebted.

- Don't suffer from double vision. Make sure that your vision for the joint company is compatible with your Chinese partner's vision.

- Expect that the relationship with your Chinese government partner will, at best, amount to "peaceful coexistence."

- Never trust a Chinese feasibility study. It will be aimed at attracting your interest, not defining the real opportunity. Do your own study.

- You can't do too much due diligence on prospective partners. Understanding your partner's political and family connections is essential. Forget "face," get the facts.

- Start with harmony at home. Headquarters politics kill as many joint ventures as do disagreements with the Chinese partner.

- Contract details matter less than the personal relationships developed in negotiations. The person who will run the business should negotiate the contract.

- Stress respect and equality with your Chinese partners and employees. Insults and slights are never forgotten, and retribution is a certainty.

- Place both your expatriate and Chinese executives on an equal footing.

- Fairness, honesty, and strong personal relationships will overcome inevitable differences.

- Chinese employees are looking for leaders. Choose capable and strong-minded mentors, not dictators or risk-averse bureaucrats, to run your China business.

- Eliminate revolving doors in the executive suite. Choose expatriate managers who have a deep interest in China, and keep them in place for an extended period.

- Roll up your sleeves. There are no passive investments in China. Expect that revenue and profits will not justify the high-level management time required for the first several years.

- Don't hire the party secretary's kid. Those political connections can also be turned against you and spoil your corporate culture. If you need such help, consulting contracts with time limits are best.

- Don't mistake language ability with business or management competence. The savviest and smartest Chinese managers often don't speak English or have a Western university degree.

3

Eating the Emperor's Grain

China's relationship-driven system is often incompatible with honesty. This peasant tycoon's journey into the dark heart of China's endemic corruption shows how it works and outlines your options.

T WAS A LAST ROLL of the dice, thrown out of desperation but not despair.

His brothers and sisters, in-laws, nieces and nephews, and hundreds of close friends and valued employees were being detained, interrogated, and threatened with long jail terms or death sentences. His wife was in the Vancouver exile home, on antidepressants and feeling hopeless, while their three teenage children watched kung-fu movies or played computer games.

But for the man once known as "the Boss" and "the Detective," the man who went from ditch digger to celebrated tycoon, from model citizen to most-wanted fugitive, there was always the hope his luck would turn in Canada's honeymoon capital of Niagara Falls, Ontario.

In an eighty-four-day spree at Casino Niagara, Lai Changxing, unaware he was under surveillance, tried to stretch the last of his money as far as he could. His bets totaled $5.7 million. On his best day, Lai won $237,500. On the worst, he lost $85,400. But he was never one to quit when he was ahead, especially now when he desperately needed to build a pile of cash that might save his own life.

It had been the same in business. Lai always saw too many opportunities. There were too many ways to profit from China's booming economy, too many ways to exploit the many cracks between China's mismatched political and economic systems. There were too many officials to befriend and buy their protection and too many people in his impoverished hometown to whom he felt obligations to provide schools, medical facilities, and even monthly sustenance checks.

With his losses totaling $445,735, Lai's gambling spree ended on November 23, 2000 when the Royal Canadian Mounted Police arrested him outside his hotel on a charge of falsifying information on his application for refugee status. His next gamble would be for his life, fighting extradition to China in the Canadian courts. The premier of China had already declared that Lai should be executed ten times over.

Lai Changxing fell into this terrible predicament because he had jumped aboard the roller coaster of Chinese economic reform at the very beginning and had taken it for the full ride, right into the dark heart of the Chinese political and economic system. Lai built a remarkable web of protective relationships that reached from the misty coves of the southern China coast to the offices and living rooms of China's secretive military intelligence and national police bosses in Beijing. He was so connected at the top of the Communist Party hierarchy that he could drive his stretch Mercedes right past the guards into the Chinese Kremlin, the leadership compound known as Zhongnanhai, in the old Imperial Palace grounds. His private Red Mansion entertainment palace in Xiamen was renowned for its collection of the most exotic and compliant beauties from throughout China. And now he stood accused of running the biggest smuggling operation in the history of China, slipping some $6.4 billion in oil, cigarettes, and automobiles past Chinese customs and evading $3.6 billion in taxes and tariffs in the process.

Overview

Balzac might have been writing about modern China when he said that behind every great fortune stands a great crime. In the past twenty-five years China's burgeoning economy, driven by legions of entrepreneurs like Lai Changxing and guided by the Communist Party's economic reforms, has created tens of thousands of great fortunes. Behind most of them are crimes great and small. Aided and abetted by government and Communist Party officials, people like Lai have pocketed vast amounts of state-owned assets and government money.

So pervasive is the mentality of government corruption in China that it is embodied in an ancient adage, *Chi Huang Liang,* which means, "eat the emperor's grain." In imperial times, with the emperor controlling most things of value, seeking favors or skimming from the system was the proven path to wealth. Then Mao made it a glorious act to confiscate properties from the wealthy, and ownership of the "whole people" prevailed, so nobody owned anything. Today any one of the "people" can be convinced that they have a right to their share of the spoils as China goes through the messy process of privatizing state assets.

The sad fact is that the Chinese system today is almost incompatible with honesty. Certainly, there are upright and honorable government officials who try to follow the government's dictates of maintaining selfless socialist ways. The government's anticorruption campaigns like the one detailed in this chapter are not cynical exercises, but China has a system of checks and no balances. The party wants to root out corruption at the same time that it allows the families of the ruling elite to accumulate assets so they can remain the ruling elite in a country dominated by commerce. The Communist Party also wants to employ laws and the courts to prosecute offenders while keeping the party's ruling elite above the law unless their behavior or party politics necessitate making an example of them. In short, if you have the right pedigree, building assets quietly is quietly accepted. The result is an unspoken policy of "don't ask, don't tell."

Everywhere one looks in China there are state-enterprise bosses and government officials sporting Armani suits, driving Mercedes or Audi luxury cars, and living in apartment buildings called Park Avenue, Palm Springs, or Beverly Hills. They golf at private clubs that charge $150 a round. Many of them earn little more than $1,000 a month, but nobody asks about their assets and nobody tells. If somebody does, there is institutional impetus to bury the accusations because almost everybody is at least a little bit dirty. China has basically returned to the traditional symbiotic relationship in which merchants are beholden to officials and officials are dependent on merchants. To do business, one needs a constantly changing array of approvals, licenses, and favors from government officials. To accumulate assets for retirement and provide for the future of their family, government officials cultivate businesspeople who can help them.

Lai is like most Chinese peasant entrepreneurs. They aren't complicated people. They didn't grow up wondering whether they should be a doctor, fireman, or attorney. They grew up with too little food to eat. Ill-educated, coarse, and hyperactive, they are eternally optimistic. The future will certainly be better than the impoverished past as long as they keep scrambling for the next opportunity. And they know opportunities depend on cultivating the people in power. China has a system of organized dependency. It is your personal relationships that open opportunities and get things done. With many layers of bureaucracy and personal interests to deal with, China is not a place where individuals function alone.

As a result, the whole pattern of business relationships in China is different than in the West. Your network of family and personal relationships are more important than the rules of the road. Your network keeps you secure in the absence of a fair and unbiased legal system. Lai Changxing offers an illuminating view into this system. He took good care of the officials whose help he needed. He invested early and often in developing friendships with fast-rising government officials. Personal relationships were his company's core asset. And when his network unraveled, he fell far and fast.

Lai's rise and fall is instructive for anybody doing business in China. Dealing with China's pervasive corruption is a vexing problem for foreign businesses in China. Corruption can extend from the top of a company right through its workforce and out to officials at almost every level of government. Secretaries take kickbacks from travel agents when buying airplane tickets. Salesmen pay kickbacks to win orders. It isn't difficult for the average Chinese employee working for a General Electric or Siemens or Sanyo to decide to eat a bit of the emperor's grain. After presenting the tale of Lai Changxing, we will examine the dimensions of corruption facing foreign companies and look at ways they handle it. We will even get some advice from Lai himself.

Much has been written in Chinese newspapers—the government's propaganda machine—that paints Lai as a devious criminal mastermind. There have been a couple of books by Chinese writers living outside of China that give a more balanced picture. And there are thousands of pages of court documents in Canada that have been generated by Lai's extradition fight that give both sides' version of events. My account of Lai Changxing's saga is based on my close reading and analysis of these often contradictory materials, as well as interviews with Lai and others involved in the case. After watching corruption in China from the sidelines for many years, I've made my judgments about what rings true and what seems to be nonsense.

The Ditch Digger

Lai Changxing was born in 1958 in Shaocuo, one of many muddy farm villages nestled in the foothills near the coast of Fujian province in southeast China. Lai is the seventh of eight children, and his education ended after three years of elementary school when the Cultural Revolution closed China's schools. As a teenager, he worked the family's tiny farm plot and joined his two eldest brothers in a ditch-digging brigade at a nearby military camp. He served as an apprentice blacksmith for a farm machinery factory for two years. Lai hated the backbreaking work and he hated having bosses. He didn't want to wear out his body and end up in a hillside grave overlooking a farm field as his ancestors had for hundreds of years.

When Deng came to power and launched China's economic reforms, Lai seized the moment. He and four friends cobbled together the equivalent of $180 in 1979 and bought forging equipment to make car lug nuts and other simple parts. He soon branched out with his own small car parts factory. His gregarious personality and indefatigable energy persuaded other companies to appoint him as their national sales representative. As he bounced around the country on filthy, overcrowded trains, Lai smelled opportunity everywhere. Everybody in China was starting from zero in the business world, so he had the same chance as anybody to become gloriously rich. Car parts led to textile machinery parts, and then to his first big success. He illegally bought the blueprints for textile machinery from a worker at a state-owned factory in Shandong province for the equivalent of $2,500. He copied the machinery and became a market leader as China built the underpinnings of what would become its gargantuan garment export business.

But the life of a traveling salesman was exhausting and inefficient. Instead of going to the buyers, Lai decided that he would bring the buyers to him. He began to organize his own trade fairs. Buyers loved the opportunity to travel to the coast of Fujian, where sunshine and seafood were abundant. Lai also found it much more efficient to wine and dine buyers in groups instead of doing the nightly banquet circuit with individual customers in whatever town he happened to be in. By the late 1980s, Lai was churning out everything from calendars to garments to umbrellas. But what really intrigued him was the big money to be made in electronics. It wasn't easy to get into the electronics business. Nearly all such goods were imported into China, mostly by smugglers. With its rugged coastline,

Fujian had long been a hotbed of smuggling. Situated as it was directly across the straits from Taiwan, it was rigidly controlled by the military and police; success in the electronics business required good relations with military and police officials. Suddenly, Lai found his niche in life.

The state-run China Travel Service already had set up a lucrative business in duty-free televisions, stereo systems, and household appliances purchased by visiting overseas Chinese for their relatives in China. The visitors would obtain vouchers from China Travel Service before they arrived. They would then redeem the vouchers for the duty-free product in China and deliver it to their relatives. Lai organized and cornered a secondary market in these vouchers. Travel agents and tour guides would buy them from visitors on his behalf. Then Lai redeemed the vouchers for color televisions and household appliances by the truckload. He expanded his business by organizing cut-rate China tours for overseas Chinese who would deliver their vouchers to his travel guides. This business was centered in Shishi, a coastal city known as a smuggling center. The authorities considered smuggling a way to jump-start economic development and provide pocket money for poorly paid police and government bureaucrats. Motorcycles routinely sped through Shishi's streets carrying towering stacks of VCRs and stereos. Some police officers drove Taiwanese automobiles, whose importation was forbidden. Lai thrived in Shishi, setting up an electronics retail store in a hotel owned by the police. As police officials and their mistresses came and went from the hotel, Lai befriended them all. He quickly figured out that directly smuggling goods into China would be much more profitable than fiddling with vouchers. With the tacit approval of his police friends, he set up a small smuggling operation that brought in televisions and motorcycles.

His success brought a steady stream of officials knocking on Lai's door, their hands outstretched. Local governments gave him impressive-sounding awards and patriotic titles, then told him he should fund their pet projects. Like all Chinese businesspeople, he had no choice but to accommodate the requests. And because private enterprises were unacceptable in the early days of reform, Lai housed his businesses under local government agencies, whose officials demanded a percentage of the profits. In return, it was understood they would protect him from tax authorities. But one day, after drinking at a nearby restaurant, two tax officials armed with screwdrivers marched up to the home of one of Lai's brothers, who was a business partner. They demanded entry, intent on prying open cabinets and drawers in a search for accounting books. Lai rushed to his brother's house and threw the taxmen out, but they continued to pursue him, eventually sealing off his businesses and factories. Fed up with the legal battle, Lai left the business to his brother to sort out and headed for the big city, Xiamen, about two hours south. He took with him some $4 million in assets.

Lai didn't stay in Xiamen long. He was tired of the hassles of making small money compared to the vast wealth he saw coming from Hong Kong. He knew that if he became a Hong Kong resident he could come back to China as a foreign investor and get tax breaks and other advantages. While he may have neglected tax officials, Lai had been assiduously courting the police; now he struck a deal with them. They would help him emigrate if Lai would help them, covering accommodations, food, and entertainment expenses for Chinese police officials and intelligence operatives who visited Hong Kong. He agreed and in 1991 he moved to Hong Kong.

The Middle Man

Lai arrived just as Hong Kong's property market was beginning a spectacular rise. People stood in line all night to snap up apartments that weren't even under construction yet. For an entrepreneur like Lai, the situation was ripe for huge profits. By 1993 he had turned the $4 million he brought from China into about $40 million.

In Hong Kong, Lai hosted many groups from the Fujian and Xiamen intelligence branches of the police and the military. Before long, his intelligence contacts asked him to provide them with information about the activities of Taiwan authorities in Hong Kong. At the same time, Taiwan's network in the colony asked him to assist their intelligence gathering in the Mainland. He was even invited to join Taiwan's ruling KMT party. It was natural for a businessman from Xiamen to be sucked into the cross-straits spy war since Fujian is the ancestral homeland for some 80 percent of Taiwan's population.

Lai was the man in the middle. Mainland intelligence agencies funneled payments to a dozen spies in Taiwan through his company. He sometimes hosted Taiwan officials when they came to Hong Kong. Shortly before China resumed control of Hong Kong in 1997, Lai's car, with its special plates allowing travel between China and Hong Kong, transported Mainland agents' files on Hong Kong's civil servants across the border. Through his connections with a Taiwan spy chief in Hong Kong who wanted to defect to China, Lai received and passed along to Mainland authorities a list of names of Taiwan agents in China. In all, Lai spent more than $1 million of his own money helping the various Mainland intelligence agencies in Hong Kong.

When Lai returned to China two years later as a foreign investor, he scattered his money around various businesses. He set up a trading firm, bought a factory that made car stereos, and another that assembled personal computers. But he had seen that real estate was at the core of the fortunes of the Hong Kong tycoons. He determined to make himself the property king of Xiamen. Through his company, Yuanhua International, or the Fairwell Trading Corporation, he accumulated land in key locations in Xiamen, which had been a crossroads for smugglers for centuries.

To foster tourism, Lai built a $17 million replica of Tiananmen Square and the Forbidden City that was used as a movie studio. He purchased the city's soccer team and changed its name to Yuanhua. He even made a few guest appearances as goalie.

Lai didn't neglect his home village of Shaocuo, about two hours away by car. He built a mansion there for himself with glass walls overlooking pagodas and gold-leaf Chinese characters gracing the front door. But he also paved the road to the village and donated money to build more than thirty schools in the area, including the Yuanhua Middle School with busts of the world's great thinkers circling the schoolyard and a curriculum aimed at giving poor kids a chance to get into China's colleges. He built a retirement home and activity center for the elderly in Shaocuo and he gave several hundred people monthly "retirement" checks of about eighty-five dollars each.

The Red Mansion

Lai ruled over his growing empire from the Red Mansion, named after a Chinese classic novel about a wealthy and dissolute Chinese family. Lai built the seven-story structure in 1996 on land obtained from the Xiamen police department. From the outside it looked like any Chinese office building with faded red tiles. But inside was a different matter. Lai's office was on the top floor. Under that was a warren of private banquet rooms, a forty-seat movie theater, private karaoke lounges, sauna and massage facilities, and a half dozen guest rooms. The Red Mansion was Lai's private haven where he discreetly entertained his rapidly growing network of government friends. Everything at the Red Mansion was free. A Hong Kong master chef prepared tureens of shark's fin soup, swallow's nest, and abalone. The imported cognac and wines were the best in China. Guests at the Red Mansion would routinely enjoy a sauna, massage, and a romp in a guest room with one of the tall, slender young ladies who graced the mansion. The officials' bodyguards could work out in the well-appointed gym while waiting for their bosses. After one visit, most officials kept coming back for more. Often the mansion was so busy that managers had to borrow girls from Xiamen nightclubs. The half dozen bedrooms would be reserved for the highest officials, while those of lower rank were given rooms at two other guesthouses owned by Yuanhua International. Remembering well the lesson of the Shishi tax bureau, Lai wanted all aspects of government relations directly under his control, especially the all-important entertainment. He told friends that the only government officials he was afraid of were those without a "hobby"—either girls or money. Lai himself seldom partook of the pleasures the Red Mansion offered. He would sip beer at the frequent banquets, then slip off to his office for a bowl of rice porridge.

Lai was enterprising in helping his friends in government and the police get ahead. When Zhuang Rushun was a mere traffic cop in Shishi, Lai imported and donated satellite telephone equipment that Officer Zhuang used to set up a traffic monitoring system that became a national model. A few years later Zhuang had risen to become the second in command of the Public Security Bureau of Fujian province and one of Lai's closest friends.

One of Lai's most important associates was Yang Qianxian, the fastest-rising official in local customs. Yang had started work in the Xiamen Department of Customs in 1980 and by age thirty was head of the investigation department. By age forty, he was appointed chief of Xiamen customs and Communist Party secretary for the organization, making him the youngest customs director in China. Under his leadership Xiamen earned regular awards for being one of the best customs branches in China. Yang first met Lai in 1989 when Lai was running his textile machinery factory in Shishi. At the time he dismissed Lai as a nobody. But Lai relentlessly cultivated him. In 1993, Lai donated $12,000 to Yang to help him spread gifts around the system so he could become the director of Xiamen customs when the position became vacant. When Yang's father died, Lai called immediately and offered to go to Yang's hometown to help with the funeral arrangements. He later supplied Yang with a Lexus to drive, as well as a Huanan tiger skin worth $100,000 to hang on his wall at home. He introduced Yang to the woman who became his mistress and then supplied the couple with a house when she became pregnant with Yang's son.

Some of the Red Mansion's guests could be troublesome. Lan Fu, the vice-mayor of Xiamen, was an inveterate gambler and was always asking Lai to stake him for losses. Lai purchased a $150,000 apartment for Lan's mother in Tianjin, a $350,000 house in Australia for Lan's son, and he covered the boy's private school tuition in Singapore and Australia.

Lai's friendships reached high into the government ranks. One of the most important and frequent visitors to the Red Mansion was Vice-Minister Li Jizhou of the Public Security Bureau, who was in charge of border security and antismuggling efforts for the entire country. Lai first met Li Jizhou in the late 1980s when Lai was selling electronics from his shop in the police-owned hotel in Shishi. Over the years, they dined and socialized together whenever Vice-Minister Li was in Xiamen or Lai was in Beijing, where he always stayed in the presidential suite of the Palace Hotel, a five-star hotel then owned by the Chinese military. Vice-Minister Li dubbed Lai "the Detective" because Lai always had the freshest and most accurate political gossip, not only about who was doing what to whom in Fujian, but also in the leadership circles in Beijing. One day Li mentioned that his wife, Cheng Xinlian, had retired from her government job. Lai asked why didn't she consider doing business?

"What can Cheng Xinlian do? She can't do anything," Li said.

"I can help her do business," Lai answered.

Within a month, Lai had given $120,000 to Ms. Cheng and her friend, Liu Yan, wife of another Public Security Bureau official, to open a restaurant. Two years later, in 1996, Ms. Cheng told Lai that her daughter, Li Qian, wasn't doing very well in the United States. She was having trouble getting a green card and keeping a steady job. Lai wired $500,000 into Li Qian's California bank account.

Over time Lai earned a reputation as a sincere and simple person who offered discreet benefits and asked for little in return. He was a model citizen and celebrated Fujian success story.

Oil, Autos, and Cigarettes

Or was he? Prosecutors tell a different story. They say Lai ran a very aggressive family-managed smuggling operation that partnered with all levels of the Chinese government and military. It was a business that was based on Lai's great strength as a relationship builder and political gossip monger. The Chinese government's case against Lai and his Yuanhua group companies concentrates on the smuggling of three products—oil, automobiles, and cigarettes—all of which carried extremely high custom tariffs that made smuggling them very profitable.

Chinese prosecutors say that most of Yuanhua's six hundred or so employees were engaged in shipping and smuggling. The company purchased the goods overseas, with the oil, cigarettes, and automobiles coming mostly from the ports of Singapore and Hong Kong. When vessels carrying the contraband approached Xiamen harbor, Yuanhua sent small boats out with fake cargo manifests to exchange for the real cargo manifests. Ship captains received an envelope of cash. Upon reaching port, the goods went one of two routes. For some, duties were paid based on the low-duty items listed on the fake cargo manifests. Others were marked for transshipment to other countries, thus entering China duty free. Those items were sent to bonded storage areas that Lai and his partners in the government and military controlled.

The containers on which duty had been paid were moved into the company's distribution network. Containers that were destined to be transshipped were unloaded at night. The cigarettes or other contraband were loaded into empty containers that had already passed customs inspection. The original containers, now empty, were resealed and exported after having new customs seals affixed. The cigarettes were taken to other warehouses for repackaging, often in shoe boxes. Since Fujian is the sports shoe manufacturing capital of the world, it wasn't difficult to use established shoe shipment channels to distribute the cigarettes around the country.

The car smuggling network was more complicated. Auto sales

companies in Fujian and elsewhere would take orders for imported vehicles, which were then compiled in Hong Kong. Lai's Hong Kong associates would order the vehicles from Japan and Germany. Some were shipped directly to Xiamen. Others were first shipped to Singapore, marked for transshipment, and later forwarded to Xiamen. Again, the cargo manifests were changed as they steamed into the port of Xiamen. Bringing cars into Xiamen was especially risky because the port wasn't designated by the government to handle autos. What's more, owners of cars in China require detailed origin papers to obtain license plates. But that didn't pose any particular problems for the smugglers because many of the purchasers were government officials and military officers. Chinese police have documents called "confiscation certificates" that are issued for smuggled autos that they capture. The certificates allow the police to sell the cars into the market. The smugglers established a network to purchase confiscation certificates from the police for about $12,000 each, about 25 percent of the customs duty that would have been due. Chinese prosecutors say that they were able to trace the smuggling of 3,588 vehicles to Lai and his associates. They put the value of the vehicles at $190 million, and lost customs duties at about $110 million.

Refined oil from Singapore and Australia was smuggled using two methods. Sometimes the oil was offloaded, under the watchful and complicit eyes of the Chinese military, from small tankers onto local cargo vessels retrofitted with oil tanks. These small ships would scatter along the coast of Fujian and Guangdong provinces. Other times the oil would simply pass through customs without leaving any paperwork trail and end up in government-owned oil storage tanks. It was then sold to municipal and provincial oil companies and moved into normal government supply channels. Investigators were frustrated for months in their attempts to track the oil smuggling. They could find no unusual documents in the customs files. They finally figured out the smuggling volumes by comparing the records of the Xiamen oil storage facilities with the officially recorded volume of oil imports. They found that an astounding four million tons of oil had been smuggled into Xiamen in about a three-year period. They claimed that Lai controlled all oil smuggling in Xiamen, and others who wanted to smuggle oil had to obtain a "quota" from him to avoid customs inspection.

Wrong Place, Wrong Time

In the late 1990s, China was awash in a smuggling epidemic. The nation's economy had boomed throughout the 1990s, but Chinese customs revenues remained anemic. Even multinational companies manufacturing consumer products in China used smuggling networks to distribute their products in China because they were faster and cheaper than the domestic state-owned distribution monopolies. The smuggling hit hardest at China's oil industry. The controlled domestic oil price was almost double the going international rate and the government estimated that at least one-third of China's oil supply was smuggled into the country, mostly by the military and police. Because the People's Liberation Army is under the jurisdiction of the Communist Party, not the government, even top government officials often were afraid of confronting military officials, especially in the provinces. Protected by their party status, military and police units were fully caught up in the gold rush. In any given town the karaoke clubs, girlie bars, sauna and massage parlors, and brothels were inevitably in military- or police-owned buildings. The top luxury cars in town belonged to military officers and their families, conspicuous by their distinctive white license plates.

In March 1998, Premier Zhu Rongji came into office, determined to crack down on smuggling and get the military out of business. It had been one of his favorite causes as vice-premier, albeit a lonely one. The military had fiercely opposed the vice-premier, arguing that it needed income from business to supplement inadequate funding by the government. While still vice-premier, Zhu gathered evidence of Lai's Yuanhua smuggling operation and its ties to the military. He took that evidence to Admiral Liu Huaqing, who was vice-chairman of the party's Central Military Commission. But

Admiral Liu knew Lai through Liu's daughter, who worked for a navy company that partnered with Yuanhua in some smuggling operations.

Liu told Zhu to back off. "Little Lai is not bad at all," he said.

Now, as premier, and with the explicit public backing of President Jiang Zemin, Zhu was looking for the big case that he needed to expose the extent of smuggling and the connections between smugglers and the police and military. Early in 1999 he found it.

Lai Changxing says his undoing started with one of the hundreds of associates he had in various enterprises early in 1999. Here is his version of events: Zhu Niuniu, who manufactured fake Kodak film, partnered with Lai in some smuggling operations. But Zhu wasn't a particularly reliable partner. Working through a defunct company that he had owned in partnership with Lai, Zhu borrowed some $1.8 million from a company owned by the Chinese military. To get the loan, he forged Lai's signature. A chronic gambler, Zhu lost the money and began pressuring Lai to help him repay it. Lai, tired of his erstwhile partner's screwups, refused. An enraged Zhu tried to blackmail Lai, who brushed him off. Then Zhu prepared a seventy-four-page report on Lai's smuggling, naming officials who accepted bribes from Lai. As Lai tells it, the report was full of fabrications. Zhu sent the report to officials in Xiamen, where Lai's friends promptly kept it under wraps. Then Zhu sent the report to the Communist Party's Central Commission for Discipline Inspection. To insure that it got into the right hands, acording to Lai, Zhu Niuniu paid a $3,500 bribe.

On March 29, 1999, the details of the Zhu Niuniu report were passed on to the party leadership. With evidence implicating Lai and Vice-Minister Li, Premier Zhu finally had the big case he needed, and a chance to cripple a huge smuggling operation while exposing corruption at the highest levels of the police and military. Events began to move quickly. The investigation officially began on April 20 when President Jiang Zemin created the "4-20" task force to go after Lai. Jiang ordered investigators to look into the involvement of senior leaders, but to keep that information secret, and to distinguish between those local officials who helped the smugglers and those who were simply negligent in their duties. He also ordered that all the details be reviewed by the party's internal discipline committee and the party's ruling politburo.

When the investigation began, Lai worked his network furiously. Investigators wanted to find Vice-Minister Li's mistress, Li Shana, whose testimony would be instrumental in connecting the vice-minister with Lai. Lai was hiding her in one of his Xiamen villas. But Li Shana wouldn't stop calling her friends, whose phones were tapped by Chinese investigators. Lai moved her twice more, but she kept making calls. Police tracked her to a remote safe house in Henan province and she was taken to Beijing to build the case against Vice-Minister Li.

On June 13, a team of twenty investigators quietly infiltrated Xiamen, only to run into a brick wall. Most of the main suspects they were planning to put under surveillance had already fled the country. Xiamen government officials had been warned the investigators were coming and had their stories prepared. The investigators searched meticulously through Xiamen's customs declaration documents, but found nothing about Lai's Yuanhua group. It was clear that Lai knew their every move even before they made it. Shaken, the police retreated to Beijing to reorganize the investigation.

Tipped off to the investigators' impending arrival, Lai had retreated to Macao, leaving his oldest brother, Lai Shuiqiang, to try to liquidate assets and clean up Yuanhua. As he often did when under stress, Lai sought solace in Macao's gaudy casinos while continuing to work his contacts in Beijing by phone. He desperately needed his friends in the military and intelligence circles to vouch for him. He still believed that he could escape punishment if central authorities were aware of his work for Chinese intelligence services. He believed that Premier Zhu wanted to stop smuggling without publicly unearthing past smuggling scandals involving the military. He failed to grasp that Zhu needed to implicate high officials if his fight against smuggling was to be successful.

In early August 1999, an army of some three hundred investigators from Beijing descended on Xiamen, taking over the entire Wanshou Guesthouse and arranging for it to be guarded by four hundred soldiers. At the same time, Lai had hit a winning streak in the Macao casinos. Emboldened by his lucky streak, Lai secretly returned to Xiamen on August 9 to figure out what remained of his business empire. While in Xiamen, he got phone calls from two friends—Zhuang Rushun, deputy head of the Fujian province police, and Yang Qianxian, director of Xiamen customs—warning him that Chinese investigators knew he was back and were preparing to arrest him. The port, airport, and major highways out of town were all under close surveillance. Lai ordered one of his drivers to get a plain sedan with tinted windows and pick him up near a highway entrance. They easily passed through a police roadblock on the highway that was checking only luxury cars. They drove straight to Shenzhen, the Chinese city that shares a border with Hong Kong. With the help of police friends, Lai boarded a boat to Hong Kong. A few days later, tipped off by a Hong Kong immigration official that China was arranging to have him arrested in Hong Kong, Lai; his wife, Zeng Mingna; and their three children boarded a plane to Canada.

Canadian Exile

As Lai and his family arrived in Canada, the Chinese government-controlled media exploded with a campaign portraying him as public enemy number one. Using numbers from the Zhu Niuniu report, they accused Lai of smuggling $6.4 billion in goods and avoiding $3.6 billion in taxes and tariffs. Authorities came down very hard on his family, arresting nearly all of his adult relatives. At first, the investigators merely called them in for interrogation and then let them go home in the evening. They were told that punishment would be lenient in return for providing information. The oldest brother, Lai Shuiqiang, who had been only briefly involved in Lai's smuggling operations, trusted the police and convinced thirteen people, including relatives and Yuanhua employees, to return from abroad and cooperate with the police. They were promptly arrested, tried, and convicted.

Lai had been a master at keeping his companies at arm's length from the actual smuggling transactions, which were in the name of partner companies. Investigators never built a strong paper trail, instead mostly relying on confessions obtained by interrogating family members, employees, and arrested officials. In the end, it took a thousand investigators twenty months to compile the case against Lai. Chinese prosecutors said that Lai partnered with an array of companies owned by the Chinese military, the Fujian provincial government, the Xiamen city government, and various national police and national security agencies.

At first, Lai lived in a Vancouver mansion that he purchased for about $1.5 million. He had a driver and a big sport-utility vehicle at his disposal. But almost all of his money was tied up in Xiamen real estate, which the authorities had confiscated. When they also traced and froze his various bank accounts, Lai's lifestyle deteriorated quickly. He moved his family into a three-bedroom apartment in a working-class section of Vancouver.

Armed with two new mobile phones, Lai worked his network in China, asking friends he had helped over the years to send him cash. He also established phone contact with his older brother, Lai Shuiqiang, who was trying to help Chinese authorities persuade Lai to come back to China. Investigators camping in Lai Shuiqiang's home opened a regular dialogue with the fugitive, assuring him that he would be treated leniently if he returned. They tried, unsuccessfully, to get him to meet them in Singapore. Finally, three investigators and Lai's eldest brother flew to Vancouver. They lied to the Canadian government, obtaining business visas by pretending to be a Chinese government business delegation. Lai talked to them for three days in their hotel rooms, which he paid for. They carried a written promise that he wouldn't be executed, that his wife wouldn't be arrested, and that part of his confiscated assets would be set aside for his children, who would be free to live where they wanted. Lai didn't believe them. If he wasn't executed outright, he told them, he would die a violent and unexplained death in jail.

The Chinese investigators refused to accept his novel argument that he hadn't damaged China's finances. "Although my company didn't follow regulations strictly, I didn't betray my country," he told them. "I would never steal money from the treasury. I only made money before it went into the treasury. It hadn't become the country's money yet."

Political Refugee or Common Crook?

The investigators went back to China empty-handed. Lai applied for refugee status in Canada on June 8, 2000, claiming that he had a "well-founded fear of persecution" because of his political opinions and his membership in a particular social group. He contended that he had been caught in a power struggle and that as a wealthy entrepreneur he is a member of a class of people in China that the government persecutes and discriminates against.

The Chinese government has put tremendous pressure on the Canadian government to return Lai to China. Canadian officials say the subject came up in every senior-level meeting. The Chinese could not understand why Canada didn't simply turn over Lai.

"They never, never, never got it that we could not interfere in our own court system, that we could not force the outcome, right up to Zhu Rongji and the highest levels," said a senior Canadian official who was a participant in many of the discussions. "It was beyond their comprehension. They just did not believe that we cannot tell our courts what to do."

During all this time, and up until publication of this book, the Canadian courts have been slowly moving the case along. After their arrest in November 2000, Lai and his wife, Zeng Mingna, were in and out of Canadian jails for almost two years. Their hearing before the Canadian Immigration and Refugee Board lasted for five months, by far the longest in Canadian history. Witnesses ranged from exiled Chinese dissidents criticizing the Chinese political and legal system to Chinese prosecutors detailing Lai's crimes.

In June 2002, the board ruled against Lai, essentially finding in favor of the Chinese government that Lai was not a political refugee but a criminal subject to extradition. On February 4, 2004, Lai lost his first appeal in the Federal Court of Canada. But Lai's lawyer, David Matas, Canada's leading human rights attorney, said appeals could continue for several more years. In essence, Matas intends to put China's legal and court system on trial in Canada. He said Lai has a well-founded fear of persecution because he likely faces an unfair trial, torture, and death back in China.

"That fits the legal definition of a refugee," Matas said.

Consequences

Lai's family is in shambles. His brother who ran the cigarette business, Lai Changbiao, is back home in Shaocuo, a paraplegic as a result of a bar fight. Lai Changtu, the brother who ran the automobile operation, is serving fifteen years in jail. Lai Shuiqiang, the trusting elder brother who inadvertently lured thirteen other participants home to be prosecuted, was given a lenient sentence of seven years for his cooperation. Two years into his sentence he died in a labor camp at age fifty-four. Officials said it was a heart attack. One of Lai's nephews, Chen Wenyuan, is serving a life sentence after officials suspended his death sentence. Lai's father-in-law and mother-in-law were jailed for sending Lai money for his legal defense.

Beyond Lai's immediate family, the toll from the Yuanhua case has been enormous. Nearly four hundred government officials were caught up in the case, including two ministers, twenty-six provincial officials, and eighty-six county officials. A total of 159 officials faced criminal charges, while 196 officials with senior party rank were punished according to party discipline. Fourteen people received death sentences. Four people committed suicide.

Yang Qianxian, the head of Xiamen customs, received a death

sentence for taking some $170,000 in bribes from Lai. The sentence was suspended and Yang given an indeterminate jail sentence in return for his cooperation in implicating Lai. Zhuang Rushun, the rising star and deputy chief of the Fujian province police, was sentenced to death, but the sentence was changed to an indeterminate jail sentence because he cooperated in the case. Lan Fu, the greedy vice-mayor of Xiamen, was charged with taking bribes totaling some $600,000 and sentenced to death. It was later commuted to an indeterminate jail sentence after he confessed and helped investigators.

Li Jizhou, Lai's close friend and vice-minister of the Public Security Bureau, was sentenced to death. The sentence was reduced to jail time because he "showed repentance." In his written confession, Vice-Minister Li said his major problem was neglecting his political study, "seldom reading the books of Marx, Lenin, and Mao." He also said he had spent too much time with businessmen.

"According to the old saying, Government officials shouldn't have too many friends," he wrote. "That makes sense."

Lai need not feel lonely. Just three months after he fled China for Canada, Forbes magazine published the first-ever list of China's richest people. Cobbled together from bits and pieces of ten years of accumulated newspapers and other public documents, the Forbes list soon became known in the Chinese media as the "death list" for the government scrutiny that it focused on entrepreneurs who had been less than scrupulous in amassing their wealth. As other lists of rich Chinese appeared in the popular media, the Chinese government acknowledged that some four thousand Chinese government officials were on the lam in foreign countries after stealing an estimated $5 billion in government and state-enterprise assets.

As one senior Chinese official with twenty years of working at top levels in Beijing told me: "Being corrupt is not a big deal. Everybody is corrupt. But you can't be corrupt and be politically incorrect at the same time. You don't have to be clean as long as you are loyal to your political protectors above you. Honesty in China will always lose out to piety and loyalty."

In August 2001, under the orders of Premier Zhu Rongji, Lai's now-infamous Red Mansion was opened as an anticorruption exhibit. It would, officials said, serve as "an alarm bell that has to keep ringing and ringing." It was a huge hit. People flocked to Xiamen to see the double-size bathtubs in which generals had cavorted with prostitutes, the dance hall and movie theater, and Lai's own bullet-proof car. A month later, even as travel agents were being flooded with tour requests, the exhibit closed. The public's reaction, recorded in the visitors' book, had shocked the leadership.

"Such a big case, so many corrupt officials, how come it has dragged on for so many years before being discovered?" asked one visitor. "This is a problem with the system."

Ruminations from "the Boss"

I met Lai Changxing in Vancouver in the summer of 2003. I expected to encounter a sleazy, somewhat scary guy. Instead I found the nicest international fugitive you would ever want to meet. Sitting on the balcony of a modest Hilton Hotel near his home in the blue-collar suburb of Burnaby, Lai looks like a Chinese worker on a North American holiday. Dressed in a T-shirt and khaki slacks, he sports a flat-top crew and the ruddy face of a peasant. He doesn't look at all distressed but he chain-smokes Chinese Double-Happiness cigarettes and fiddles with two mobile phones. As they did in Yuanhua's heyday, the phones ring every few minutes. But it's no longer Chinese generals and top party officials on the other end. It's his demanding and distraught wife, who wants him to cook dinner and warns him that he must be home before the 6:30 P.M. curfew that Canadian officials have imposed as part of his house arrest.

There's little for Lai to do these days except ruminate over his ordeal. He doesn't understand why his methods have failed so miserably. He built visible friendships with senior officials, but he seldom asked them for anything in return. He counted on those highly visible friendships with senior officials to reassure lower-level officials that they could safely become Lai's friend and help him out just as he helped them. Lai says that he followed this tradition, merely exploiting the natural inclinations among the lower-level officials he befriended. He explained it to me with this convoluted reasoning:

"I didn't give government officials money in exchange for their help with my business. I wouldn't do this. If I regard you as a friend, when you have difficulties, I will help you. If you have requests, and I am capable of meeting those requests, I will help you. But I won't ask you to repay me. It is a mutual exchange. With these friends you can know which business you can do, and what you can't do, which areas you can make money in and which areas you can't. There is no harm in having these friends, right?"

Lai hates that he is known across China as a gangster. He sees himself as an average businessman who did everything right. He treated people fairly. His employees were paid higher-than-market wages. Many had free lodging and free food. He fired only one employee in all his years in business. The man was a drunk, so Lai continued to send a monthly stipend to the man's wife and child. There were other smugglers besides him, Lai told me, but they were from prominent families. They were quietly put out of business and given protected government or military positions, not a bullet in the back of the head.

"I had no grand plan. I pursued the businesses where I thought I could make the most money. Everything that has happened was just a coincidence," Lai said as he gathered his cigarettes and mobile phones to head home before his curfew time. "Now I see how dark the system is. I would have been better off to stay a vegetable farmer. Nobody will interfere with you. Nobody will be jealous of you."

What This Means for You

While this is a dark tale, and China still has many, many dark corners, this episode occurred in the 1985–95 "smash-and-grab" decade when people like Lai's nemesis Zhu Niuniu got themselves into the middle of government deals and made piles of money. Many of these ill-educated but powerful slugs and thugs of the system are now retired, enjoying their luxury cars, countryside villas, multiple mistresses, and focusing on lowering their golf handicaps.

With the spectacular rise of private Chinese companies, often funded by venture capital or stock market listings, the business environment is more transparent and marginally more law-abiding. But China still doesn't pay civil servants enough to expect honesty, and the government workforce is so vast that to hike salaries to keep up with the private sector could bankrupt the government. Young people today, both in government and the private sector, are also aware that they are at the tail end of the Chinese gold rush, so many are eager to feast on the "emperor's grain" while they have the chance.

How does this environment affect your company in China, and how do you deal with it without going broke or going to jail? As a foreign company in China you are in the same boat as Chinese companies: you depend on approvals and favors from officials in order to conduct business, and you sell and distribute your product into a system that is lubricated by graft. The practices I have seen employed by foreign companies in China can be categorized as good, bad, or ugly.

Let's start with the good. Do not succumb to the notion that all Chinese people are corrupt and the system requires corrupt behavior. There are many companies that insist on strict ethical standards and develop higher-level methods and relationships to survive in China. Large multinationals can operate above the muck because their deals are often very large, very visible, and they are interacting with senior government and party officials. They often win business in China as they would anywhere else in the world by selling top-quality products that China needs and bringing in state-of-the-art manufacturing capabilities and know-how. While operating in China, these companies try to focus on helping their Chinese partners, suppliers, and customers become more sophisticated and international.

In the 1980s and 1990s, it became widespread practice, considered ethical and acceptable, to arrange overseas tours for Chinese business and government counterparts, mixing facility tours, business seminars, and training courses with generous opportunities for tourism and relaxation. Many officials and state-enterprise managers don't have the money or the permission to travel overseas for learning or tourism on their own, so this formula is still effective today. In the late 1980s and early 1990s, AT&T essentially trained the hierarchy of China's telecom bureaucracy and engendered lots of goodwill along the way. It is important to have company officials accompany these delegations, from start to finish, because the true personal friendships developed on these trips are invaluable.

Many of your Chinese business counterparts these days are well funded and well traveled, so free trips and business tours have little allure. But these individuals are focused on building internationally competitive companies. Exchange programs in which Chinese business partners work temporarily in a series of headquarters departments or home-country manufacturing operations are very effective. Equally useful are high-level training opportunities. Perhaps the best example of this is General Electric, which invites senior executives from Chinese partners, suppliers, and customers to attend ten-day management courses with simultaneous Chinese translation at GE's highly regarded executive training facility in upstate New York. GE also regularly assembles Chinese executives at hotels in China to attend GE training seminars, at which top GE officials give seminars and mingle with the executives. Chinese executives who participate feel that they are part of the GE family and also members of an exclusive club.

Now the bad. Once you get below the level of big multinationals doing large deals, China becomes a swamp. If you are selling your product or services to the Chinese government and state-owned enterprises, you often have to decide how much of your soul you also want to sell. The procurement process in China is usually corrupt at every level. Whether it is factories purchasing equipment, retail outlets agreeing to purchase and display your product, or companies seeking professional services, kickbacks are often required.

American companies and executives are forbidden from engaging in any form of bribery by the Foreign Corrupt Practices Act. Europeans generally face similar but looser restrictions. Companies from elsewhere in Asia often consider such fees a normal and accepted part of doing business. The solution chosen by many companies is to engage Chinese consulting firms or agents who act as middlemen in such transactions. The Chinese entity will often introduce an agent or consulting company to the foreign company to advise them on the deal. This is the foreigner's version of "don't ask, don't tell." Kickbacks or payoffs are never discussed or acknowledged because the foreign executives can't "knowingly" be engaged in bribery. It is simply acknowledged that certain agents and consultants can be helpful in creating business opportunities. What happens after that, nobody wants to know. American attorneys hate this practice, but many of them help multinationals draft contracts that do what they call "papering over" the FCPA. In general, the process involves paperwork that demonstrates that you have done your due diligence, that there is a business reason for using this agent or consultant, that the entity wasn't created for this specific transaction, and that the operators and shareholders of the contracted entity can't be traced back to a decision maker or government official. You also have to be able to make the case that you aren't overpaying for the service. "But once you go through that process, you want as little information as possible," said a veteran China attorney. One European company I know has a unique twist on this. Its contracts with middlemen are restricted to only one copy and that is printed in black ink on red paper, thereby making it impossible to photocopy. The company's China boss keeps that one copy in his office safe so that if internal auditors begin an inquiry, he can destroy the contract quickly.

In recent years, as the global economy cooled and China became the hot spot, the headquarters of multinationals sometimes pressured their China operations to make up for the lack of growth elsewhere in the world. Faced with rocketing revenue expectations, these China bosses had a tough choice to make: embark on career suicide by keeping their business clean and revenue low, or engage in aggressive kickback practices to meet their numbers. To preserve their sanity, some foreign executives go out of their way to not know what goes on inside their sales departments. I have several American executive friends who couldn't wait to escape from their China assignments because selling their soul or wrecking their career was an unspoken daily dilemma.

Another not infrequent step to the south side of the ethical line is the quiet funding of college education and living expenses for the sons and daughters of Chinese officials and state-enterprise bureaucrats. In some cases this is handled through foundations and similar entities so that the fingerprints of the company are not evident. In other cases, it is as blatant as depositing money in an overseas bank account in the student's name and giving that bankbook to the official who is involved. This is a routine practice for some Taiwanese and Hong Kong companies.

Finally, the ugly. When you are working at the grassroots level in China, direct bribery is all too often the path to success. I have Taiwanese friends who regularly deliver suitcases of cash to factory purchasing bosses in order to make sales of their manufacturing equipment. The retail business in China is riddled with store buyers who require kickbacks in exchange for stocking your merchandise. Again, this process is made convenient by distributing consumer goods through Chinese agents who deal directly with the retailers. In some cases, if you pay sufficiently, the buyer will block your competitor's product from the store. In a similar fashion, with China's newspapers, magazines, and television stations all under government control, local advertising agencies engage in a carnival of kickbacks to China's media managers.

A friend of mine who sells equipment to factories in the provinces explained the science of arranging kickbacks in China.

First you get an information source in the company who can tell you who really makes purchasing decisions and how they are made. Then you cultivate that person, or group of people, and wait for the signals. "The moment they give you their home phone number, you know you are in," my friend said. Salespeople are happiest when it turns out that there is a single powerful person who can *gaoding*, or "fix," the purchase and clandestinely distribute the cash to his colleagues. If it turns out that multiple people in multiple departments make the decisions, then the salesperson will likely cultivate relationships through nighttime entertainment, much like Lai at the Red Mansion, and bankrolling group holiday excursions. One friend calls this the "3G system": girls, golf, and gambling. In a weird twist of ethics, cash bribes signal a bond of trust between the people involved because they have to feel comfortable they won't be exposed.

A more traditionally Chinese way of seeking business favors is to bestow gifts. During Chinese New Year, it is expected that businesspeople will visit Chinese officials and executives at their homes and deliver gifts. In the past, cartons of cigarettes or bottles of expensive liquor were common. Today, laptops, golf clubs, home entertainment centers, and even automobiles can be on your holiday gift list. Chinese listed companies often work in a similar way. One of the main duties of the secretary of the board of directors is to make sure that board members are provided with automobiles, vacations, gifts, and expense accounts at expensive restaurants to keep them happy and beholden to the CEO.

What do you do? As China becomes more wealthy and sophisticated, it is getting easier to avoid corruption. There are many foreign companies that have policies of zero tolerance for corruption in China, and still enjoy good business because their products are the best and in demand. The Chinese market recognizes and seeks quality.

The travel, training, and education for partners discussed earlier is a proven way to operate on a higher plane in China, but this also has to be accompanied by strict internal company policies. Some companies require employees to sign code of conduct agreements. I did this with our employees at Dow Jones, and clearly told them that any violations would not only lead to their dismissal, but that I would also notify the police. We never had a problem, but we weren't selling widgets to factories in the boondocks, either.

Corruption has been a huge problem for the sourcing companies that act as middlemen between Chinese factories and foreign buyers. Their biggest problem was not with the Mainland Chinese but with Taiwan and Hong Kong factory bosses in China. They are often quick to offer envelopes of cash to sourcing company quality inspectors. One sourcing company run by a friend of mine stopped this through strict rules for their inspectors that include no entertainment or meals at night with factory officials. If a factory offers bribes, the sourcing company immediately cancels all orders. "If you cancel orders a few times, word gets around that you are serious," he said. Other companies arrange meetings at which they pull together all of their suppliers and announce they will blacklist permanently any supplier offering bribes or gifts to their buyers. Many Chinese factories react positively because it takes the guesswork out of transactions.

As for internal company management, your CFO must be somebody you trust completely, and you should apply transparency to your sales and procurement systems through CRM software and other technology solutions that remove power from individuals. Some of the better-managed Chinese companies shift their procurement managers every six months because they figure that is how long it takes for the sales and procurement people to develop close enough personal relations to arrange kickbacks.

The Little Red Book of Business

- If you decide to sell your soul and succumb to China's corruption, get a good price and focus on charity work in your old age.

- China's modernization is aiming at "rule by law" not the "rule of law," so relationships and personal power reign supreme.

- China is all checks and no balances. Chinese government anticorruption drives are not cynical exercises, but the effect is minimal because the overall system is almost incompatible with honesty.

- Your Chinese employees and partners have a confused ethical and moral framework, the result of a society turned upside down by reform in a country led by a party that has shifted from wealth repudiation to wealth creation.

- The gold rush of privatizing government industries in China is ending and officials and entrepreneurs are focused on snapping up state assets. Young people, sensing the end to easy money, may be more eager than their elders to "feast on the emperor's grain."

- China has returned to its traditional symbiotic relationship between the merchants and mandarins. Officials clear the way for business. The businesspeople pave the way for officials to accumulate assets.

- Senior party members in China seldom engage in direct corruption, preferring nepotism as the means to building family wealth. For the ruling elite, gathering family assets quietly is quietly accepted.

- To help your lawyer sleep at night, adhere to "don't ask, don't tell." Choose legitimate agents and consultants to obtain licenses and approvals, and seek as little information as possible about how they obtain them.

- Don't bribe. Nobody stays bought and the Chinese know it is against American law. Instead, invest in long-term, mutually beneficial relationships with customers including training, travel, and recreation opportunities.

- At its core, Chinese society is all about self-interest. It is very strong on competition but very weak on cooperation.

- In China, a conflict of interest is viewed as a competitive advantage.

- Draw bright lines for your employees. In Chinese culture, there is an indeterminate line between a gift and a bribe.

- Pay your employees sufficiently well to warrant their honesty, have them sign a code of conduct, and let them know there are real consequences for violations.

- Treat your entire company as if it were the finance department, installing CRM software and other technology solutions to promote data control and transparency, removing power from individuals.

- Assume your procurement department is corrupt unless proven innocent. Rotate procurement officials frequently into different products.

- Move boldly to confront scandal in your company. Prosecute wrongdoers rather than pay them to go away.

- *Guanxi,* the oft-cited Chinese word for relationships or connections, is overrated, temporary, nontransferable, and resides in the hands of the individual who has it. Never, ever put your business in the position where you are dependent on one individual for access to government officials.

- Inform your suppliers that they will be eliminated from consideration if they try to bribe your employees. The suppliers appreciate being let off the hook.

4

Dancing with the Dinosaurs

Powerful bureaucratic opponents can be beat if you have China's interests at heart. Dow Jones and Reuters demonstrate how using China's own tactics can be useful.

THIS MEANS WAR!

To be honest, my initial reaction to the new decree from the Chinese propaganda agency Xinhua wasn't that violent. The first paragraph merely indicated that Xinhua would "supervise foreign wire services . . . to safeguard state sovereignty."

No problem, I thought. We can work around that. All foreign businesses in China fall under the nominal supervision of one or another Chinese government entity.

But the next paragraph was more ominous. "Government departments at all levels, enterprises, and institutions . . . are not allowed to purchase economic information directly from foreign wire services . . ."

That can't be right. That would mean we would lose *all* of our customers.

Then it got worse. Xinhua "will examine and approve . . . economic information to be released in China."

That's censorship! What sense does that make for financial and business information used by financial market traders?

"Xinhua will determine subscription rates."

Wait. They're setting prices? No way!

Then the final straw: Foreign news organizations had three months to register with Xinhua or "be punished in accordance with the law."

I threw the directive onto my desk and looked out the window of my Beijing office at the cracked and filthy cement wall fifteen feet away that was my only view. It was January 16, 1996.

"This is going to be a real shitty year," I told the wall.

Xinhua was pulling a classic Chinese government power grab. It wanted to force news agencies—specifically financial information providers, such as my company, Dow Jones, and our biggest competitor, the British news agency Reuters—to teach Xinhua our business, hand over our customers and technology, and then stand aside as it pocketed the profits from the $35 million financial news and data businesses that we had created from scratch.

I had seen similar situations when I was *The Wall Street Journal*'s China bureau chief. Every so often a Chinese bureaucratic dinosaur would emerge from its regulatory swamp to stomp on a successful foreign or private Chinese enterprise and claim the business territory for itself. As a reporter, I enjoyed the drama of these battles. They were grist for great stories about what made China tick. But now I was the chief executive of Dow Jones's businesses in China. It was my head under the fossil's foot and my company's business in China was in mortal danger. This would be a fight for life.

Overview

China can be a scary place to do business. The legal concepts that govern Western business practices—the sanctity of contracts, the separation of regulators and competitors, and the protection of intellectual property, for example—simply don't exist in any dependable way in China. Despite significant economic reforms that have partially opened China's economy to foreign companies, the government and the Communist party remain all-powerful. Confronted by an order from the Chinese government, the normal businessperson's instinct is to accommodate and avoid conflict. It's difficult not to. The directives of the Chinese Communist government today still often carry the same forbidding tenor as the edicts of the Chinese emperors, whose orders ended with the phrase "tremble and obey."

Yet conditions for doing business in China are improving as the nation becomes more exposed to global business practices. Senior government officials, many of whom are well-versed in global economics and politics, continue to order the necessary adjustments for China to become an increasingly powerful and important player in the world economy.

I learned a lot of lessons in our two-year pitched battle against the Xinhua news agency and its shadowy ally, the powerful Communist Party Propaganda Department. I learned that if your business is doing what is right for China, you can win a battle against the most entrenched and ruthless government foes. You have to be extremely tough, persistent, and patient—and very creative in working both the Chinese and Western political systems. I and my collaborators from Dow Jones and Reuters made up our strategy as we went along, relying on our instincts of how China operates and knowledge of what the country's leaders want to accomplish. We also stayed carefully within one very basic parameter: When fighting battles and fixing problems in China, you can't embarrass the system. If possible, it is helpful to portray your opponent as doing so. But your arguments, especially as a foreigner, must be wrapped around what is good for China, not what is wrong with the Chinese government. If you are looking for justice and fairness in China, remember that the Communist Party, like the two thousand years of imperial rulers who came before it, considers the ultimate justice in China to be whatever maintains the system and its stability.

Unfortunately, this story is not one for the history books. The vast Chinese bureaucracy will continue to have a Jurassic Park of bureaucratic dinosaurs plodding around for many, many years, all seeking ways to feast on foreign and local businesses. Intel, Broadcom, and other world chip giants recently won a protracted struggle over a completely bogus Chinese wireless communication standard that would have allowed twenty-four designated Chinese companies to gain access to their technology and business secrets. DHL, FedEx, UPS, and their counterparts in the courier business are fighting with the Chinese post office, which on a crisp December day in 2001 got the government to decree that the most profitable part of the international courier business would be handled by the post office in China.

My friends in those industries have asked me from time to time for advice on dealing with their struggles and adjusting their strategies. I tell them the story of our scrap with Xinhua and the lessons we drew from that. This chapter is an expanded version of that conversation.

Left in the Dust

The modernization of China was leaving Xinhua in the dust. In Mao's day, the agency had been a glorious and powerful workplace. The nation's best and brightest college graduates were sent to work for Xinhua. With more than ten thousand cadres, Xinhua crafted the propaganda that shaped the thinking of China's masses. Its reporters also produced secret investigative reports that informed the party bosses about what was really happening in the country. Xinhua reporters stationed in Chinese embassies around the world filed news reports while also serving as intelligence agents and analysts. Money, or at least a profit, wasn't a concern to Xinhua in its heyday. It was amply funded by the government.

As rigid Communist doctrine began to give way to economic reform efforts, Xinhua's influence waned. Budgets grew tighter. The agency tried to bail itself out by getting into business. But the two hundred or so business entities it created, ranging from real-estate interests to the sale of Motorola pagers, were mostly money losers, created more to provide Xinhua officials with cars, expense accounts, and other perks than to generate profits. Still, the agency had gotten a taste of the money to be made in financial information with the advent of China's stock markets. Xinhua created two successful stock market newspapers, the *China Securities Journal* and *Shanghai Securities News,* in the early 1990s. Companies listed on the two exchanges were required by law to publish their earnings announcements in the papers and the ads often ran to several full pages. True to its propagandistic heritage, Xinhua usually wrote glowing stories about the companies to accompany the ads.

Xinhua also had a profitable operation in Hong Kong. China Global Public Relations Co. employed Xinhua's propaganda techniques and distribution network for commercial companies. The man who headed this business, a skinny, quick-witted Xinhua bureaucrat named Ma Yunsheng, was a rarity in the Xinhua bureaucracy, an entrepreneur. He inadvertently would lay the groundwork for Xinhua to come after Dow Jones's business.

With the exception of its stock market newspapers and the public relations business in Hong Kong, Xinhua was on the sidelines as the demand for financial news and data exploded in China in the early 1990s. At that time there were four global providers of comprehensive real-time financial news and data. Three were American—Dow Jones, Knight-Ridder, and Bloomberg—and the fourth was Britain's Reuters. Dow Jones and Reuters essentially split the China market, with Reuters having the larger share. Bloomberg had a minuscule presence and Knight-Ridder wasn't in China at all.

By the mid-1990s, China's economic reforms were entering their Wild West days. Unlicensed exchanges trading everything from soybeans to steel were popping up all over the country. We couldn't keep up with the demand for financial and economic data and news. Our terminals carried price feeds from the fourteen main Chinese commodity exchanges, as well as from the two Chinese stock exchanges. Our international information covered every important financial market in the world. All told, our terminals had sixty thousand pages of constantly refreshed real-time information, and Reuters's system was even larger. Chinese banks were installing our terminals by the hundreds, each at a cost of $2,000 a month, so that their traders, like those in financial firms around the world, could spend their days and nights staring at the screens, watching world events and news stories drive prices up and down.

Xinhua, of course, saw all this happening and began to lust after the obvious profits in the financial news and data business. It was stymied, however, by China's banks and trading firms. With some $100 billion in foreign exchange reserves at the time, China was becoming a significant player in world financial markets. Traders in Beijing's banks needed real-time access to the same market-moving data and news as their competitors in Bonn, Boston, or Bangkok. Dow Jones and Reuters supplied the data and news that were the lifeblood of the markets. China's banks and commodity trading firms didn't want Xinhua in the middle of their information flow. They figured that Xinhua's censors would slow news delivery and kill controversial stories that China found distasteful but nonetheless moved financial markets where Chinese traders had positions to defend.

The Hong Kong Huckster

As Xinhua sank into its bureaucratic swamp, Ma Yunsheng, who was running the agency's Hong Kong public relations operation, began thinking about how the Internet might be a way to make some real money. He teamed up with two U.S.-educated Hong Kong Chinese entrepreneurs. James Chu was a UCLA computer science graduate who had bounced between real-estate sales and mail order marketing. Peter Yip was a computer engineer with an MBA from the Wharton School and had experience in strategic planning at KPMG Consulting in the United States. Together the trio dreamed up a plan for Xinhua to use its political clout to gain monopoly control of the Internet in China. The plan was to create the China Wide Web, a separate network walled off from the global Internet's World Wide Web. The Internet in China would be a closed user group with paid-only access under the control of a Xinhua subsidiary to be called China Internet Corporation, or CIC. CIC would filter any information from the Internet that crossed into China's border, ridding it of unwanted political and social content, and translating it into Chinese. Given China's focus on economic development, CIC's key content would be business information. CIC would build a twenty-thousand-square-foot complex in Shenzhen and hire platoons of Chinese translators to fill it. Fantastic financial projections were assembled, with estimates of more than one million customers and hundreds of millions of dollars in revenue within a few years. Xinhua, desperate for more revenue, bought the entire scheme. In 1994, the agency registered China Internet Corporation (CIC) in Hong Kong as a wholly owned subsidiary of the Xinhua News Agency.

While Ma and Chu worked on getting political permission to control the Internet, Peter Yip set out to raise capital among Hong Kong's tycoons. A short but sturdy man with a square head, perfectly coifed hair, pin-striped suits, and Gucci shoes, Yip is a master salesman who knew what the Hong Kong tycoons wanted to hear. They were eager to cultivate Mainland China relationships. CIC's Xinhua parentage was a powerful calling card. The name "Xinhua" inspired fear in Hong Kong because the agency's Hong Kong office was staffed with diplomats and spies busily laying the groundwork for the July 1, 1997, transfer of Hong Kong to China from British rule. Hong Kong's wealthy businesspeople were desperate to do anything to curry favor with their future sovereign. Yip talked his way right into their pockets, easily raising $25 million to get CIC started.

Dow Jones and Reuters provided proprietary information to paying subscribers and thus had little to worry about from CIC, even if it were able to control the Internet in China. What we didn't know at the time was that James Chu had prepared a "white paper" to justify CIC's efforts to control the Internet. In "A Vision for the People's Republic of China's Internet Development" he likened information to "viruses." An uncontrolled Internet spreading dangerous viruses would threaten China's national sovereignty.

"When new ideas are brought into another culture, it [sic] will sometimes destroy the old existing one and create social unrest," Chu wrote. The paper concluded that "there are ideas that . . . should be stopped at all cost."

Xinhua rewrote Chu's white paper and then passed it to the party propaganda department, which sets strict content guidelines for all media and cultural entities in China. The nation was still reeling from the horrible global publicity that resulted from the Tiananmen Massacre in 1989. Ding Guangen, China's propaganda czar and one of Deng's poker pals, loved the idea of protecting China from outside information and ideas. But before the authorities could figure out how to implement the controls, young Chinese entrepreneurs had already set up Internet service providers and Yahoo-like Chinese websites, and the nation's universities had established a network of international links to the Internet. It was too late to control the Internet. But Chu's arguments about protecting China from outside influences had given Xinhua the weapon it needed to achieve another goal. The agency convinced the State Council—roughly the equivalent of the American president's cabinet—that foreign news and data providers in China needed to be better controlled. The result was the January 1996 directive that, if enforced, would drive Dow Jones and Reuters out of business in China and, not coincidentally, put China's entire economy in danger.

The Chinese government at this time was in many ways very primitive. The various agencies and departments were rigidly controlled from the top down, with little or no coordination among them. Xinhua had obtained the State Council's approval of its new regulatory powers by working almost exclusively within the Communist Party Propaganda Department. Xinhua's leaders hadn't consulted with the ministries of foreign trade, foreign affairs and finance, the stock market regulators, or the central bank. Had they done so, someone would have made it clear that an order effectively muzzling the free flow of financial information in China and jeopardizing the nation's financial institutions wouldn't be well received in the rest of the world.

Suddenly, China was in the midst of a firestorm of accusations and questions from abroad. Headlines across the globe condemned the order as a step backward for China. The Clinton administration, the European Union, and the World Bank all questioned how China could successfully take over the international financial center of Hong Kong if the country's leaders didn't understand the financial markets' vital need for the free flow of news and data. More troubling for China, Xinhua's decree raised questions about how ready China was for possible membership in the World Trade Organization. China desperately wanted to join the WTO. Pride was part of it—membership would be an important recognition of China's place in the world economy—but membership also would help China's leaders make further economic reforms within the country. China's vast export machine also needed the practical protections that WTO membership would provide. Without membership, any of its many trading partners could simply shut its doors to Chinese products at the slightest provocation. Chinese officials who were deeply involved in the WTO negotiations and in the return of Hong Kong had been blindsided by Xinhua. They took their complaints directly to the State Council.

It wasn't long before Guo Chaoren, the president of Xinhua, found himself before the State Council, explaining and offering self-criticism. Guo, whose given name translates as "superman," had significant political clout as a member of the Communist Party's central committee but no understanding of financial markets. He had made his name as a reporter extolling China's suppression of the Buddhist rebellion in Tibet in 1959. Now he told the State Council that the directive was intended to protect China from American cultural domination, which he said might make the Chinese forget their heritage. The State Council said they supported Guo's goals but ordered him to fix the problem. That was easier ordered than done. Guo couldn't simply cancel the decree. The loss of face for him, for Xinhua, and for China would have been intolerable. But as he found over the next two years, enforcing the decree wasn't much of an option, either. Both Dow Jones and Reuters had determined that they were neither going to tremble nor obey. The battle was on.

Divide and Conquer

Typically, China's bureaucrats bring an industry to heel by dividing and conquering. Sure enough, at my first meeting with Xinhua officials to discuss the new rules, they said that Reuters was the real target. They complained that Reuters had too much market share and that Reuters's news service carried much more political news than the Dow Jones service. It was probably true that Reuters was their principal target. The company had a gold mine in its foreign exchange terminal, through which 60 percent of the world's foreign exchange transactions took place. Chinese bankers were snapping up those terminals as fast as Reuters could install them.

What the Xinhua officials didn't know, however, is that Reuter's China boss, a gentlemanly and intelligent British Sinologist named Richard Pascoe, was one of my closest friends. Both Richard and I were journalists in China before taking over the business side of our respective companies. As a journalist, you see a dark side of China that is usually hidden from foreign businesspeople. We had been forced to live in diplomatic housing compounds where our phones were tapped and our apartments bugged. Our secretaries, translators, drivers, and even our children's baby-sitters were foreign ministry employees who were required to report on us. In tense times, people we talked to casually on the street were hauled in for questioning. Whenever I took a reporting trip outside Beijing, I was followed by a dozen or more plainclothes agents. The frustrations of living under such circumstances probably added fuel to our urge to fight Xinhua. I was much more emotional and angry than Richard as the battle began. One day I pitched a fit about a particular Xinhua official who was both duplicitous and arrogant. Richard told me to relax and put the matter in perspective.

"Jim, you have a car and driver," he said. "You live in a big house and take vacations in Thailand. These guys ride bicycles to work in the morning and they live in shitty apartments owned by Xinhua." I was much less self-righteous after that.

There was a temptation among Dow Jones Telerate executives in Hong Kong to cooperate with Xinhua and knock Reuters from its dominant market position. However, the idea was immediately vetoed. Both Peter Kann, Dow Jones's chief executive, and Reuters's CEO, Peter Job, believed that taking a stand against Xinhua was vital to both companies' global business interests. Kann and Job were both former journalists who believed that the unfettered distribution of news and data was key to the success and stability of global financial markets. They also worried that if China won this battle, both Dow Jones and Reuters would face similar attacks from other developing countries.

"It's the free flow of information, not just Reuters's information, that China finds threatening," Kann said in a memo quashing Telerate's suggestion. "Thus, my general view is that we and Reuters are better off hanging together on this issue because the alternative, almost surely, is to hang separately."

Richard and I made a pact. Our companies were fierce competitors. We admitted that we couldn't tell each other everything, but we also promised not to lie to each other. We agreed to share information and plot common strategy to fight Xinhua. Within China, we could cooperate only behind the scenes. If foreign companies publicly band together in China to challenge the government, it can quickly trigger paranoia and insecurities left over from the 1800s, when foreign powers carved up China. It is best to work these kinds of issues behind the protection of an industry or trade association. But we had none. Instead, Richard and I would meet late at night in my home or in the quiet corner of a hotel lobby to plot strategy before and after meeting separately with Xinhua.

Within a month of the State Council directive, Dow Jones and Reuters had worked out a list of common principles that would guide our negotiations with the Chinese government. First and foremost, we knew we had to respect China's sovereignty by acknowledging the government's right to a "border check" on news. That simply meant that we acknowledged their right to read incoming news stories on our wires. We explicitly denied that they had any right whatsoever to change the stories or to otherwise censor them. The second most important principle, and the one that became our mantra, was that Xinhua could not be both our regulator and our competitor. Unfortunately, that is very often the case in China. What the West routinely views as a conflict of interest, the Chinese simply see as a competitive advantage. As China prepared for entry into the World Trade Organization, however, the government knew that separating regulators from business management was imperative.

Somehow, Xinhua missed that memo.

Beyond that, we stuck to basic business principles: allow the market to set prices, ensure equal market access for all—no restrictions on developing new customers and launching new products—and full protection of our intellectual property.

The Reuters lawyers were very clever. They viewed the Xinhua directive as an opportunity as much as an obstacle. Like many businesses in China at the time, we were operating under undefined legal authority. The legal philosophy in China is opposite of the United States. China has a presumption of government control, so unless something is expressly permitted by law or regulation, you can't do it legally. In America, the presumption is one of individual freedom, so unless something is expressly restricted, the people have the right to do what they want.

There was nothing in Chinese law that said we could, or couldn't, conduct this business in China. Operating in such gray areas is quite normal in China, but this isn't a comfortable place to be when the government decides to target your company. So we made it a goal to get a written clause that explicitly gave us permission to operate as financial news and data providers in China.

Having a set of high principles to guide your negotiations in China is fine. They're necessary. But it's also necessary to pursue what our Chinese lawyer, Gong Jun, calls the "iron-ass strategy" when negotiating. The Chinese are very patient negotiators. That isn't surprising if you know China. The Chinese people grow up enduring nonstop speeches from teachers and lengthy propaganda lectures. They can tolerate endless nonsense. Foreigners, on the other hand, often become impatient, which puts them at a disadvantage. It's best when negotiating to develop an oratorical loop that you can politely repeat time after time while sitting in your chair for hours. He who breaks first loses.

I won one of those small victories at an early meeting with Xinhua. The Xinhua officials across the table were angry and befuddled at the uproar their edict had created. They hoped to calm things by backpedaling and telling us what they thought we wanted to hear. They promised "no interference in our business," only "minor management fees" and "strengthened protection of intellectual property rights." In turn, we politely blanketed them with lists of detailed questions about how the policy would be implemented. We went around and around until a Xinhua official named Yang Zhen had had enough.

"We are in charge," he snarled, shaking a finger at me. "You will do what we say. You have no right to question any of this."

Yang's outburst was telling. There are, of course, many extremely sophisticated and intelligent people and organizations in China. But there are also many who still operate in a world that is best described as a "thugocracy." Decades of social chaos, political purges, and wrenching Maoist manipulation created a government operating culture in which bludgeoning your opponent into submission and then taking the spoils is a way of life. Xinhua was chockful of heavyweight thugocrats like Yang. We knew we couldn't beat them through intellectual argument alone. We had to be just as thuggish as they were. My next chance to hit them hard came a few weeks after our meeting with Yang. My weapon was a Xinhua sales brochure.

We were back at Xinhua on a chilly February morning for more discussions. A dirty gray blanket of sooty coal smoke hovered over the frozen concrete of Beijing. Sleepy Xinhua staffers, long underwear protruding from their pants legs and shirtsleeves, shuffled through the barely heated halls cradling jars of hot tea. We settled around a table pockmarked with cigarette burns in a dimly lit meeting room where tattered red curtains blocked any natural light. Four Xinhua officials filed into the room, offering wide smiles and friendly handshakes. As we sat down, a man with disheveled hair, a jumble of stained teeth, and a rumpled white shirt opened a pack of Chinese cigarettes and leaned across the table to offer us a smoke. Discussions started when the Xinhua boss lit up an imported Marlboro and demanded: "When is Dow Jones going to register with Xinhua?"

Instead of answering, we launched into our now familiar back-and-forth litany about Xinhua being both our regulator and competitor. We said that as regulator and competitor Xinhua had a clear conflict of interest. As always, the Xinhua officials swore up and down that there was a clear division between Xinhua's regulators and Xinhua officials who were launching competing businesses.

After a half hour of back and forth, Xinhua took the argument in a new direction. They accused me of "ulterior motives." They said that I was trying to destroy Xinhua's reputation for integrity. That was what I had been waiting for. We knew that salespeople from a new Xinhua subsidiary company were already calling on our clients in southern China, telling them to cancel the "illegal" foreign services and subscribe to the new "authorized" Xinhua service.

I apologized "for causing any misunderstanding." Then I conducted an informal survey. Smiling, I pointed at each of the four Xinhua officials one by one, asking a question: "Are you our regulator or competitor?"

"Regulator," they each responded.

Then I lifted my briefcase onto the table and slowly pulled out a brochure that the new Xinhua subsidiary was distributing to our clients. I opened it to a photo of smiling Xinhua executives.

"Then who are these guys?" I asked.

The photo was of the four Xinhua executives sitting across from me. They were the leaders of the company Xinhua had created to take away our business.

All four stared down at the photo without saying a word. After fumbling to light another Marlboro, the leader announced that this meeting would end so that they could "conduct further research." They left the brochure on the table and rushed out of the room. I had caught them in an outright lie. Their loss of face was enormous. But then again, we were fighting for our survival.

Letters, Lobbying, and Delays

We had been given three months to register with Xinhua. Our plan was to delay registering until we could obtain a written agreement that narrowed the scope of the regulations to those with which we could live. We looked for different ways to keep Xinhua off our backs. One tactic was to scare them with the complexities of our business. In a series of letters, and a product demonstration in our office, we pointed out that if Xinhua signed contracts with our customers, Xinhua would have the legal liability to collect our money from deadbeat customers. We also let them know that they could be the defendant in lawsuits filed by our third-party information suppliers whose information was being stolen by Chinese competitors. I launched into a complex explanation of technology issues, some of which I made up as I went along. The man in charge of trying to understand all this was a kindly Xinhua sports editor named Wang Yongsun. He had been called back from retirement to handle this project because he could speak English. As he sat in our office getting increasingly befuddled by our product demonstration, sweat beads formed on his forehead and he nervously shuffled his shoes back and forth on the floor beneath the desk. Clearly he was going to have a hard time explaining these complexities to the bosses.

The delays gave us time to organize a massive lobbying and letter-writing campaign that would take advantage of the international attention that Xinhua had brought on itself. Within China we had plenty of tacit support from our banking and trading company clients, but they all declined to take any action. In China, Xinhua held the ideological high ground. The Communist party's deep-seated belief in the need to control information—and Xinhua's well-known ties to Chinese intelligence agencies—made it politically risky for Chinese companies to actively oppose the new regulations. Our Chinese bank customers basically wished us luck and settled down to watch the show.

We knew from the outset that we had to enlist the U.S. government on our side. Dow Jones hired a Washington, D.C., law firm that was headed by President Clinton's close friend Vernon Jordan, who was also a member of Dow Jones's board of directors. I had been a reporter on Capitol Hill during the Reagan administration, so I knew how both Washington and Beijing worked. It would be my job to focus on tying together our lobbying efforts in the two capitals.

Our strategy was to insure that every time a Chinese official or minister met with a foreign politician or government official— whether in China or overseas—the Xinhua issue would arise. Richard Pascoe and I became letter-writing machines. We churned out letters for our bosses to send to everybody from top Chinese leaders to European Union officials to important members of Congress and Parliament. I personally wrote letters that, after editing by their aides, were sent out over the signatures of U.S. Trade Representative Mickey Kantor, Treasury Secretary Robert Rubin, Senator John McCain, Undersecretary of Commerce Stuart Eizenstat, and many others. A letter in March from Dow Jones Chairman Peter Kann to Chinese Premier Zhu Rongji was aimed at educating him on our viewpoint that the regulations were bad for China. The flurry of letters reached an absurd stage. At one point I drafted a letter that was sent over the signature of a U.S. government official.

Then I helped the Chinese recipients of the letter to draft the response.

We had friends in high places. Shortly after Xinhua announced the new regulations, U.S. Trade Representative Mickey Kantor warned the Chinese ambassador that Xinhua's power grab might be embraced by the anti-China lobby in Congress and used as a weapon to fight the Clinton administration's efforts to ensure annual renewal of China's MFN trade status. Kantor's office invoked a "standstill" agreement in which China had pledged not to enact restrictive regulations on foreign businesses while negotiating for WTO membership.

Pieter Bottelier, the World Bank's chief representative in Beijing and a trusted adviser to the Chinese government, stirred up the Chinese financial bureaucracy with letters and personal meetings. Bottelier was genuinely outraged by the Xinhua directive, calling it "the most regressive step China has taken since it began economic reforms." His actions were key in framing the issue for China's financial policy makers.

We also used the law to elevate what was really a domestic political fight to the level of an international legal dispute. We searched for all the laws and agreements we could find that had even a remote bearing on our case. We found a July 1984 Chinese law that ordered "every entity and individual" with access to foreign information to collect "important scientific and technological intelligence materials" and hand them over to the Chinese military. That was evidence, we said, that Xinhua was basically under orders to steal our technology. We also used "fair and equal competition" clauses in trade agreements between the United States and China to demand that Xinhua give us all of their price lists, customer lists, the technical specifications of their financial information business, and all the other details they were requiring that we hand over to them.

As these legal issues bounced back and forth in letters, senior officials in the Chinese ministries of foreign affairs and foreign trade became helpful strategic advisers to us. They told me which American officials should send letters to which Chinese officials. They helped me think through the most palatable way to present our arguments. The sophisticated officials in these ministries viewed the Xinhua moves as a regressive money grab that was detrimental to China's accession to the WTO. They wanted the Xinhua issue resolved and off the table so they could focus on WTO.

The Old Versus the New

Three months after the Xinhua directive came down, in my role as chairman of the American Chamber of Commerce in China, I led a group of twenty-five American business executives who had operations in China on a lobbying trip to Washington to seek renewal of China's MFN trading status. Following the 1989 Tiananmen Massacre, Congress used the annual renewal of China's MFN status for a wide-ranging congressional debate on China that covered everything from human rights to missile proliferation. Every year, legislators introduced bills to deny renewal of China's MFN status. If passed, the result would have been punitive tariffs that could derail China's economic growth because the United States was China's dominant export market. Our annual AmCham lobbying trip was aimed at educating Congress, the White House, and even the Pentagon that the more business done with China the better.

Xinhua had assured me before I left for Washington that implementing regulations for its January decree would not be published while I was away and that when issued they would reduce the scope of Xinhua's regime to "minimal interference." On April 15, 1996, I escorted several American executives to meet with the editorial board of *The Washington Post* to make our case for the renewal of China's MFN status. That night I returned to my hotel to find a flurry of phone messages and faxes from Beijing. Xinhua had not only announced the enforcement regulations, but the details were extremely onerous. This, to me, was strong evidence that Chinese security officials were the ultimate backer of this information control regime. The trade minister, foreign minister, central bank governor, and even the Chinese WTO negotiators were not in favor of these Xinhua regulations, but here was Xinhua storming ahead at full speed.

A reporter from *The Washington Post* called me to ask if I felt like a fool for leading business executives to lobby for China on Capitol Hill while China's main news agency was stealing Dow Jones's business. I was extremely angry, but I figured it was better to get even than get mad. I spent the next two days giving a series of press interviews, saying how this just bolstered the business community's case on Capitol Hill. I framed it as the Old China fighting the New China. We were on Capitol Hill to argue for free trade and increased business ties because we believed this would lead to reform in China. With these regulations, Xinhua was just showing how economic reform forced the dinosaurs of Old China to thrash around for footholds in the new commercial world. The *Post* did a lengthy feature story with two photos. My mother liked it. Xinhua hated it. When I went to the Chinese embassy to talk to Ambassador Li Daoyu about the issue, he burst into laughter. He understood how dumb Xinhua was to give me such a prominent platform to publicize the issue in Washington.

When engaged in disputes, the Chinese government often tells foreigners that they have "hurt the feelings of the Chinese people." When I got back to Beijing in May, I told Xinhua officials that they had "hurt the feelings of all Dow Jones employees." I told them I had lost face at headquarters because I had assured my bosses that the implementing rules would be delayed. As a result, I told them, I could no longer be involved directly in the negotiations; all decisions would now come from "higher authorities" at Dow Jones in New York. Now I could really drag my feet. I felt great. I was mastering Chinese negotiating tactics.

The Endgame

The negotiations, lobbying, and letter-writing campaign seemed to go on forever with little progress by either side. But in April 1997, Xinhua made a fatal mistake. From time to time, both Dow Jones and Reuters had talked about flexing our collective muscle by cutting off China's news and data feed. Without the constant updating of our screens, Chinese traders would be left with billions of dollars in market positions and no information. It would be like suddenly going blind in a high-stakes poker game. But the idea never got serious consideration from Dow Jones. It was the equivalent of having a nuclear bomb; it gave us perceived strength, but it was a weapon we couldn't use and still retain our credibility among traders. Reuters executives kept open the possibility of cutting off their news and data feed if China went after Reuters's immensely lucrative foreign exchange dealing system.

For its part, Xinhua had clearly thought about simply shutting down our businesses if we refused to register. They decided to demonstrate their muscle by closing down one province. Many of our customers had been installing satellite dishes without bothering to get licenses. In Guangdong, a dispute between the provincial Department of Radio, Film and Television and the Radio Management Committee over which agency would collect fees for satellite dishes resulted in a survey of rooftop dishes. Xinhua got the locals to prod our customers to show proof that they were legally registered with Xinhua. The deadline was May 30. One month later, according to the official notice, those who weren't registered would be "penalized." Xinhua officials told us this meant that Dow Jones and Reuters customers in Guangdong province would have their satellite dishes confiscated and thereby their signals cut on June 30, 1997, unless they were registered with Xinhua.

The Guangdong threat was part of a carrot-and-stick strategy Xinhua launched to try to force our hand. The carrot that the agency offered was to drop its demand to collect management fees from the foreign news services, which had originally started out with Xinhua seeking 40 percent of our revenue. All other regulations, Xinhua said, "will be rigidly enforced."

Now we had them.

Consumed as it was with internal political maneuvers, Xinhua apparently never lifted its head to look at what else was happening on June 30. At midnight on June 30, 1997, the British government would hand Hong Kong back to China. Some five thousand journalists were gathering in Hong Kong, many of them looking for stories to illustrate how China would or would not screw up Hong Kong. Xinhua was scheduled to cut off access to the world's financial markets in China's most financially sophisticated province, the one closest to Hong Kong, on the very day Hong Kong would be returned to China.

I hyped the hell out of their mistake. I flew to Washington and briefed officials at the USTR, State, Treasury, and Commerce departments and informed key members of Congress. In Beijing, I complained to the ministries of foreign affairs, foreign trade, finance, and several others. Xinhua was bombarded with so much criticism that I expected officials to be wearing helmets the next time I met them.

The battered agency backed off. The Hong Kong handover went off smoothly without a Guangdong information cutoff. Xinhua was now less determined to bludgeon us into submission. They tacitly acknowledged that we could be as thuggish as they could. Now they only wanted to make the problem go away. Within two weeks of the Hong Kong handover, Xinhua agreed that an exchange of letters between U.S. and Chinese government officials would be a convenient vehicle to forge a solution. Richard Pascoe and I were told to back off and exchange no more correspondence with Xinhua. This was now considered a government-to-government negotiation.

The U.S. letter—one that Pascoe and I helped draft—raised an extensive array of questions and concerns. Five months later, a letter came back from Chinese officials specifying that Xinhua would receive no fees, no profit split, no details of our financial arrangements with customers, and no specifications for our software and hardware. Xinhua would have two duties: a nominal registration procedure and the ability to monitor our news. That letter became the vehicle for a negotiated agreement between the U.S. and Chinese governments, and its provisions also applied to Reuters and other non-American international information providers. We called it an "interim solution" to protect ourselves globally. We didn't want what happened in China to set a precedent in other countries. The "interim solution" nomenclature allowed us to get on with our business. We planned to later permanently nullify the Xinhua regulations through "national treatment" language in the WTO agreement.

On October 29, 1997, nearly two years after Xinhua first proclaimed the directive, the White House announced that China and the United States had reached an agreement that allowed foreign financial news and information providers to operate in China "on acceptable terms."

That didn't mean, however, that Xinhua accepted those terms. I've since learned that after President Jiang returned from his U.S. summit meeting, a senior Xinhua official went to the Ministry of Foreign Trade and Economic Cooperation and said, "Can we go after them now?" He was bluntly told that Xinhua would abide by the terms of the agreement. Nonetheless, even today Xinhua officials insist that the exchange of letters was merely a "clarification" and it doesn't constitute an official agreement. Reuters and Dow Jones officially registered with Xinhua in December 1997.

Xinhua is now split by internal battles between those who want to engage in more business, and purists who want to restrict the agency to its propaganda mission. FIAC, which was supposed to take over our business, now consists of a few junior clerks sitting in a cement room, watching international news scroll across a screen all day. FIAC officials summon Dow Jones and Reuters executives from time to time to criticize them for publishing news stories that Xinhua doesn't like.

Are You "Yipping" Me?

While the thrust and parry of our negotiations played out, Xinhua learned a more modern way of doing China business from Peter Yip (whom we met earlier in this chapter), a model that is now often employed in many variations by Chinese bureaucracies in search of cash: hype and list. Once Yip realized that China Internet Corporation couldn't control the Internet, he decided to turn CIC into an international business information service for China. But the company's association with Xinhua, and Yip's reputation for hyping CIC as he talked to different potential partners, made it difficult to get any traction. When CIC purchased equipment, company press releases called the supplier a CIC "partner." Multinational executives who answered letters from Yip found themselves listed on brochures as "advisers." Everybody was told a different story. He would tell Reuters that he had a deal with Dow Jones. He would tell Dow Jones that he had a deal with Reed Elsevier. He would tell the *Financial Times* that he had a deal with *The Wall Street Journal*. It didn't work. The big media companies were all talking to one another about the Xinhua situation and Yip's reputation preceded him. He became a comic figure. Some of us used "yip" as a verb that loosely equated with lying, as in "Are you yipping me?"

But Yip was nothing if not persistent. He quickly changed strategy again and purchased the URLs for china.com, hongkong.com, and taiwan.com and promoted himself as China's Internet king. He renamed the company Chinadotcom and talked his way into public listings in New York and Hong Kong at the peak of the Internet bubble. He continued to hype the China dream to raise nearly three-quarters of a billion U.S. dollars from public listings for Chinadotcom and affiliates in eight months in 1999 and 2000.

In the next four years, Chinadotcom, with Yip at the helm, blew through about $500 million. When he wasn't tending to his racehorses or socializing with fellow tycoons, Yip bounced around the world, from one idea to another, from one deal to another. In the year 2000 alone, Chinadotcom spent $190 million to purchase some fifty companies. Almost all imploded. Chinadotcom never became a serious player in the Chinese Internet, but Xinhua finally got its hands on some cash. During the initial share offerings, some $90 million were directly pocketed by Yip, Xinhua, and other shareholders. Subsequent share sales earned Xinhua another $35 million, according to an agency official. Xinhua still holds a 7 percent stake in the company.

What This Means for You

There are some aspects of our prolonged fight with Xinhua that were unusual. For example, there was no room for any real compromise between the two sides. The financial news and data business simply cannot exist if it is being censored or used to peddle propaganda. Xinhua couldn't accept a role as a silent partner in a business that often published information that angered or upset China's leaders. So we had a fight to the finish. If Xinhua had come to us with proposals similar to deals forced on us years earlier by the governments of Malaysia and Indonesia—state news agencies in those countries got a 5 percent revenue share from Dow Jones and Reuters—we likely would have gone along.

If a Chinese bureaucracy makes a move on your business, the best thing to do at the outset is ask yourself if there is a deal that can be done. Put yourself in the shoes of your new potential competitor. Is there a way to give them what they are seeking and still maintain a reasonable and independent business in China? If there isn't a reasonable compromise that appears obvious—and be prepared to accept only an absolutely reasonable compromise—then prepare for battle.

The key to winning a fight with the bureaucrats is to appeal to the more confident and reasonable side of China. Carry the struggle over the heads of your bureaucratic adversaries. If your business spans the entire nation, that means to the president, premier, and other politburo members and ministers. But don't go there for anything less than a world-class dispute. At the senior levels, the Chinese government is very focused on the larger issues, not petty pick-pocketing or the maintenance of inefficient monopolies. If you do take the fight to the highest levels, tread very carefully around issues of sovereignty or foreign domination. China is paranoid on those subjects and its extensive network of military and security forces is a formidable foe. If your problem involves a provincial or munici-pal agency, the local governors, mayors, and Communist Party sec-retaries are the people to target for help, but don't hesitate to go over their heads should they be in cahoots with your adversary.

We felt we had little choice but to take our fight to the top and we knew we would find allies there. The premier and president wanted to build accountable and stable domestic financial markets and maintain the country's ability to gather billions in foreign capi-tal through overseas listings of Chinese companies. Even so, we had to nullify the arguments of China's security forces by acknowledg-ing from the start that China had the right to monitor the informa-tion we were providing. We went to pains to emphasize that the data and information we were supplying were going to closed trad-ing rooms and was not to be distributed publicly.

We were fortunate that China was desperately seeking entry to the World Trade Organization. We were able to become a minor roadblock in their way, one they badly wanted cleared. We also were able to capitalize on Xinhua's stupid mistake in threatening to shut down our information and data feeds to Guangdong province on the same day that Britain was scheduled to return Hong Kong to Chinese rule. Don't count on being handed a weapon like that.

As I look back on our strategies and tactics, I realized that by simply following our instincts on China, Richard Pascoe and I fought a very Chinese battle against our Chinese adversaries. There is a universal fear by government officials that something they do could be criticized for not upholding the country's interests. We quickly and loudly—and truthfully—portrayed Xinhua's plan as a selfish land grab that would be seriously detrimental to China's national interests. We also used the law as a political weapon, just as the Communist Party does. We searched through international and domestic statutes and trade pacts to find language we could turn into noble weapons that put us on the side of the angels. We chose language that called for protection of intellectual property, fair competition among businesses, transparency in regulations, and similar issues that were stated Chinese government objectives and things they had agreed to in trade pacts. We weren't building a legal case. We didn't have a clear one. Instead, we used this assemblage of legal clauses to frame our political arguments and our propaganda campaign.

Except when going toe-to-toe with Xinhua in negotiations, we kept our message positive. We educated the relevant bureaucracies and business groups, from top to bottom, in the United States, Europe, and China on our point of view. Within China, without realizing it at the time, we employed the Communist Party's favorite tactic of political struggles by isolating our adversaries and then attacking them politically. Our modern adjustment was to attack Xinhua as "counterproductive" not as "counterrevolutionaries."

Finally, we took our case to anyone outside China who might be willing to help. Given the constant flood of foreign officials to Beijing and the relentless globe-trotting of Chinese officials, there are abundant opportunities to have your issue come up in conversation. Because of the circumstances surrounding our dispute, we were able at various times to enlist some very powerful players, including President Bill Clinton, Treasury Secretary Robert Rubin, Senators Phil Gramm and John McCain, and Federal Reserve Chairman Alan Greenspan. You may not be able to recruit such heavyweights, but your congressmen and various business associations and trade groups can make their voices heard. Draft the letters for their signatures. The easier you make it for the politicians, the more they're willing to help.

My advice is that you write letter after letter after letter. China is ruled by the pen, not the sword. Blanket the bureaucracy and leadership circles with polite and professional letters that poke holes in your adversary's action by asking questions and raising issues that will bolster your point of view. When Chinese bureaucracies get letters, they feel compelled to respond. Make them squirm with tough questions. You can get away with some pretty outrageous questions and rhetorical hyperbole by playing the role of the dumb foreigner. The Chinese in their hearts believe that their system is so nuanced and complex and inscrutable that foreigners cannot fathom how it really works, so use that to your advantage. Asking process questions that would necessitate your Chinese interlocutor explaining their system to you is a good way to tie them into knots.

In the end, this sort of government advocacy is an art, not a science. There are no magic formulas. You must rely on the instincts of your most experienced China hands and business executives to decide when and how hard to push. You can't be too hard, but if you're too soft you'll get nowhere. Indeed, you need to exercise caution about which weapons you do use. Had we chosen to flex our muscles by shutting off our information flow to China's banks and trading firms, plunging them into chaos, we would simply have confirmed that foreigners could have a stranglehold on a vital sector of the Chinese economy. The focus would have shifted instantly from economic development to state security. That's a battle no foreigner will ever win.

My best advice for handling these crises is to anticipate that they are coming and spend the money for comprehensive and proactive government relations in China. Many companies hate to do this because the costs can't be directly attributed to profits. You can be certain that if you are doing business in China, whether your company is big or small, you will run into political problems, large and small. You may not end up in a debilitating battle as we did. But with one part or another of the Chinese government having its fingers in every aspect of business in China, if your regulator is not your competitor, it is likely that your regulator is dedicated to helping your Chinese competitors.

The Little Red Book of Business

- Be tough. The Chinese respect it. Never "tremble and obey" if doing so will damage or destroy your business in China.

- If engaged in a heated battle, remind your Chinese counter-parts of their own proverb: *Bu Da Bu Xiang Shi,* "Without a fight, you don't get to know each other."

- Remember that while China is confident, reasonable, and eager to become a world-class competitor, many Chinese politicians remain deeply paranoid and insecure about the outside world.

- Avert crises by spending the money necessary for a com-prehensive and proactive government relations program in China. You might even help shape your industry's regulatory environment.

- Before engaging in a fight with a hostile regulator, determine if a fair deal can be done. Is there a way to satisfy what they are seeking and still maintain a reasonable and independent business in China?

- If you must fight with the bureaucracy, take your fight to the highest possible level, where officials are the most reasonable and focused on China's larger interests.

- Frame your arguments to show how your business is good for China, not what is wrong with the Chinese government. You can't make the system look bad.

- Government officials can lie to you, but you must never lie to them. Exclude information, but don't provide false informa-tion.

- Be prepared to educate the bureaucracy from top to bottom to prove that your proposition is better for China than that of your government adversary.

- Persistence pays. Make yourself a major nuisance by blanketing the bureaucracy and leadership circles with polite and professional letters asking tough questions and raising issues bolstering your position.

- Patience pays. The Chinese are waiting for your attention to wander or your headquarters to grow weary of battle. Adopt your own "iron-ass strategy" by developing an oratorical loop you can politely repeat while sitting in your chair for hours.

- Play the "dumb foreigner" when necessary. Tie your opponent in knots by asking detailed questions about how the system works. The Chinese believe that their system is so nuanced, complex, and inscrutable that foreigners could never understand it.

- Don't rely exclusively on the law in China. You will lose. Use laws and regulations to enhance political and business arguments in favor of your position.

- Understand and use the fact that most Chinese government officials live in fear of being criticized for not upholding China's interests.

- Enlist your home government, relevant international organizations, and trade associations to fight for your cause. Show your adversaries who you are by who you know.

- Never go toe-to-toe with the cops. They have immense power and you will always lose. Instead, go around them and find ways to disarm their arguments.

- If you decide to purchase Chinese listed company stocks, beware of "hype and list" businesses.

5

Caught in the Crossfire

Government lobbying must be a key part of your China business plan, especially for technology companies that might be squeezed between hot competition and the Cold War.

AS THE WHINE OF Air Force One's jet engines died, nearly all eyes in the crowd gathered at Beijing's airport were on the doorway through which Richard M. Nixon would step. The president of the United States had come to Beijing on this chilly February day in 1972 on a "journey for peace," seeking rapprochement with America's die-hard Cold War enemy. It was an historic occasion. But one group of spectators was far more focused on the Boeing 707 that had brought Nixon to China than they were on the president himself. They were some of the top officials in China's struggling aircraft industry and they had been invited to examine the jet while it was parked on the tarmac. They were impatient. The sooner Nixon came down the stairs to shake hands with Premier Zhou Enlai and get in the limousine, the sooner they could get aboard the sleek white aircraft.

For years China's aviation industry had been stuck in a time warp, using primitive machinery to build rickety aircraft based on outmoded Russian technology. That was all that was available because of the West's Cold War restrictions on technology transfer. The only break they had gotten over the years was when a Pakistan

Airlines Boeing 707 crashed in western China in 1971. Chinese government engineers carefully dismantled it. Using reverse engineering techniques, they built two copies of the design that they called the Yun-10. Alas, primitive manufacturing techniques, lax quality controls, and a lack of advanced avionics resulted in a plane just as shoddy as the Russian planes China had been building for two decades.

Now they had a chance to examine the best commercial airliner that money could buy and technology could build. After all, this Boeing 707 had just brought the American president to China. He wouldn't travel in anything less than the best. The Chinese aviation officials were impressed by the workmanship and technology. The plane's interior was comfortable but not luxurious. But the cockpit, that was almost overwhelming! It had everything an aviator could dream of: radios, navigational equipment, and gauges that measured any parameter you could think of were all laid out in orderly clusters for the pilot, copilot, and flight engineer. Outside, the plane's smooth skin and almost seamless fairings were evidence of the tight tolerances and precision machining that went into its construction.

Nixon's trip was a huge success. Years of hostility were put to rest, diplomatic relations began to thaw, and trade ties were encouraged. Within weeks of the trip, China's top leaders, acting on recommendations of their aviation engineers, ordered ten 707 airliners from Boeing, promising to pay for them with U.S. dollars, despite the country's dearth of foreign currency reserves.

Overview

That initial order for ten aircraft set in motion a complex series of events. It marked the beginning of China's desperate and relentless effort to repair and renew its technological and industrial base with advanced Western technology. It touched off a commercial race among the world's aircraft manufacturers to dominate a potentially huge market. Immediately behind them came the world's satellite makers and aerospace companies seeking to harvest new profits in a market that grew so quickly that success or failure in China determined a company's future. As China struggled to build a modern aviation and space industry, American and European companies wanted both to help and to exploit the effort. Amid the competition for the China market, the Cold War–era export control agreements on technology crumbled. China's race to obtain advanced technology triggered political warfare within the U.S. government between those who wanted to severely limit what China could purchase and those who favored advanced technology sales and cooperation with China as both a political and commercial strategy. Many businesses were caught in the middle.

This is a two-part story. The first is about how McDonnell Douglas desperately tried to save its commercial aircraft business by assembling airplanes in China while diligently trying to satisfy the often conflicting requirements of the U.S. and Chinese governments. The second part is about how Hughes, Loral, and other American satellite makers got caught in a frustrating catch-22. They were forced to launch their satellites in China because the American government curtailed launch capacity at home. As Chinese rockets failed and their satellites exploded on the launch pads, the U.S. companies felt compelled to provide technological help, but at the risk of being accused by Washington of aiding a potential enemy.

McDonnell Douglas's failure went beyond politics. The company neglected business fundamentals and failed to keep pace with China's constant and rapid changes. The satellite companies, in contrast, got their business and politics right, but were pummeled in Washington because conservative Republicans needed a weapon to attack the Clinton administration.

Today the U.S. government is in danger of following in the footsteps of McDonnell Douglas by failing to keep pace with China's constant, rapid changes. Many U.S. politicians and policy makers don't recognize fundamental changes in the global technology marketplace and ignore the fact that the voracious China market can now determine which companies win globally. The Cold War has given way to hot competition, but not everyone in Washington understands that.

The China Expert

Gareth Chang wasn't quite sure why he had been invited to the meeting being convened by Douglas Aircraft President John Brizendine in Long Beach, California. Chang, a thirty-six-year-old engineering executive in McDonnell Douglas's St. Louis headquarters, knew that Brizendine had recently returned from a trip to China looking for market opportunities for McDonnell Douglas's commercial airliners. Sure, Chang had been born in China and he was known as something of a whiz kid around the company, but he had left China as a small child and his reputation was based mostly on some important advances he had made in the esoteric realm of military reconnaissance technology that had nothing to do with commercial aviation.

Brizendine was excited. He told his assembled executives that China had asked if McDonnell Douglas would be interested in setting up a factory in China to coproduce 125 commercial airliners a year. That was more than the Long Beach factory was making! A deal like that could be the key to reversing McDonnell Douglas's fortunes. And they were fortunes in dire need of reversal. Immediately after World War II, Douglas airplanes represented 90 percent of passenger aircraft in the United States and Europe. But as Brizendine returned from China, Douglas held less than 20 percent of the market. The McDonnell Aircraft Corp., founded in 1939 by James Smith "Mac" McDonnell to make military planes, had purchased Douglas in 1967 to diversify into the commercial airplane market. The midwesterners running McDonnell from its St. Louis headquarters had never gotten comfortable with the Californians running Douglas. They suspected that the Douglas executives lived too well and managed too loosely. Brizendine resented St. Louis's oversight. He was determined to break free of the executive handcuffs and revitalize Douglas.

Few of his executives shared Brizendine's enthusiasm. At best they were intrigued, but cautious. Nixon's groundbreaking China trip in a Boeing 707 had instantly made Boeing the preferred supplier and market leader for commercial aircraft in China. A joint venture in China might break Boeing's lock on that market. Among all the skeptics, one voice was enthusiastic. China had abundant scientific and engineering talent, Gareth Chang told the other executives, and it had a rudimentary aircraft manufacturing industry. The joint-venture idea was very promising, he said, but he warned against being too optimistic. "We'll be lucky to be able to build ten airplanes a year," he predicted.

That was good enough for Brizendine. Gareth Chang quickly emerged as the company's China expert. He had left China at the age of six when his father, a Nationalist Party police official in Shanghai, fled with the family to Hong Kong as the Communists seized power. Now handsome, poised, and articulate, Chang certainly had the look and bearing of a young Chinese ambassador or executive. If his McDonnell Douglas colleagues thought he was a China expert, then he'd be a China expert.

The proposal that McDonnell Douglas sent to China was mostly a general outline of how McDonnell Douglas made airplanes. It suggested that a China coproduction facility could start by assembling kits of parts that would be sent from Long Beach. The group drafting the proposal knew it had to focus on two realities: China would have to commit to purchase enough airplanes for the deal to make economic sense, and McDonnell Douglas would have to be prepared to license significant technology to China.

The proposal promptly disappeared into the Chinese government's labyrinthine bureaucracy. Only after two years of silence did a fax appear from China asking to begin talks. Suddenly the scramble was on. Ideas were being passed back and forth when Chinese Premier Deng came to the United States in 1979 on a groundbreaking state visit to mark the resumption of formal United States–China diplomatic relations. China had just ordered three Boeing 747 airliners and Deng had requested a tour of the massive 747 production line in Seattle. Chang was crushed. Boeing was becoming more deeply entrenched in the China market.

China followed Deng's trip with a delegation of thirty officials and industrial bureaucrats who toured the United States for a month, looking for business opportunities and studying American capitalism. Chang deftly maneuvered to make himself a coordinator of the second visit, working out details between the State Department, Commerce Department, FBI, and Chinese organizations. The Chinese delegates had naïvely planned to play McDonnell Douglas and Boeing off against each other and head home with a letter of intent for airplane coproduction in China. They didn't realize the time and effort that American companies put into such complex deals and they went home empty-handed. They did, however, return to China with Chang's assurances that McDonnell Douglas was eager to become a partner.

Convinced that China was a huge opportunity, Chang headed there to push things along. He found a warm reception. Most of China, especially military bases and factories, was still closed to foreigners, but Chang was escorted to a dozen of the military's aircraft factories. They were all the same, fashioned from the Soviet industrial cookie-cutter mold in the 1950s. Behind high walls guarded by soldiers, Chang saw sprawling compounds replete with schools, hospitals, worker housing, and dozens of huge but tattered buildings housing dusty machine shops and airplane assembly areas.

As he visited the plants, Chang was delighted to discover groups of English-speaking engineers who had been educated at MIT, Princeton, Harvard, and other top universities prior to 1949. They were excited about the prospect of building modern airplanes. Chang also became a popular tutor on the American system for senior Chinese officials. In sessions that usually went late into the night, Chang would sit in conference rooms adorned with Mao's photo and brief senior generals on how the Pentagon worked with

U.S. defense contractors or answer questions from senior political leaders about the details of American family life. How much was his income? Tax payments? Spending on food, medical care, and other necessities? The officials took copious notes. They were amazed. Decades of anti-American propaganda had left them convinced that in the United States the government controlled everything. Chang was not only making himself a China expert, he was becoming a trusted insider among China's elite.

Chang returned to Long Beach to report that he had found a potential partner in government-owned Shanghai Aviation Industrial Corporate (SAIC), which had an airplane factory at a World War II–era airfield twenty miles outside of Shanghai. It had little aviation work to do. Many of the factory's four thousand workers were making aluminum bus bodies. Chang suggested that Douglas start small, testing the ability of Chinese workers with a contract to manufacture MD-80 landing gear doors. The Chinese were befuddled and worried by the five-hundred-page contract that McDonnell Douglas lawyers drafted to seal the $1 million deal. The Shanghai factory director looked forlornly at Chang as he signed it. "I am signing this because I trust you," he said. At the end of 1979, Chang was promoted to president of McDonnell Douglas Asia/Pacific and opened the company's China office in two rooms of the Beijing Hotel. He didn't move to China, preferring to commute from California.

Pounding Rivets

Formal negotiations for the larger coproduction project opened in 1979 and continued for six tedious years. McDonnell Douglas directors worried about the risks of doing business in China. After all, Boeing was selling more and more planes to China and it didn't have production facilities there. To reassure the directors, Chang told them he foresaw China helping McDonnell Douglas cut costs by producing parts there. He also convinced the Chinese to buy five MD-82s built in Long Beach to show good faith and to give Chinese airlines a chance to get accustomed to the airliner. The initial dream of producing 125 airliners a year shrank to a 1985 contract that called for SAIC and McDonnell Douglas to coproduce in Shanghai twenty-five MD-82s that would compete head-to-head with Boeing's extremely popular 737. SAIC held an option for twenty-five more. McDonnell Douglas would license SAIC to assemble MD-82 kits. The planes would be produced on the same production lines in Long Beach as all the other MD-82s. But before they reached the final assembly area, the nose, fuselage, wings, tail, and other major components would be crated and shipped to Shanghai for final assembly.

While far short of what had been envisioned years earlier, the agreement, touted as a $1 billion deal, was the largest commercial deal ever between U.S. and Chinese companies. It established a pattern that China would follow for decades: in exchange for market access, foreign manufacturers would transfer technology and produce at least some of the product in China. Chang was an instant celebrity. *Fortune* magazine dubbed him "The Billion-Dollar Man."

The factory in Shanghai was a shambles. It had been built to produce a simple jet trainer, but now was mostly idle. The dilapidated building with a dirt floor the size of ten football fields had to be refurbished to accommodate McDonnell Douglas's high-tech assembly line. Over a period of months the factory was transformed into a replica of Long Beach, right down to the numbered tools and safety slogans. Less than two years after the project began, the first coproduced MD-82 was FAA certified. It was, by any measure, an amazing achievement. The Chinese engineers and production workers learned quickly. Pressured by its Chinese partners, McDonnell Douglas spread its technology around, contracting for some MD-82 parts from other Chinese airplane factories.

Chinese managers gradually took over key positions in the production process. They adapted well to such American manufacturing techniques as "total quality management," a rigorous system of statistical measurements, problem solving, and continuous quality improvements. But it was expensive to make the kits because of the extra steps for packing and shipping. Indeed, it cost as much to pro-duce a finished MD-82 in Long Beach as it cost to produce a kit for shipment to Shanghai. To reassure the Shanghai venture that it wouldn't be undercut by Long Beach, McDonnell Douglas agreed not to sell finished MD-82s from Long Beach in China. Instead, it sold the kits to the Shanghai factory at a steep markup. Because Shanghai had an iron-clad agreement that the Civil Aviation Administration of China (CAAC) would buy the first twenty-five planes, it then added its own markup. Chang wasn't worried about what it cost CAAC to buy the MD-82s. After all, from the Chinese point of view, the whole purpose of the coproduction agreement was to improve the Chinese aircraft industry, not to provide a few dozen cheap airplanes.

Cutting Costs, Courting Customers

By the late 1980s, the Chinese aviation world was changing fast as China dismantled its Soviet-designed industrial sector. The govern-ment monolith with which Chang had arranged the original MD-80 deal was splitting into pieces and dividing up responsibilities. One result was a proliferation of airlines formed by local and provincial governments. In the middle of China's eastern seacoast, the city of Xiamen founded Xiamen Airlines in 1984. In the far northwest, Xinjiang Airlines came to life in 1985. Zhejiang province, just south of Shanghai, jumped in with Zhejiang Airlines in 1986. By the early 1990s, China had eleven separate airlines, all government owned, but each with its own bottom line.

Boeing treated the regional airlines like royalty. Indeed, without Boeing the regionals may never have been created. Boeing's generous training programs for pilots, flight engineers, mechanics, and ground crews, as well as significant investments in parts depots and flight simulators in China, were the foundations that got the airlines off the ground. Boeing also flew the airline executives—local govern-ment bureaucrats, most of whom hadn't traveled much in China, much less abroad—around the world to visit Boeing in Seattle to place orders. The sales trips included lengthy layovers in Hawaii and other tourist hot spots. By the end of 1989, Boeing had sold ten 707s, thirty-four 737s, thirty-three 757s, ten 767s, and three 747s to the Chinese airlines. In the same period McDonnell Douglas had produced about a dozen MD-82s in Shanghai.

Chang largely ignored the airlines, confident of the ultimate power of his backers in the Chinese leadership. The original contract required CAAC to purchase the airplanes, so CAAC was constantly twisting arms, trying to force the Chinese airlines to buy the MD-82s. But they resisted. If the aircraft was made in China, then clearly it was inferior to the American-produced Boeings. Price was an issue, too. Because of the markups that McDonnell Douglas charged the Shanghai venture and the further markups that Shanghai charged CAAC, the MD-82s from Shanghai cost several million dollars more than a comparable Boeing 737. It didn't help that the best McDonnell Douglas could offer was a sales trip to Shanghai while Boeing took its customers hopscotching around the world.

Despite weak sales, Chang was proud of his accomplishment. The MD-82s assembled in Shanghai were every bit as solid and reliable as those produced in Long Beach. Chang figured that once the airlines realized this they wouldn't be so reluctant to buy. Meanwhile, he was focusing on the cost advantages that McDonnell Douglas might eventually wring from its Chinese partners. His goal was to employ China's inexpensive engineering and manufacturing talent to bring down Douglas's production costs. It was, after all, the argument that had finally convinced the McDonnell Douglas board to go ahead with the original project.

In 1987, China asked Boeing, McDonnell Douglas, and the rapidly growing Airbus Industrie to submit proposals for coproducing medium-range passenger airplanes to serve domestic routes and feed passengers into hub airports in major cities. In its first phase the project to build what was called the Trunkliner envisioned 150 airplanes valued at $4.5 billion. The Chinese goal was for 75 percent of the Trunkliner airframe to be produced in China. The plan dovetailed nicely with Chang's long-term goal to shift much of

Douglas's global component manufacturing to China to reduce costs. It was the natural second stage of the existing coproduction project. This time inexpensive Chinese labor would allow the joint venture to undercut the price of Boeing's planes imported into China. Chang pressed hard to win the Trunkliner business.

Suddenly, though, the honeymoon in U.S.-China relations ended with the Tiananmen Massacre. American images of cuddly Chinese pandas gave way overnight to grim views of corrupt and evil Communist dictators with no regard for human rights. President George H. W. Bush froze military technology transfers, weapons sales, and military-to-military contacts with China. Military officials who had long worried about China as a future threat suddenly were getting plenty of ink and airtime. Congress demanded that any advanced technology going to China be thoroughly scrutinized to insure that it wasn't "dual-use" technology that China might use to improve its military capabilities.

As China's people hunkered down to avoid the crackdown and Chinese leaders dithered between Marx and open markets, McDonnell Douglas continued to struggle with its commercial airliner business. The company was now a distant third in the global market behind Boeing and Airbus, saddled with $4.8 billion in debt and laying off seventeen thousand workers. Boeing, in contrast, had just delivered a modified 747–200 to the White House to replace the Boeing 707 that had delivered Nixon to China. In 1990, China placed one of the biggest aircraft orders in Boeing's history, a $9 billion order for thirty-six planes and options on thirty-six more. To win the order, Boeing agreed to produce cargo doors and other non-crucial parts in China.

Nevertheless, in 1991, China selected McDonnell Douglas for negotiations for the Trunkliner project. Only a few months later Deng, who had retired but was still the Communist Party patriarch, publicly upbraided his successors in Beijing for backtracking on economic reforms, reigniting the reformist agenda. China went back to work. In March 1992, McDonnell Douglas signed an initial agreement with the China National Aero-Technology Import &

Export Corporation (CATIC) to coproduce forty upgrades of the MD-82 known as the MD-90. The MD-90 would be a transition to building the MD-95, a smaller one-hundred-seat aircraft that China would produce itself with McDonnell Douglas technical assistance under the Trunkliner program. Meantime, China was taking delivery of its hundredth Boeing.

The Trunkliner would be an enormously complex project that would require major technology and manufacturing upgrades to China's aviation industry. It would utilize four Chinese factories, some of which already were making parts for Boeing or the MD-82. In 1993, as preparations for the MD-90 were under way, Gareth Chang received a phone call from Michael Armstrong, the chief executive officer of Hughes Electronics Corporation. Armstrong had read press clips about Chang's China success and he wanted him to head up Hughes Electronics International, where he would be responsible for developing DIRECTV in Japan and building the satellite business in Asia. Coincidentally, Chang had just completed a corporate strategy study for McDonnell Douglas that concluded there was little long-term future for the company's commercial aircraft business. He accepted Armstrong's offer.

The Big Hitt

With Chang's departure, the Trunkliner deal landed in the lap of Bob Hitt, a dedicated Douglas production boss. Hitt had joined McDonnell Douglas in 1982 and had progressed steadily with production management jobs before becoming U.S. operations manager for the China coproduction program under Chang. At first he oversaw production of the MD-82 kits for Shanghai, but soon was spending much of his time in China, working to map out the Trunkliner production, logistics, and assembly.

When Chang left, Hitt faced a job that was beyond daunting. His mission would be to produce flawless parts and components at several rusting Chinese airplane factories controlled by indecisive bureaucrats who had just been cut loose from the military. He had to teach the precise ballet of component delivery and systems integration to people for whom coordination and cooperation were an alien concept. These people took orders from above and passed them down to someone else. To work with other factory bosses as equals was unthinkable. How, for example, could the managers at Xi'an, the largest and most capable factory, even think about listening to requests from the arrogant and self-important Shanghainese?

But Bob Hitt had the fortitude and temperament for the job. What's more, he loved China and the Chinese loved him. At six foot four, with thick glasses and an obvious paunch, he stood out sharply against his Chinese colleagues. But he had traits the Chinese admired: a fierce chain-smoking habit, a constant stream of good-natured profanity, and the ability to guzzle beer and trade shots of *mao-tai* late into the night with any banquet companion foolish enough to challenge him. He was a real leader who had the real knowledge that his Chinese counterparts craved. As he rode in cars and buses on country roads going to and from isolated airplane factories, he was endlessly amused by the sights and sounds of China. Watching a bicyclist wobble down the road with a live hog on the handlebars and a dozen squawking chickens bound to the back, he would laugh out loud. "Every day in China you see something you don't see every day" was one of his favorite remarks.

Hitt had studied *Chinese Negotiating Style*, a classic study of Chinese official behavior and negotiating techniques originally written for the U.S. military by MIT Sinologist and political psychologist Lucian Pye. Hitt took great delight in identifying various behaviors while negotiating with Chinese executives or government officials. Late at night after punishing rounds of *mao-tai* toasting, a Chinese counterpart might begin pressing Hitt for more details.

"Ahhh, the creative use of fatigue," he would announce.

Chinese negotiators might use flattery to get Hitt to reveal technical information they needed.

"Okay, this looks like the 'enlighten the uninitiated' ploy."

And when the Chinese would inevitably launch into an impassioned recitation of China's problems and how they were all the West's fault, he would chuckle. "Oh, not the imperialist guilt thing again."

The never-ending banquets that are a fixture of China business were like an amusement park to Hitt. Many of the Chinese aviation executives spoke English and Hitt constantly entertained them with stories or jokes, often laced with profanity. He was willing to eat anything, so the Chinese put more and more exotic dishes in front of him. One of his favorite banquet dishes was "surprise soup." The first time he ate it, he flipped open the silver lid on the bowl and said: "Fuck, wheels up, there's a bird in the surprise soup!"

One of his Chinese companions giggled. "No, that's not the surprise. The surprise is that there is a date and a nut inside the bird."

Hitt loved that kind of stuff.

The Fifth Factory

McDonnell Douglas's direct counterpart in the Trunkliner agreement was the China National Aero-Technology Import & Export Corporation (CATIC), the export-import arm of the Aviation Industry of China (AVIC). CATIC would help McDonnell Douglas coordinate the work of the four factories involved in the Trunkliner project. With the factories gearing up for Trunkliner production, CATIC was in the market for equipment. And it just so happened that a McDonnell Douglas screwup could be useful to CATIC. In its quest to cut costs, McDonnell Douglas had purchased an old Rockwell factory in Columbus, Ohio, but then decided it wasn't needed and announced it would be closed. Its huge stretches, presses, and machining and milling tools would be auctioned off for whatever McDonnell Douglas could get. Most of the machinery had been built in the 1960s and even the newest tools were a decade old.

CATIC soon got wind of the tool sale. The Chinese are deeply attuned to seek bargains and this had the odor of a true bargain basement sale. A delegation of Chinese engineers dispatched to Columbus in September 1993 to inspect the equipment was met by epithets from the workers who knew they would soon lose their jobs. Some workers even threw bolts at the delegation while others tried to block their video cameras. The Chinese decided to buy the equipment, but negotiations to seal the deal lasted for almost half a year as the Chinese fought to drive the best bargain.

In February 1994, CATIC agreed to pay $5.4 million in an all-or-none deal for 278 items, ranging from metal presses large enough to shape an airplane wing to desks, hand tools, and even wastebaskets. The Chinese would have to pack and ship the goods and have the factory cleared by July 5. McDonnell Douglas had hoped that CATIC's purchase of the tools would make it easy to close the Columbus factory, but they didn't reckon with the complex regulations governing the sale of machinery for export. The U.S. Commerce Department wanted reams of information before it would issue export licenses.

The licensing requirements were part of a long and schizophrenic effort by various U.S. government departments to control the spread of technology around the globe. During the height of the Cold War the restrictions had been extraordinarily tough, with the United States, Europe, and other non-Communist allies cooperating to block advanced technology and weapons from reaching the Soviet bloc and China. But technology had grown more complex with the advent of silicon chips, supercomputers, and satellites. American companies complained that the restrictions were hurting foreign sales. After Nixon's trip to China, the United States eased technology and weapons export controls to that country. By 1987, the U.S. military was permitting the export of fuse and detonator assembly lines, counterartillery radars, and antisubmarine torpedoes. Grumman even won a $550 million program to upgrade the avionics in Chinese fighter jets that were copies of Soviet MIGs.

The Tiananmen Massacre changed everything. Even as China

resumed its efforts in the 1990s to remake its economy, the U.S. military was butting heads with the U.S. Commerce Department over technology exports. Commerce officials thought the Defense guys were paranoid; the Defense guys pegged Commerce as naïve and beholden to corporate interests. In 1994, European and Japanese companies began selling whatever technology and equipment they wanted—with the exception of weapons—to whomever they wanted. American companies stood alone under tight technology export restrictions for China.

Hitt put John Bruns, a Chinese-speaking American who had grown up in Taiwan, in charge of getting the export licenses. Bruns was a shrewd but unassuming thirty-year-old with a flop of hair across his forehead and a constant mischievous grin. He found China just as entertaining as Hitt did. He had started as an intern in the China sales group of McDonnell Douglas in 1986 and had worked his way up to become Hitt's troubleshooter for the China coproduction projects.

Bruns and Hitt continually pestered CATIC to provide them with the detailed information the United States required. The most sensitive pieces of equipment were six big five-axis machine tools that could perform complex simultaneous motions: the typical horizontal, lateral, and vertical movements, as well as rotation around two perpendicular axes. Computer-controlled five-axis machines could be used to produce a variety of sophisticated products, including huge propellers for submarines that turned almost silently underwater. Not surprisingly, the Pentagon was generally opposed to the export of such machines to China.

CATIC assured the Americans that the information was coming, but it also told them about another decision it had made. Fearful of being left out of the skimming and kickback opportunities inherent in running a Chinese factory, CATIC officials had decided it would keep the most sophisticated machinery for itself in a fifth factory that would make the most complex parts for distribution to the other four factories.

Hitt liked the idea. It would be much more efficient than having the Chinese duplicate the capability in each of the four factories. But he also warned that the change in plans would delay the export license applications since some of the equipment would now be going to a different location than originally envisioned. He reminded CATIC that it would be responsible for all storage costs for the equipment until the licenses allowed export to China. CATIC suddenly woke up and faxed the necessary information.

McDonnell Douglas in May 1994 filed twenty-four export license applications covering thirty-two pieces of equipment. Internal U.S. government debates delayed the application for months. Commerce finally obtained consensus by adding conditions to the licenses, including one particularly burdensome requirement: McDonnell Douglas must provide quarterly reports to the U.S. government about the location of the machine tools and how they were being used. CATIC soon hauled its bargains off to China. Meanwhile, China's aviation industry was purchasing some two dozen state-of-the-art computer-controlled five-axis machines from Europe and Japan.

On March 24, 1995, Bruns set off on the first of the government-mandated quarterly inspections of the equipment CATIC had bought. He took photos of crate numbers and checked them off his list, but he couldn't find six of the machines. He asked his CATIC escorts where the machines were. Avoiding direct eye contact, they muttered, *Bu tai qingchu,* which literally means, "That is unclear." It really means, "I can't tell you." Bruns would have to talk to their bosses.

Bruns was furious. He had spent four months pestering CATIC executives and cobbling together information for the license applications. He had held their hand throughout the whole process, dealing with information that was usually confusing, vague, and late. From the day he joined McDonnell Douglas's China operations it had been drilled into his head that all U.S. government laws and licenses had to be strictly followed. Bruns stormed into CATIC's Beijing office the next day and confronted the program managers. He grew angrier and angrier as they continued to evade his questions. At first, they were also muttering *bu tai qingchu*. But Bruns kept pushing. His company's integrity was on the line. He simply had to find those missing machines. Suddenly the Chinese discovered that the equipment had been sent to Nanchang, a city in southeast China.

"We ran out of storage space and sent them to Nanchang," a CATIC official said.

Bullshit, Bruns thought, something else is going on here. But what really pissed him off was that the Chinese were being so cavalier about it all. They didn't take the export license conditions seriously. In China, the art of getting licenses and approvals is to tell the government whatever it wants to hear, and then do whatever you want after permission is granted. You can always work around the system in China. What a mess, Bruns thought.

Bruns and Hitt, anxious about the apparent violation of the export license conditions, immediately reported the problem to the McDonnell Douglas export control office. A McDonnell Douglas letter on April 4 notified the U.S. Commerce Department that six machine tools had been diverted without McDonnell Douglas's knowledge to the Nanchang Aircraft Company.

It took until August for Hitt and Bruns to get permission from the Chinese government to visit Nanchang. There they found just another sprawling, dilapidated, and filthy Chinese factory. Five of the big machines were still crated, but a sixth, a ten-year-old stretch press, was uncrated and being installed. The huge metal-bending contraption was so big that the Chinese had to knock down a wall of the old brick factory to get the machine into it. The installation wasn't going well. The Chinese workers who had dismantled the equipment in Ohio had made meticulous notes and diagrams and had numbered each component and part so the machines could be reassembled in China, but they had placed all that paperwork in the crates with the tools. While in transit, water had seeped into the crates, turning all those meticulous notes into so much soggy pulp. Looking at the partially assembled machine, Hitt and Bruns could only laugh.

"How can this fit anybody's definition of high-tech?" Bruns asked.

The Chinese weren't laughing. They had bought tools to build their aircraft industry and they had received junk. The head of the Nanchang plant wrote a letter to Hitt in September apologizing for violating any U.S. regulations but also expressing surprise that the secondhand tools were so tightly regulated. He had purchased far more advanced machinery from Europe without having to obtain any licenses.

Hitt and Bruns deduced that CATIC and its bureaucratic counterparts at the four factories were engaged in the usual infighting and harebrained business schemes of Chinese government companies. CATIC, eager to amass profits, had added a healthy markup to the tools it intended to sell to the four factories, but the factory managers refused. They wanted state-of-the-art equipment, not America's hand-me-downs. Meanwhile, CATIC's planned fifth factory never got off the ground. CATIC was stuck with the tools.

Hitt and Bruns never determined exactly how the tools wound up in the Nanchang factory. They were relieved that it didn't seem to matter. The Commerce Department apparently considered it a case of Chinese commercial chicanery rather than a serious national security violation by McDonnell Douglas. McDonnell Douglas forced CATIC to box up the metal press and ship it along with the rest of the tools to the Trunkliner factory in Shanghai. In February 1996, the Commerce Department amended the export licenses so that McDonnell Douglas could use the tools in Shanghai. But McDonnell Douglas engineers considered the machines outdated and unusable. They were rusting in their crates a decade after leaving Columbus.

Rocket Science

While Bob Hitt and John Bruns slogged through the machine tool mess, Gareth Chang had his own technology troubles at Hughes, troubles that had started even before he joined Hughes. In December 1992, a Chinese Long March rocket carrying the Hughes-manufactured Optus B2 satellite exploded forty-eight seconds after liftoff from the remote Xichang launch center in western China.

Hughes had turned to China because there was no other way to get its satellites into space. To justify its enormously expensive space shuttle plans, the U.S. government had decided to phase out expendable rockets and use the shuttles to deploy satellite and other payloads in space. But then the space shuttle *Challenger* exploded in 1986. NASA prohibited the use of shuttles for commercial payloads at the time when satellite demand was soaring as the digital age brought advances in satellite television and telecommunications and global data distribution. The United States had some 90 percent of the market share of commercial satellites, but if Hughes, Loral, and Lockheed Martin couldn't get their birds into space, they would be out of business. Russia had some launch capacity available, but the U.S. government wouldn't allow American satellites to be launched from the Soviet Union. The European launch consortium Arianespace had no extra capacity. China, however, had plenty of rockets and was looking for business.

Like other forms of complex technology, satellite launchings suffered from American schizophrenia. The Tiananmen Massacre prompted Congress to prohibit the launch of U.S. satellites on Chinese rockets unless the president issued a "national interest" waiver. For the next several years the waivers were alternately granted or withheld, depending upon the state of political relations between the United States and China.

Hughes's investigation of the Optus B2 failure determined that the problem was a design flaw in the nose cone that protected the satellite. It had split open. That finding caused lots of problems. Chinese officials denied any responsibility. They couldn't have their Communist Party bosses thinking that they were building shoddy rockets. It was a matter of money, too. China had insured the rocket and Hughes had insured the satellite. With rockets and satellites running $100 million or so each, the insurance companies didn't want their clients blamed. And with satellites waiting in line for launch dates, China wanted to protect its cash cow.

After much finger-pointing, Hughes agreed in May to sign a memo stating that "there is no design or manufacturing or integration flaw in the launch vehicle or the fairing . . ." Once that face-saving document was signed, the Chinese launch company, Great Wall Industry Corporation, went ahead to fix the nose cone, as Hughes suggested, by using stronger rivets. The U.S. Air Force colonel who had been monitoring the investigation approved in writing the transfer of a simplified and sanitized version of Hughes's failure analysis to the Chinese. In August 1994, Hughes's Optus B3 satellite was successfully launched in China.

The success was short-lived. In January 1995, a Chinese Long March rocket launching Hughes's Apstar 2 satellite exploded fifty seconds after liftoff. Instrumentation showed once again that the nose cone had failed. Great Wall hadn't done the full modification that Hughes had recommended. And, once again, the Chinese refused to accept Hughes's conclusion. Great Wall was desperate to cover up any flaws in the Long March rocket for fear that insurance companies would refuse to underwrite future launches. In the end, both sides would blame wind shear for the accident. It had been windy that day, and Hughes engineers were willing to stipulate that the nose cone could work on a calm day. The Chinese placed partial blame on the coupling between the rocket and the satellite so that both sides could share responsibility.

Chinese and Hughes Satellite officials issued a joint press release in July 1995, citing "two possible causes for the failure." Hughes said high winds had affected the nose cone and the Chinese cited problems with the coupling between the rocket and the satellite. After getting approval from the Commerce Department, Hughes released to the Chinese rocket makers its own investigation blaming the nose cone.

Within months of that compromise a Long March rocket launching a Loral Space Systems satellite tipped over as it was being launched. It flew sideways into a nearby hillside, destroying a farm village and killing or injuring more than one hundred peasants. The insurance industry went ballistic. Political compromises and face-saving explanations wouldn't cut it. If Loral and Great Wall couldn't pinpoint the cause, and fix it, insurers would not only refuse to pay claims, they would quit backing Chinese launches. The Chinese quickly explained that their investigation had determined that a broken wire in the guidance system had caused the failure, but insurance executives didn't buy it. They wanted an independent investigation. Great Wall asked Hughes and Loral to lead the investigation. The team's report concluded that flaws in the electronic flight control system caused the crash. The committee made general recommendations for improved design, quality control, and launch safety procedures for the Chinese rocket. A meeting with Great Wall was scheduled for June to refine details of the recommendations.

Political Problems

Suddenly Hughes and Loral found themselves trapped in a fierce bureaucratic battle pitting the Pentagon and the State Department against the Commerce Department. The battle had started three years earlier when President Clinton transferred the State Department's authority for export controls on some commercial satellites to the Commerce Department. He later granted Commerce authority over all satellite exports. The State Department was left with export controls over technical assistance provided to foreign governments for rockets and satellites. Barely two months after that decision, China test-fired M-9 missiles in waters off Taiwan on the eve of Taiwan's first presidential election. It was a brutally obvious warning to Taiwan about who was really boss. Chinese missile and rockets were suddenly a sensitive subject in Washington.

Using its remaining power to regulate "technical assistance," the State Department, along with the Pentagon and CIA, launched an investigation into the Loral failure review. An export analyst in the Pentagon's Defense Technology Security Administration decided that the Loral and Hughes investigators should have obtained a "technical assistance" export license from the State Department to conduct the review. The State Department ordered them to halt the investigation of the Long March malfunction.

Anti-Chinese sentiment rose in the summer of 1996 when news stories began appearing, alleging that several Chinese-American hustlers had raised significant funds for Clinton's 1996 reelection campaign from overseas Chinese and Mainland Chinese sources. Republicans in Congress, intent on embarrassing Clinton, questioned whether he had been making it easier for U.S. satellites to be launched in China because Loral CEO Bernard Schwartz and Hughes CEO C. Michael Armstrong were heavy Democratic Party donors. With House Speaker Newt Gingrich and his allies pummeling the White House on the issue, the Pentagon determined in 1997 that "Loral and Hughes committed a serious export control violation by virtue of having performed a defense service without a license . . ." The companies were accused of helping China determine the true source of the missile failure (a power amplifier in the guidance system) and exposing China to Western diagnostic processes that could lead to reliability improvements in all Chinese missile and rocket programs. In May 1997, the case was turned over to the Justice Department for possible criminal action.

Even as Special Prosecutor Kenneth Starr was filling the headlines with his probe of Clinton's affair with Monica Lewinsky, Gingrich in June 1998 formed a "select committee" to investigate whether China had illegally received sensitive U.S. missile and space technology from companies that had received favorable treatment from Clinton. The House committee of five Republicans and four Democrats was chaired by conservative Republican Representative Christopher Cox of California. The McDonnell Douglas machine tool case got swept into the investigation, as did alleged security problems and possible espionage at U.S. nuclear weapons labs. As the committee gathered testimony from more than 150 individuals and sifted through tens of thousands of pages of documents, Washington was seized by Chinese spy mania.

On December 30, 1998, the Cox committee approved its seven-hundred-page classified report. Gingrich and Cox were unable to make a declassified version of the report public before Clinton's upcoming Senate impeachment trial as they had hoped. But Cox and other Republicans were very eager to tell reporters that the committee concluded that China was sucking up U.S. technology secrets.

The "Donorgate" scandal turned out to be a case of four Chinese Americans, dishonest, low-grade hustlers, who used aggressive and poorly policed Clinton-Gore fund-raising for the 1996 election to enrich themselves by pocketing much of the money or promoting themselves as White House insiders to Chinese officials and businesses in Asia. But the scandal had raised the specter of Chinese Americans being willing to sell out their country. Leaks from the Cox committee hearings further inflamed public sentiment. A Department of Energy intelligence analyst told the committee that a 1995 Chinese underground nuclear test indicated that China may have obtained the design of a miniature nuclear warhead from American's weapons labs and suggested that a Chinese American scientist at the DOE's laboratory in Los Alamos, New Mexico, was a prime suspect.

Two days after a *New York Times* story detailed the accusation, Energy Secretary Bill Richardson fired Taiwan-born scientist Wen Ho Lee for "failing to properly safeguard classified material . . ." The FBI didn't have sufficient evidence to bring espionage charges against Lee, but continuous FBI leaks and elaborate theories spun by Clinton's opponents led to a media barrage that artfully blended administration approval of the Chinese satellite launches, the "Donorgate" campaign contributions, and the accusations against Wen Ho Lee. The implication was clear: the Clinton administration couldn't protect America's secrets and had solicited campaign contributions in exchange for giving U.S. and Chinese companies favored treatment.

Paying the Price

In April 1999, Bob Hitt was summoned to Washington for six hours of questioning by federal prosecutors investigating why the six machine tools had been rerouted to Nanchang without approval. Hitt was relieved when at the end of the session the U.S. attorney who had been questioning him said he had no worries.

"You really didn't have anything to do with this," the prosecutor told him.

A month later, the unclassified version of the Cox report was published. The narrative sections on the individual Loral, Hughes, and McDonnell Douglas cases were sober and factual. But the report's analysis and conclusions were laughable to anyone who knew anything about modern China. The report portrayed the Chinese government as a monolith in which the Communist Party politburo controls all aspects of industry and commerce with the aim of challenging U.S. interests around the world. The report said that the "main aim for the civilian economy is to support the building of modern military weapons and to support the aims of the PLA [People's Liberation Army]."

It was in this atmosphere that in the summer a new group of Justice Department prosecutors took over the McDonnell Douglas case. On October 19, 1999, a sixteen-count indictment was filed against McDonnell Douglas and CATIC. Hitt personally was indicted in the first count, which alleged that he and two CATIC employees—Hu Boru, a CATIC buyer, and Yan Liren, who had inspected the tools in Columbus—conspired to violate the laws of the United States. Suddenly Hitt faced a potential $250,000 in fines and five years in jail. McDonnell Douglas and Hitt pleaded not guilty.

The hastily drawn indictment was full of factual errors and creative legal theories. Hitt, for example, had never even met Yan Liren, his purported coconspirator. Investigators had simply taken Yan's name off a list of inspectors who had journeyed to Columbus. Prosecutors wove together theories of "collective knowledge" and "conscious avoidance." Even if no individual at McDonnell Douglas had committed a "willful and knowing" violation, the company's "collective knowledge" amounted to a "willful and knowing" violation of export laws. Beyond that, the prosecutors said, McDonnell Douglas had ignored signs that CATIC might not build the Beijing machining center and in doing so had practiced "conscious avoidance" of information. That, in turn, led to the submission of false information on the export license application forms. The indictment clearly was aimed at appeasing the Pentagon and conservative Republicans in Congress rather than enforcing the law. McDonnell Douglas lawyers, filing massive discovery motions, used the indictments' shortcomings to force the government to reveal the uninformed and inconsistent operation of the export control system.

Hitt was relieved in May 2001 when a federal appeals court dismissed the indictment against him. His attorneys had successfully argued that the five-year statute of limitations had expired because his alleged conspiracy with Chinese officials would have ended with the September 1994 export license approval, which was just over five years before his October 1999 indictment. Hitt, diagnosed with lung cancer three months after the indictment was dismissed, retired in December 2002.

When the Clinton administration left office, the rabid hatred of the president that had propelled the investigations dissipated. Prosecutors wanted to clean up the messy export control cases. Charges against CATIC were settled in May 2001, with the Chinese company pleading no contest to export law violations and paying a fine of $2.3 million. In November 2001, all criminal charges against McDonnell Douglas were dismissed. The government acknowledged that the company had engaged in no wrongdoing and had made no false statements to the government. To settle separate civil charges, the company agreed to pay a fine of $2.1 million for its liability for acts and statements by the Chinese.

No criminal charges were filed against Loral or Hughes. In January 2002, Loral paid $14 million as part of a civil settlement with the government. The company didn't admit any wrongdoing, but did agree to spend $6 million to strengthen its compliance with export laws. Hughes in March 2003 agreed to pay $32 million in penalties to settle civil charges. The company expressed "regret for not having obtained licenses that should have been obtained."

To reach the settlements in both the McDonnell Douglas and Hughes cases, the government had to negotiate with Boeing, which now owned them both. The airplane giant had purchased McDonnell Douglas in August 1997 and later closed down the MD-82 and MD-90 lines because they were direct competitors to the Boeing 737. The company offered to honor the agreement with China for forty of the MD-90s, but the Chinese demurred. They didn't want to purchase an out-of-production airplane. Only two of the MD-90s were produced in China. At the Shanghai coproduction facility, the Chinese began working to build their own Trunkliner aircraft using technology from Brazil. In 2002, Boeing celebrated its thirtieth year of doing business with China by announcing that more than three thousand Boeing airplanes were flying with parts made in China. The company also estimated that the China market would be good for another 2,300 planes over the next two decades.

Boeing had purchased the space and communications business from Hughes Electronics (a subsidiary of General Motors since 1985) in January 2000 for $3.75 billion. At the time, the company had a backlog of orders for thirty-six satellites valued at $4 billion. During the late 1990s dotcom boom, however, fiber optic cables were strung across the world and the market for satellites collapsed not long after the purchase of Hughes. The U.S. machine tool industry suffered, as well, as Japanese and European companies supplanted American dominance of the industry.

Sorry About That

The FBI arrested Wen Ho Lee in December 1999, nine months after the Cox committee's allegations were leaked to the press. He was charged with fifty-nine counts of mishandling classified information and violating secrecy provisions of the Atomic Energy Act. He was put in solitary confinement and forced to wear leg shackles during exercise period. The resulting paranoia about Chinese spies made life miserable for the huge numbers of ethnic Chinese scientists and researchers at U.S. universities, government research institutes, and in private companies. Representative Cox and other Republicans involved in the investigation that had triggered the anti-Chinese racism in the United States did little to quell the furor because the specter of widespread Chinese spying made Clinton look bad.

The case against Wen Ho Lee began to crumble in August 2000 when the FBI's chief investigator admitted that he had provided inaccurate testimony about Lee in hearings. Embarrassed prosecutors scrambled to negotiate a settlement. On September 13, Lee walked free after pleading guilty to one felony charge of copying files from a classified computer to unclassified computer tapes. The simple fact was Lee had taken some work home with him. Lee agreed to drop a racial discrimination suit he had filed against the government. In accepting Lee's plea, U.S. District Judge James Parker said that top U.S. government officials "have embarrassed our entire nation" by their shameful treatment of Lee.

For Gareth Chang and other leaders of the Chinese American business community, and new Mainland Chinese immigrants to the United States, the Chinese spy mania was a wakeup call to become more active in U.S. politics. In California, the home state of Congressman Cox, the Chinese business community already had significant clout. Many Chinese Americans there were disgusted with Cox for using racism as a political tool. Cox paid the price in May 2001. President Bush decided not to nominate Cox to the federal bench after Chinese American leaders let friends in Congress know that they would vehemently oppose his nomination.

Cox tried to bury the hatchet. His staff arranged off-the-record meetings in late 2002 and early 2003 with Chinese American business leaders. Cox told them he was sorry that his committee's report had fueled anti-Chinese racism. He blamed the CIA and the Clinton White House for introducing distortions in the final declassified report. He said he realized that China was changing through economic reforms and hinted that being in the China-bashing camp in Congress was no longer a politically profitable place to be.

The Chinese Americans were invariably polite and respectful to Cox. But Cox had already made his bed; as one attendee said later, "We didn't buy any of it."

What This Means for You

Since the United States reestablished diplomatic relations with China in 1979, the relationship between the two nations has been schizophrenic. When a Chinese fighter jet collided with an American EP-3 spy plane off the coast of China, I was one of three former chairmen of the American Chamber of Commerce in China asked by the membership to determine the political repercussions of the incident.

In Beijing, we saw Chinese of all ages, including our own U.S.-educated employees, condemning the accident as another example of the American policy of trying to keep China weak. Since the Tiananmen Massacre, the Chinese government fostered a spirit of nationalism focused not on China's many achievements but on the resentment of "foreign elements"—chiefly the United States—who were conspiring to keep China poor and weak. When the U.S. Congress railed about Chinese human rights abuses, opposed China hosting the 2000 Olympics, or threatened trade sanctions, the Chinese press adeptly framed the actions as American attempts to "contain" China. The May 1999 U.S. bombing strike on the Chinese embassy in Belgrade that killed three Chinese journalists was a tragic gift to Chinese propagandists. The United States blamed it on a CIA targeting mistake, but I have yet to meet one Chinese who believes that. The spy plane incident added more fuel to anti-American nationalism.

The situation in Washington was little different. Democratic Senator Dianne Feinstein of California angrily pulled out a news article accusing her of being a "China sympathizer" because her husband had business interests there. A former top Defense and State Department official told me that the spy plane accident happened after the United States increased the number of patrols along the Chinese coast from several times a month to almost every day. The spy planes' mission, he said, was to briefly, but deliberately, violate Chinese airspace to set off Chinese radars and other electronic defenses. The spy planes mapped them to find blind spots for U.S. bombers and fighters in the event of war with China. We were told that Defense Secretary Donald Rumsfeld had a "get the Reds" attitude toward China. A White House official told us that the Bush administration considered China a "second-priority country" in Asia, and that Japan, South Korea, Thailand, the Philippines, and Australia—all of which shared America's "goals and priorities"— would get more attention. An intelligence official told us that the Belgrade embassy bombing had been a watershed. Before that, he said, China had bought weapons to look resolute. Now, he said, "they are putting together operational systems that are aimed at Taiwan."

We returned to Beijing with a very pessimistic report—and the realization that there are more than a few people in Washington who still want to "contain China." We predicted that it could be years before the Bush administration thawed. Then came 9/11. The destruction of the World Trade Center towers by Al Qaeda terrorists gave the Bush administration a new public enemy number one and China suddenly became one of America's best friends.

This was one of the quickest and most extreme reversals in the always contentious U.S.-China relationship. Most American businesses weather these storms without serious damage beyond fending off Chinese attempts to use political tensions as a weapon to extract better commercial terms. But the exception is technology. American technology companies, from aircraft manufacturers to software designers, are directly at the crossroads of lingering Cold War distrust between the two countries.

China understands that technology is the key to its military and commercial modernization. But the ludicrous caricature in the Cox report—of all-powerful Communist leaders organizing Chinese officials, businessmen, scientists, and students to act like an army of robots gathering U.S. secrets as they visit or reside in the United States—reveals more about U.S. thinking than Chinese actions. Certainly China has no shortage of spies and scientists who work to get their hands on advanced technology in the United States and elsewhere. But asserting as the Cox report did that modernizing China's military is "the main aim of the civilian economy" is simply stir-fried Kremlinology. China today is not the Soviet Union of yesterday.

The Cox report revealed the thinking and attitudes of a powerful alliance of old Cold Warriors and younger neo-conservatives in Washington. With a similar alliance alive and well in Beijing, American technology businesses will continue to find themselves squeezed and in danger of losing the global competition to companies from countries that don't view China in the same way.

Ignore the hyperbole and look at the facts in the Cox report and it's very clear that any serious effort to "contain" China is a fool's mission. The China market is simply too voracious, the Chinese economy too powerful, and the political allegiances and alliances of the Cold War that could even attempt such a thing no longer exist. The Cox report shows how China is able to purchase almost any commercial technology it desires from Japan, Israel, Russia, or the European Union, all of which heartily disagree with America's notion of a "China threat." Europe sees the rise of China as a natural result of its twenty-five years of reform, and many in Europe and elsewhere welcome a more powerful China as a necessary balance in a world dominated by the United States.

The commercial implications of outmoded ideas and policies are ominous. As McDonnell Douglas, Hughes, and Chinese American scientist Wen Ho Lee learned during the Clinton administration, Washington politicians will roll right over any company or individual who steps into the middle of a down-and-dirty political fight. Unless the business community helps the United States—and Europe, Japan, and other significant players—devise informed and intelligent technology trade policies and build a consensus that recognizes China as a powerful global player, American technology companies could find themselves scrambling to maintain global competitiveness as Cold War thinking generates policies that allow others to capture the China market.

In the next decade, defense contractors will become mired deeper and deeper in this issue. But almost any technology company could fall victim. Many software companies may one day wake up to face strict U.S. government restrictions on China sales because of American political opposition to China's use of modified American software to censor the Chinese Internet. We can see from the McDonnell Douglas saga why the United States slipped behind in the machine tool industry. I recently visited one of the ultramodern multibillion-dollar silicon chips plants going up in Shanghai. All the equipment was from Japan or Taiwan, the result of U.S. export controls.

Executives from Hughes and McDonnell Douglas told me that one lesson they learned was that technology companies doing business in China require significant investments in proactive government relations in Washington. The mission isn't only to make friends, but to educate officials. The American bureaucracy from top to bottom—and lawmakers who rely on business support—must understand that blocking U.S. technology that is freely available from Europe or Asia undermines the global competitiveness of U.S. companies because China is such a huge market.

American technology companies operating in China must realize the vulnerability of Chinese American employees. Openly discuss the issue and how to deal with it within the company. Only through such discussions can companies develop corporate policies and contingency plans to protect their employees from political assault in the United States or manipulation by Chinese officials.

There is no doubt that Gareth Chang and tens of thousands of people like him have made great contributions to China's development. They do so partly out of emotional ties to their homeland. They want to make China a better place, but they mostly do it to make a buck. China is one market where they feel they have a competitive advantage. The many hundreds of Chinese Americans whom I have known working in China are among the most patriotic Americans I have ever met. The attitude of new Chinese immigrants in the United States isn't much different. They leave China for America because they believe it is a better place to learn and live and prosper. But, like overseas Chinese, when they return to China, they are often not completely trusted because they are considered tainted by their time in the West.

A final lesson is that basing your business on special deals from the Chinese government is foolhardy. The Chinese government offers special deals because you have something they want, not because they want to help build your business. Unless there are clear and competitive commercial underpinnings, you will lose, no matter what the government has promised. Cultivating relationships with Chinese officials is very important, but basing your business on those relationships is a formula for disaster. The market will always win in China. Kiss the cadres, but embrace the customer, as Boeing did.

The Little Red Book of Business

- Trying to "contain" China as a national or corporate strategy is nonsense.

- Technology companies that don't make government relations and education a key component of their China business plans could find their business short-circuited by political storms.

- China is moving fast and changing faster, an environment in which few Western companies are structured to compete. Your China business model must be configured for constant changes in every aspect of business and politics.

- Never use the Chinese market as a last resort to save your business. The Chinese can smell desperation and will take advantage of your weakness.

- Exploit your advantage in China. A country that practices information and thought control stifles innovation. Transfer what knowledge you must, but hold back the rest.

- If the Chinese have a strategic objective to obtain a certain technology, they will get it from somewhere. The only solution is to innovate rapidly when Chinese companies use your technology to compete against you.

- Cultivate relationships with Chinese officials, but don't base your business on those relationships or special deals from the government. Kiss the cadres, but embrace the customer.

- Don't bring home the Chinese way of going around rules to get things done. Follow explicitly all of the rules of your government. Taking shortcuts will come back to haunt you.

- If your company or industry gets caught up in the middle of a political battle in Washington concerning China—or a dispute between Washington and Beijing—duck, shut up, and call your attorney and senator. The facts alone will not protect you.

- Politics no longer drive everything in China. To understand where China is headed, focus on analyzing the country's business and commerce more than deciphering *People's Daily* headlines.

- Acknowledge that your overseas Chinese employees can become pawns in political battles. Openly discuss and determine strategies to prevent China from taking advantage of them and the United States from accusing them of disloyalty.

- Relations between the United States and China are caught up somewhere between the Cold War and hot competition. Recognize that underlying the diplomatic and business cooperation between the two countries are strong political forces on both sides that see the other as a future enemy.

- China constantly erects political or regulatory roadblocks aimed at limiting foreign business opportunities and helping domestic companies. Don't confuse your administrative victories in these battles with genuine business accomplishments.

- Get your own copy of Lucian Pye's classic text, *Chinese Negotiating Style,* and read it. It's still very relevant.

6

The Truth Is Not Absolute

The Communist Party believes it must control information to stay in power, but China needs an informed citizenry to compete in a global economy. This leaves the media, from Rupert Murdoch to a crusading Chinese journalist, searching for the size of their cages.

RUPERT MURDOCH isn't a man accustomed to cooling his heels, but there he was on a crisp day in October 1997, pacing back and forth at the top of the steps at the north entrance to the vast Great Hall of the People on Tiananmen Square, looking skinny, nervous, and unimportant. He was anxiously awaiting permission to walk the last mile of his tortuous journey into the good graces of the Chinese Communist Party. Aides to Communist Party propaganda czar Ding Guangen would escort him to an audience with Ding, the man who had worked for years to derail Murdoch's effort to break into the China media market.

Murdoch had earned the enmity of China's top leadership four years earlier when the Australian media mogul said in a speech that advances in communications technology had "proved an unambiguous threat to totalitarian regimes everywhere." Murdoch had been referring to Russia and Eastern Europe, but the Chinese took his warning as a dire threat. The speech came just two months after

Murdoch bought control of STAR TV in Hong Kong, a new free-to-air satellite television network that reached every corner of China. A month after Murdoch's September 1993 speech, Premier Li Peng struck back, banning the private ownership of satellite dishes in China.

Murdoch had been seeking to make amends ever since. He had tried numerous avenues in an apparent attempt to curry favor. Highly paid consultants proved useless. Murdoch made donations to a foundation headed by Deng Xiaoping's handicapped son, he purchased expensive art from one of Deng's daughters, and his publishing company entered into a lucrative book contract for another daughter. He even ordered his executives to remove the British Broadcasting Corporation programming from the STAR transponder that covered China, a signal he was interested in entertainment, not news, for China.

Liu Changle, a former army officer with his own media aspirations, finally opened the door to the inner sanctum for Murdoch. He convinced the Chinese government that he could partner with Murdoch and keep him under control in China while building a station that would broadcast the Chinese viewpoint to the world. With the leadership's blessing, Murdoch and Liu eighteen months earlier had launched Phoenix Satellite Television in Hong Kong. Now Chinese President Jiang Zemin was about to visit the United States and Ding wanted to ensure that Murdoch's Fox network and his U.S. publications would treat Jiang kindly. Today Murdoch would be granted absolution for his speech four years earlier.

But first he had to be reminded of his status in China. Hence the wait at the north entrance. When he and his small party were permitted past the soldiers guarding the doorway, Murdoch still had a long trek through a maze of red-carpeted hallways to his meeting at the opposite end of the sprawling complex. As they walked, Murdoch rehearsed his presentation: There had been misunderstandings, but we shouldn't dwell on the past. Make it clear that we are very influential and want to be the Chinese government's friend. We want to make money in China, not trouble.

On they trudged, past ornate meeting halls, some bigger than football fields. Up some stairs, then down a long dark corridor leading to the cavernous Chinese parliament meeting hall. Down more stairs, then past the five-thousand-seat banquet hall. When he finally entered the meeting room Murdoch found Ding, with China's senior media mavens, sitting in overstuffed chairs. Murdoch settled into the chair next to Ding while his lieutenants filled the other seats.

"I understand you are an Australian company," Ding said to Murdoch. "Tell me what you do."

The polite putdown didn't bother Murdoch. Speaking unnaturally slowly for the translator's benefit, he said he had been fascinated with China since childhood. He said that he understood that China has strict rules and regulations for the media, and that he would follow them completely. Murdoch suggested that he and Chinese government media outlets should work together on non-controversial projects to build mutual trust. When Murdoch began reeling off the many and varied holdings of his conglomerate, News Corp., Ding interrupted when he heard the word "Fox."

"Fox, Fox movie studios," Ding said. "I used to love watching Tyrone Power movies when I was a university student."

The incongruity changed the course of the conversation and Ding turned to Murdoch's absolution. Ding signaled that bygones were bygones by pointing to the officials assembled on his left: the director of the Press and Publications Administration; the minister for Radio, Film, and Television; the director of the *People's Daily*; the head of the State Council Information Office; and the president of CCTV, the national broadcaster.

"I understand that you have been talking to my people, and it would be a good idea for us to make a fresh start," Ding said. "For the future, here are the people who manage the media businesses in China. All your future dealings should be through them."

Murdoch was off the blacklist. It seemed a much shorter walk on the way out.

Overview

Murdoch wasn't the first foreign executive to make that long march through the Great Hall of the People. It is a routine part of the political pageantry intended to give senior Communist leaders an aura of omnipotence and to remind visitors of China's dynastic tradition going back two thousand years. The clear message to executives is that they should be grateful to be able to do business in China. The humbling process begins when a foreign business executive gets the last-minute summons to the audience that his minions have been trying to arrange for months. As the otherwise powerful foreign executives step over the raised doorstep, their shoulders slump and they seem to shrink. When they finally greet whichever Chinese leader awaits them, what I call the "slobbering CEO syndrome" begins.

"China is such a magnificent country."

"I'm so impressed with China's progress."

"Your leadership is so inspiring."

And on and on. The Chinese have them precisely where they want them as the real negotiations begin.

To his credit, Murdoch was far from slobbering. Sure, he had stumbled on his way into China, but he eventually figured out the place. With Liu Changle's help, Murdoch had transformed himself from perceived menace to generous mentor for the Chinese television industry.

This chapter is about the Chinese media gold rush, the breakneck commercialization of the Chinese print and broadcast media. It's also about the Communist Party's struggle to control information while informing its people sufficiently to compete in a global economy, and to use the press as a tightly leashed watchdog to police its roiling market economy. All of this has happened as China's creaky propaganda machine has continued to churn out its outdated dogma. It is important for foreign businesses to understand the inner workings of the Chinese media and the country's propaganda machine. China's modernization has been guided by Deng's mantra of "reforming and opening" except for the media, which the government wants to reform, but not open. The unintended byproduct is that foreign companies in China are open targets in a journalistic free-fire zone. Chinese reporters are so restricted in what they can report about China that they sometimes feel fully licensed to say anything they want to about foreign business.

But this story also shows how China makes progress. The huge misconception in the West is that China moves forward and changes because all-powerful officials at the top issue orders that everyone follows. It isn't like that at all. Instead, it is all about networks of like-minded people creating a web of protection for the reform. Deng began the transformation of China in 1979 because he was empowered and protected by thousands of officials who, like him, had suffered personal political persecution under the tight grip of Mao's feudal politics. This story follows the careers of two Chinese journalists who have had the greatest impact in improving the news business in China. They have followed different paths to reach similar results. Liu Changle, under Murdoch's mentorship, is transforming Chinese television news behind the banner of improving China's overseas propaganda efforts. In contrast, magazine editor Hu Shuli has crashed straight through all obstacles in her crusade to bring integrity and objectivity to print journalism in China. The success of both depends on their network of supporters and the fact that China desperately needs what they are offering. Along the way, we see Murdoch learn that foreign businesses in China also need to build networks of supporters and friends. It isn't all about cozying up to the guy at the top.

The Blaring Loudspeakers

The loudspeakers were never silent. From lampposts in virtually every city, town, and village in the Mao days, the speakers blared out an unceasing line of propaganda, leaving no room for silence, lest that silence be filled by the people's own ideas. Until Deng cracked open the door to a market economy in 1978, the media in China had been firmly under the heel of the Communist Party. When Deng launched economic reforms at the end of 1978, China had only 186 newspapers and thirty-two television stations, all government owned. Most media content emanated from the Xinhua "news agency," which distributed government announcements, filtered and refocused all international news, and, most importantly, disseminated a steady barrage of government propaganda.

But the rapid transformation of China's socialist command economy into a market economy created the need for an informed citizenry. In the wake of Deng's reforms, many Chinese journalists and progressive government officials began using China's newspapers and magazines to focus and refine China's impatient emergence from the grinding poverty, political chaos, and inhumane cruelty that had gripped the country during most of the 1960s and 1970s. The press was even given a short leash to act as a watchdog on government corruption, all under the guidance, of course, of the Propaganda Department, which allowed reporters to unveil the details of corruption cases that the government wanted to use as examples to frighten others into behaving.

While the idealists saw the press as a way to push for reform and government accountability, the Communist Party officials who served as the country's newspaper editors and TV station directors realized they were sitting on a gold mine. Advertising had disappeared under Mao when the government funded the media. Within weeks of Deng's pronouncement of economic reforms, Shanghai's *Wenhuibao* newspaper carried the headline "Restore the Good Name of Advertising." Two weeks later, Shanghai TV ran an advertisement for medicinal wine, and two months later *Wenhuibao* and Shanghai TV carried the first foreign advertisements with ads for Rado Swiss watches.

Advertisers knew a good thing when they saw it. Chinese consumers were a blank slate. Virtually no Chinese brand names had survived the decades of communism. Suddenly everyone from Japanese appliance makers to American baby food producers opened their wallets to introduce their products to the Chinese consumer. Television programming was a boring procession of Chinese operas interspersed with patriotic variety shows. But the commercials, now that was entertainment! Surveys showed that viewers eagerly watched well-produced commercials, then wandered off to the kitchen or bathroom during the regular programming. As people became more affluent, advertising taught them how to groom and dress, what to eat, and which electronics or automobiles to purchase to show their sophistication and prosperity. It quickly became apparent that Chinese sodas, soaps, and appliances were no match for products from Coca-Cola, Procter & Gamble, and Hitachi. A Gallup poll in the mid-1990s showed that of the ten best-known brands in China, six were Japanese (Hitachi, National, Toshiba, Toyota, Suzuki, and Honda), three were American (Coke, Mickey Mouse, and Marlboro), and one was Chinese (Tsingtao beer). More than any other consumers in the world, the Chinese equated the quality of a given brand with the quantity of the advertising for it. The reason was simple: when they purchased the products that were advertised, the products turned out to be good.

To catch this wave, hundreds of enterprising bureaucrats and businesspeople opened new newspapers, magazines, and television stations. By the early 1990s, China had more than two thousand newspapers, seven thousand periodicals, and some seven hundred fifty local television stations that either produced their own programming or acted as relays for CCTV. Major cities were wired for cable TV. By 1993, Shanghai cable had 700,000 household subscribers who received twelve channels for the equivalent of one dollar a month. The little old ladies who in less-affluent times served as Communist Party watchdogs in their neighborhoods now became effective saleswomen for the government cable operator. Sprawling Soviet-style factories wired their huge compounds to VCRs to build their own entertainment stations. At the end of 1993, Chinese consumers were purchasing 20 million televisions per year and 97 percent of urban families had at least one television.

The rapid growth alarmed the party. The media was getting out of control. In October 1993, Li Peng signed State Council Proclamation 129 banning the purchase or possession of satellite dishes by ordinary Chinese citizens. Editors and TV station directors were told that their main goal was not to make money, but to "educate the people about patriotism," "promptly defuse sensitive issues," "guide public opinion correctly," and "don't speak in a middle position" (i.e., don't be objective).

Midlife Renewal

For Murdoch, China was both a midlife crisis and a renewal. Since his company's near collapse in 1990, caused by a wild acquisition spree and heavy debt, Murdoch's wife had been pushing him to slow down, to ease toward retirement, to temper his ambitions for building the first global media empire. Instead, Murdoch came out fighting. He sold off a slew of his U.S. magazines, gathered more cash by floating a few properties on the stock markets, and continued his global march with the purchase of STAR TV in Hong Kong, investments in television networks in Japan and Germany, and the purchase of more U.S. stations to add to his Fox network.

The STAR TV purchase was a problem. Murdoch thought he had been bamboozled. He had paid Hong Kong tycoon Li Ka-shing and his twenty-eight-year-old son Richard Li nearly $1 billion for the fledgling network, even though the Li family had spent only about $100 million to build it. According to a former News Corp. executive, STAR TV had led Murdoch to believe that it had a tacit agreement with the Chinese government for landing rights in China. That wasn't true. News Corp. executives learned after the purchase that STAR TV had told Chinese officials that STAR TV's signal wouldn't go much beyond Guangdong province, adjacent to Hong Kong. Instead, it covered the entire country and the Chinese were furious. Worse, much of the advertising on STAR TV disappeared soon after the sale was completed. Unless STAR could get a toehold in China soon, Murdoch's investment would continue to bleed millions of dollars each month.

At first, Murdoch was genuinely befuddled by China. As one

STAR TV executive put it: "He sort of thought the Chinese would give him the key to the biggest backyard in the world. Why wouldn't they want him? He figured that he would be a trusted person for them. Rupert had a slightly colonial view of the Asian masses and all the things the white man could bring to them."

During the Cold War, Murdoch had been a fierce anti-Communist. Now he wanted to help China and he thought he should be welcomed. As he told biographer William Shawcross: "I don't think there are many Communists left in China. There's a one-party state and there's a Communist economy, which they are desperately trying to get out of and change. The real story there is an economic story, tied to the democratic story."

While Chinese leaders shut him out, Murdoch began meeting with Chinese entrepreneurs. The more he visited China, the more he admired and enjoyed the people. China was a nation of people like himself, aggressive risk takers, practical people who focused on making money and were willing to adhere to whatever political line was necessary to do it. Around the time of his meeting with Ding, Murdoch met a STAR TV executive named Wendi Deng at a cocktail party. Murdoch was sixty-five. Wendi was twenty-seven, tall, thin, intelligent, energetic, and aggressive. Wendi began serving as Murdoch's translator on trips to China, but it wasn't all business. In May 1998, Murdoch separated from his wife, Anna, and his relationship with Wendi became public.

Wendi enlightened Murdoch about China. She explained to him how Chinese officials thought and what motivated them. Murdoch began repeating her explanations to News Corp. executives, who dubbed them "Wendi-isms." Wendi was the perfect match for Murdoch at this point in his life. She shared his aggression and love of the business deal. She didn't want him to slow down and retire. She wanted to join him in conquering the globe. And she was every bit as opportunistic as Rupert. The daughter of a state factory director in Guangzhou, she had parlayed an affair with a married American executive working in China into a short-lived marriage and a "green card" that allowed permanent residency in the United States. She went on to earn an MBA from Yale University. An internship at STAR TV in Hong Kong became a full-time job building distribution on cable systems in China for STAR's music channel. Murdoch and Wendi were married in June 1999 aboard his yacht in New York harbor. Wendi left the company, but she continued to serve as an ambassador for Murdoch in China.

As Murdoch's attitude toward the Chinese changed, so did their attitude toward Murdoch. In the wake of the London speech scare, the Chinese government began to accumulate a massive file on Murdoch. At first, officials were convinced that he was going to spend billions to force his way into China. They suspected that he had ties to the CIA and wanted to use satellite technology to destabilize the Chinese government. They watched his every move. At one point Ding boasted to a News Corp. executive about Murdoch's budding relationship with Wendi: "We even know what is going on between the two of them in the hotels."

Not surprisingly, the more the Chinese learned about Murdoch, the more they admired and understood him. It didn't take them long to conclude that Murdoch was a carbon copy of the typical Chinese tycoon. The indecipherable, labyrinthine structure of his global holdings and cross-holdings, which allowed him to flit between tax jurisdictions and regulatory restrictions, was standard operating procedure for the overseas Chinese tycoons who were teaching China how to do business. Equally familiar was the management structure of News Corp. Struggling to understand how Murdoch's far-flung empire was governed, one Chinese official asked a News Corp. executive to draw a management chart of the company. The executive drew a large circle with a small circle in the middle.

"That's Rupert in the middle," the executive said, "and all along the outer circle are the people who run the various businesses. Murdoch controls everything personally." With Murdoch's children serving as key executives, the Chinese tycoon model was complete.

The Chinese also learned that Murdoch's conservatism was only business-deep. True, in Washington he aligned himself closely with Newt Gingrich and the Republican right and his *New York Post* helped build and promote the political careers of Republicans like Rudolph Giuliani. But it also supported Democrats like Ed Koch and his British friendships spanned the political spectrum to insure he was close to whoever was in power.

He was also relentless, a quality the Chinese respect. Ding had ordered the State Council Information Office to keep Murdoch busy with low-level meetings and to prevent him from talking directly to senior leaders. But by working through Australian diplomats, Murdoch arranged to meet Chinese Vice-Premier Zhu Rongji in July 1997, using the pretext of a trip by Zhu to Australia. They got on well. During the meeting, Zhu momentarily confounded Murdoch. "I see you became an American citizen so you could operate a television network in the United States," Zhu said. "Would you be willing to become a Chinese citizen to get into the television business in China?" Murdoch looked pained. But then he joined in the gales of laughter that accompanied Zhu's little joke.

China could be comfortable with Murdoch. If he agreed to something, it would happen. It was so disappointing to deal with multinational media CEOs like Time Warner's Gerald Levin. Levin spent much time developing a personal relationship with President Jiang Zemin, but he couldn't control his company's news operations. No matter how friendly Jiang and Levin were, CNN and *Time* magazine continued to do stories that angered the Chinese leadership.

Murdoch finally reached the top on December 10, 1998, when he met with Chinese President Jiang Zemin. The meeting was front-page news in China. Xinhua said that Jiang "expressed appreciation for the efforts made by world media mogul Rupert Murdoch in presenting China objectively and cooperating with the Chinese press over the past two years." Once Murdoch got his chance to tell his story to Chinese leaders face-to-face, they saw eye-to-eye, dictator-to-dictator.

From Menace to Mentor

Murdoch had gone from menace to mentor. One immediate lesson China learned from Murdoch: control the gateways. To ensure CNN, HBO, and other foreign channels beaming into China reached only the authorized audiences of hotels and housing compounds for foreigners or the Chinese elite, propaganda officials required that all foreign broadcasts coming into China be transmitted through a designated Chinese satellite. This consolidation of signals also made it possible for Communist Party censors to monitor all broadcasts twenty-four hours a day and cut the signal when reports authorities don't like are shown on CNN and the other foreign channels. CCTV also created a dozen domestic specialty channels, ranging from sports to economic news to children's programming, and required all the new cable systems in China to carry them. Within a few years, Chinese citizens had access to several dozen domestic television channels. The government had worked hard to fill up the pipeline to stave off the foreign broadcasters. Throughout this buildup, Murdoch offered a helping hand. He sponsored delegation after delegation of Chinese officials and TV station executives to visit his television operations in the United States and Europe. Murdoch showed them how to use satellite technology to maintain control. It was Murdoch's control of the Asia satellite gateways that led Liu Changle to his door.

Liu was born in Shanghai in 1951. His parents were government cadres who followed the army there. In 1953, his family moved to Beijing, where his father, an educated and cultured man, eventually worked his way into the upper ranks of the Communist Party Organization Department, which selects and assigns officials for leadership roles throughout the country. During the Cultural Revolution, Liu was sent to the countryside to work with peasants. But within a year, his father used his pull to get Liu a coveted slot in the PLA to escape the chaos. In 1979, when China and Vietnam engaged in a series of vicious border battles, Liu was assigned to China Central Radio, the government's monopoly national radio broadcaster, where he made a name for himself as a fast thinker and fast talker with a knack for narrating live events. When he went to the Beijing Broadcasting Institute in the mid-1980s to polish his professional skills, he found some of his broadcasts were being used as models for students.

By 1988, Liu was a colonel and in charge of all military news broadcast on Chinese radio. While he loved the broadcast media, Liu wanted to gain more experience as well as make some money. Using family and military connections, Liu won an assignment to Sinochem, a massive state-run oil company. He was sent to a government oil trading office in Singapore in 1990, about the same time that Murdoch was scrambling to keep News Corp. out of bankruptcy. In Singapore, Liu started his own oil trading business with China, investing his oil profits in Beijing real-estate projects.

Watching Singapore's tightly controlled press, Liu began to think about returning to his first love, broadcasting. He realized that it was possible to offer quality entertainment and informative news while also providing sophisticated government propaganda that openly discussed problems, albeit from the viewpoint of an efficient and noble government's efforts to solve them. He didn't know it at the time, but Liu had found the formula for the future of television in China. He also realized that the outside world's view of China was coming from the Western press. Programs prepared by CCTV for overseas audiences were so blatantly propagandistic that they had no credibility. Like many of his generation, Liu wanted to see China modernize, to catch up to the rest of the world and earn its respect. He plunged into Buddhism, not to practice the religion, but to understand the core of Chinese traditional philosophy and culture.

About the time that Murdoch was taking over STAR TV in 1993, Liu began looking for ways to launch a Chinese-language TV station outside of China. His vision was for a station that would appeal to a global Chinese audience and beam its signal into China by satellite. At the time, the only satellite that could reach his intended audience, AsiaSat 1, was fully booked. In 1994, however, Liu heard that Mongolian state television was giving up its transponder on the satellite. STAR, which dominated the satellite, had the right of first refusal for the transponder.

Liu approached STAR about the transponder. STAR officials had seen a steady stream of Chinese entrepreneurs offering their special connections and relationships to help Murdoch out of his mess in China, but Liu was different. He was looking to build his own channel. His plan worried STAR CEO Gary Davey, who thought Liu's planned channel would compete with STAR's two Chinese-language channels. But STAR executives realized that Liu knew the Chinese media industry and its regulators thoroughly. He also had a nose for the nuances of Chinese politics. Liu and Murdoch began to talk directly. They were enough alike to be both comfortable with yet wary of each other. They both liked spicy food, taking business risks, and were willing to forgo short-term profits for long-term gain. But they also both liked to be in control. Neither plays second fiddle to anybody.

Liu wanted to control all of Murdoch's contacts with China, but Murdoch was wising up. He would do a joint-venture station with Liu to help dig himself out of his current STAR mess, but he also would continue his independent efforts for his own STAR channels in China in the future. Working with Liu appeared to be a good opportunity, but Murdoch knew better than to put all his eggs in somebody else's basket.

As they negotiated, Murdoch met his match. Liu wasn't going to give any ground on control issues and Chinese officials backed him. In the end, he convinced Murdoch to throw his Chinese-language STAR movies and STAR Chinese channels into the joint venture at zero valuation. After that, they each invested equally. The partnership breakdown was 45 percent for Murdoch, 45 percent for Liu, and 10 percent for a CCTV company in Hong Kong. When Phoenix was listed on the GEM stock market in Hong Kong in 2000, the CCTV shares were taken over by the Bank of China and 15 percent of the company's equity was floated on the market.

Launching Phoenix took enormous energy and drew heavily on

Liu's network of contacts. He courted the Information Office relentlessly, pitching the same argument to anyone who would listen. A joint-venture satellite television station between him and Murdoch would serve two purposes: he would control Murdoch in China while using Murdoch's global reach to place Phoenix on cable systems in the United States, Europe, and Asia. Liu promised that Phoenix would be a dependable and responsible "voice of China" to the outside world. In exchange, the authorities would ignore Phoenix's "gray market" distribution in China.

Liu also took pains to reassure the state-owned CCTV that he wouldn't be so much a competitor as a source of new programming. He worked his ties with the bored, discouraged editors and producers at CCTV, promising them lucrative coproduction deals and lots of foreign travel.

The Phoenix Rises

The Phoenix Chinese Channel, with its flashy graphics and fast-paced Fox-style format, burst onto the staid Chinese television scene in March 1996 with an amalgam of programming from the STAR TV Chinese and movie channels. While Phoenix didn't have legal permission to be seen by Chinese viewers, the channel was widely available in cities and even in country villages where illegal satellite dishes were proliferating. CCTV and stations in the Chinese provinces immediately copied the Phoenix shows and broadcast style.

But Liu stayed at least one step ahead. As Chinese leaders traveled overseas, Phoenix covered their speeches live and reported on the surrounding color of their journeys, something that was unheard of in Chinese television, which usually showed footage of handshakes while an anchor read dull dispatches written by the foreign ministry. Liu guessed, rightly, that Chinese leaders would be flattered by the coverage. Phoenix began getting calls from party officials requesting tapes of the coverage.

Phoenix's big break came on March 19, 1998, when Phoenix

broadcast live the annual press conference held by Chinese leaders at the end of the National People's Congress session. Newly appointed Premier Zhu Rongji was taking questions from foreign and local reporters. He interrupted the moderator and told him to call on Phoenix correspondent Sally Wu, a Taiwanese, "because I really enjoy watching her show." Sally Wu became an instant celebrity, and Phoenix had an unofficial seal of approval from the man who was now running the Chinese government. Sitting in his Hong Kong office watching the news conference, Liu broke into tears. Zhu was acknowledging that the members of the Chinese leadership were avid watchers of Phoenix because it was so much more informative than their own propaganda organs. Wu's twenty-minute news show had been an experiment. With Zhu's comments, Liu now felt safe to expand the Phoenix news output to several hours a day and Sally Wu got her own weekly special.

Later that year, Liu followed through with his initial promise to propaganda officials by launching the Phoenix Chinese News and Entertainment Channel in Cantonese and Mandarin, designed to appeal to overseas Chinese. By January 2000, the channel was widely available on cable and satellite systems in the United States and throughout Europe largely due to Murdoch's global network and assistance. To keep the state-owned CCTV and propaganda officials happy, Murdoch and Liu also began bundling the Phoenix overseas channel with CCTV's international channels for foreign broadcasters.

Liu was personally involved in every step of the news output. He instinctively knows which stories are important and what sells to a Chinese audience. He also knows just how far he can push before upsetting Chinese authorities. He created personality-driven talk shows in which stylish and witty commentators discuss current events with each other, a broadcasting innovation in China. Of course, the commentators took only marginally diverse points of view, carefully keeping their discussions within the bounds of what is permissible in China. Despite Liu's professed dislike of strident Chinese nationalism, Phoenix was bombastically nationalist in the aftermath of the U.S. bombing of the Chinese embassy in Belgrade in May 1999.

Liu's news sense is combined with the instincts of a showman. To mark the handover of Hong Kong from Britain to China in July 1997, Liu arranged for a Taiwan stuntman to jump across a sixty-meter chasm in the Yellow River in a sports car. He brought in CCTV to cobroadcast the live event.

Phoenix's impact in China sometimes surfaced in unexpected ways. Social researchers interviewing Chinese prostitutes who worked in hotels where Phoenix was available told the researchers that the only education they had on safe sex practices came from a Phoenix show, *Sex and Love Classroom.*

Establishing the Phoenix general channel and movie channels was a means to an end. Liu's goal all along was to build a twenty-four-hour Chinese news channel. In June 2000, with Phoenix starting to show profits, Liu, after overcoming Murdoch's objections, listed Phoenix on the Hong Kong GEM stock market, raising about $100 million that he used to finance his original objective of a twenty-four-hour news channel. Six months later, Liu reached his goal with the launch of Phoenix's twenty-four-hour InfoNews channel.

Liu stationed reporters in New York; San Francisco; Washington, D.C.; and Moscow. When terrorists hit the World Trade Center on September 11, 2001, Phoenix immediately canceled all advertising and went live for thirty-five hours with feeds from Fox, CNN, and others, providing simultaneous translation into Chinese along with analysis by Chinese commentators and phone interviews with witnesses in New York. In contrast, CCTV waited several hours for approval and then intermittently broadcast clips from New York supplied by CNN. For many within CCTV, this September 11 embarrassment was the last straw in their battles with the Communist Party Propaganda Department. News and talk shows began popping up on CCTV that were modeled after, albeit tamer than, the shows on Phoenix.

Soon surveys showed that Phoenix was being watched by 42 million households in China, about 13 percent of the country's viewing audience. Like all foreign stations, Phoenix is supposed to be available only in hotels and the residential compounds and offices of foreigners or high-level Chinese officials. However, with the demand for Phoenix among the Chinese elite, the station had become available in almost any modern apartment building or housing compound in China. Developers found that buyers were often reluctant to purchase apartments unless Phoenix was available in the building. The wide availability of Phoenix in the dorms and classrooms of China's universities is testimony to the government's comfort.

While they remain partners in Phoenix, Murdoch and Liu and their companies have gradually moved toward what interests them the most. While Liu focused on building Phoenix's InfoNews channel, Murdoch got busy outside of China, fathering two children with Wendi and engaging in a successful but complicated and prolonged quest to purchase DIRECTV and extend his global satellite reach across the United States. But Murdoch still keeps a close eye on his China operations, which are now based in a renovated turn-of-the-century mansion in Shanghai.

The STAR channels include Chinese versions of ESPN and National Geographic, as well as STAR-branded channels for music, movies, and sports. News Corp.'s pride and joy in China is a Chinese-language entertainment channel called Xingkong, which translates as "Starry Sky." Launched in 2002, Xingkong focuses on game shows, variety, drama, sit-coms, cartoons, and movies, much of it reminiscent of Fox programming in the United States. STAR is also building a strong network of friends at TV stations across China by contracting for them to produce shows for Xingkong and STAR's other channels. Xingkong even has a Chinese replica of *Judge Judy* that is produced in Beijing. By agreeing to distribute CCTV's international channels in the United States and Europe, Murdoch cut a deal that allows Xingkong to feed directly into several cable TV systems reaching some 2 million households in Guangdong province, adjacent to Hong Kong. This gave the media mogul his first toehold in the local Chinese television market.

In October 2003, Murdoch was implicitly acknowledged as a trusted mentor of the Chinese TV industry when he was invited to speak at the Central Party School in Beijing, where China trains its current and future leaders. Murdoch told the gathering of more than one hundred party officials, including Vice-President Zeng Qinghong and several ministers, that China should allow a market-driven media to flourish because it would further public education, increase national unity, and elevate the nation's stature. "The unleashing of the potential of the open market does not represent any loss of power," Murdoch said. "On the contrary, as the party goes from running the country's media businesses to overseeing their growth, both China's leaders and her people will be greatly empowered by the rewards."

Watchdog from the Library

Modern watchdog journalism in China began in a tiny room underneath the stairway of a shuttered middle school library in Jiangsu province during the Cultural Revolution. Residing in the room was a political outcast, Yun Yiqun, once one of China's most famous wartime reporters and the founder and director of several journalism schools. He joined the party at age twenty-one, just five years after it was founded. He served as an underground agent, gathering intelligence in Shanghai when the Communists were in the countryside and the KMT ruled the cities. That led to a twenty-year career as a top journalist for Communist publications. After World War II, he established and headed a half-dozen journalism schools in Jiangsu, Shandong, and Shanghai. At the same time, he served as bureau chief for central China for the Xinhua news agency and several national publications and edited a progressive magazine in Shanghai.

Yun had great energy and high principles, but he was trapped by the Maoist campaign to purge "rightists." Journalists like Yun were easy targets because they had years of published works that could be parsed for statements that could be construed to challenge party doctrine. Yun was locked up for ten years.

When he emerged from prison, Yun was sent to the nether regions of Jiangsu province as the administrator of the small library in a middle school. His ordeal started again within a few years when local Red Guards discovered this enemy in their midst and subjected Yun to physical and mental torture in self-criticism sessions. By the early 1970s, Yun, although no longer subject to torture, was a political prisoner living alone under the stairway in the shuttered school's library. With his photographic memory and his deep intelligence, Yun longed to talk to someone about his experiences, but he was anathema to anyone in the village. Then one day in 1973, an impatient nineteen-year-old woman in an army uniform knocked on his door. Her name was Hu Shuli, and she was trying to figure out what the hell was going on around her.

Shuli, as her friends call her, is the daughter of a trade union official father and a mother who was an editor at the trade union newspaper, the *Workers' Daily*. Shuli's parents embued her with a deep sense of moral rectitude and an unquenchable thirst for knowledge. She hewed closely to party doctrine even as a teen, eagerly leaving behind her comfortable urban existence to follow Mao's instructions to learn from the masses. As the Cultural Revolution unfolded, Shuli was sent to a dirt-poor village as an "intellectual youth." The ten students in Shuli's group cultivated barley, potatoes, and corn, but it was ideas that Shuli really harvested. She was surprised to find that the farmers were so wise and clever, yet so poor. The peasants in the village ate only breakfast and lunch and went to bed hungry to conserve their precious food supply. They got meat twice a year, during the Moon Festival and Spring Festival. They also carried no illusions and Shuli and her compatriots learned from them that the local party officials deserved no respect or admiration. It was the peasants that Shuli respected. They were no different from her. Only the accident of birth made them farmers.

Shuli returned to Beijing in 1970 with a deep respect for Chinese peasants and a deep skepticism for Chinese officialdom. She joined the army and was sent to work at a hospital in Funing County in northern Jiangsu province. For the first few years, Shuli was a cleaner. Then she maneuvered herself into the hospital broadcasting booth, a position of some influence. She took her responsibilities seriously. She woke the patients up in the morning and put them to bed at night with music. She played the radio news and made hospital announcements. It was a soft job, and the broadcast booth had a small library, so she read most of the books that appeared interesting. When she exhausted those, she quietly asked around town, looking for intellectuals or teachers who may have hoarded a few decent books from the Red Guards. She could sense that China had descended into a time of terrible personal cruelty and political nonsense. She wanted to know how that had happened.

When Yun Yiqun opened the door, Shuli introduced herself and said that she needed books to read. He asked why. She said that she had lots of time on her hands and wanted to study Chinese history. Yun welcomed Shuli like a drowning man who suddenly surfaces. He spent the next few years recommending books for her to read and answering her many questions about where China came from and how it got where it was now. He talked for hours on end about what he had seen since joining the Communist Party as an underground agent at age twenty-one. He explained how the system worked, what motivated officials, what made things happen. He told her how nobody wants to take responsibility for a big decision. He told her he still believed in the ideals of the revolution, that the wisdom of the people would rule China.

Proud Traditions

In 1978, the year that Yun died, China reopened its universities. Shuli won a slot at People's University in Beijing, where she was the only army member studying journalism. The journalism department was a cauldron of emerging intellectual ferment. Many of the professors were returning from years of imprisonment or farm-work. Mao had been dead for two years and Deng had launched economic reforms and opened up the discussion of how China could move forward. Professors taught Shuli and her classmates to be real journalists, drawing lessons from the days before Mao muzzled the press, when Chinese reporters had gathered economic and political information for the leadership during the Chinese civil war. The students and teachers openly discussed what a disaster the Cultural Revolution had been. The students were told that their role was to serve as the voice of the Communist Party, but also to act as critics and watchdogs to help the party maintain its integrity.

When she received her degree in 1982, Shuli plunged into investigative reporting, covering corruption cases for the *Workers' Daily* as it attempted to shake off the lethargy that had settled over journalism under Mao. Shuli dug right into exposés detailing the illegal personal use of government funds by Chinese officials. She worked on some stories with the most famous journalist in China at the time, Liu Binyan of the *People's Daily,* whose editors had given him permission to pursue corruption stories that the party wanted exposed. But the binge of anticorruption journalism didn't last long. Too many important people were vulnerable. The *Workers' Daily* exiled Shuli to the central China coastal city of Xiamen in 1985 to rid themselves of her constant demands for increased muckraking. Shuli made the most of her exile. She learned photography and how to drive a car. She also spent time studying English at Xiamen University when she wasn't buzzing around town in her Toyota Crown pressing local and provincial officials to talk to her.

After a journalism fellowship at the World Press Institute at Macalester College in St. Paul, Minnesota, Shuli became the international editor of the *Workers' Daily* but was suspended for participating in the Tiananmen Square demonstrations. She used the suspension to write the first postrevolution book in Chinese about American journalism. Her earlier reputation as a muckraker, combined with her book's shocking admonition that newspapers should be neutral and objective, made Shuli famous among Chinese reporters.

Back to Work

In January 1992, Deng made his "southern tour" to Shenzhen, adjacent to Hong Kong, so that papers in the British colony would carry his message for reigniting economic reform. Deng made the trip because the conservatives whom he had placed in power in Beijing after the Tiananmen Massacre blocked his attempts to get that message into the national dailies run by the Communist Party. Within months of Deng's trip, a new national business newspaper, the *China Business Times,* was launched, edited by Ding Wang, Shuli's former editor at the *Workers' Daily.* Ding appointed Shuli as international editor, a post she used to chase down and interview anyone she believed could teach her something. Officials at the new stock market regulator, the China Securities Regulatory Commission, and the foreign trade ministry were particular targets. Foreign CEOs answering their hotel room phones often found Shuli on the other end, demanding that they meet her in the lobby to be interviewed.

Then Ding Wang was ousted and Shuli quit in frustration. Politics was partly to blame. Under Ding, the paper was pushing for faster economic reforms than Premier Li Peng and other conservatives were comfortable with. But an even bigger reason was money. Ding and Shuli insisted that advertising and editorial remain separate. They wanted to pay reporters enough so that they could reasonably demand that they be honest and not write flattering articles about businesses that paid them under-the-table fees. They also opposed publishing favorable articles about companies that purchased advertising.

In 1994, Shuli won a Knight Fellowship at Stanford University. In California she studied the U.S. financial markets and the American media's role in policing those markets. She figured it would be only a matter of time before Chinese leaders realized that without the press acting as a watchdog on financial markets, China would become a paradise for stock manipulators who would leave worthless shares in the hands of small investors.

The *China Business Times* took her back as its senior reporter and Shuli found a place to continue her study of financial markets. Just down the street from her apartment in the western section of Beijing, former World Bank in China representative Edwin Lim was pulling together a team to build the country's first joint-venture investment bank, China International Capital Corporation, or CICC. Shuli began hanging out in CICC's office, relentlessly picking the brains of the Chinese who had been involved in international financial deals. She also befriended the top executives of Morgan Stanley Asia and the China Construction Bank, the joint-venture partners behind CICC. CICC was in the middle of most of the deals to list Chinese companies on foreign exchanges and Shuli worked her contacts to break the stories. Shuli set a high standard for her reporting, poring through *Euromoney, Institutional Investor,* and *The Wall Street Journal,* not only to keep abreast of international financial markets, but also to study their writing styles and standards.

In 1996, Shuli was hired as senior editor of a new business magazine called *Capital,* run by a business group under the Beijing city government. At the same time, she reunited with her old editor Ding Wang, who formed a Shanghai business magazine called *China Business Weekly.* Shuli shuttled between Beijing and Shanghai for nearly two years, writing for both magazines. Shanghai propaganda officials then closed down *China Business Weekly* for printing a photo of Taiwan President Lee Teng-hui and Shuli left *Capital* because she couldn't convince her bosses to increase the news budget and to forbid printing favorable articles for advertisers.

The Deep-Pocketed Mentors

Even before she left *Capital,* Shuli was talking about job possibilities with Wang Boming, one of China's unique characters. Born in 1955 in Poland, where his father was the Chinese ambassador, Wang in 1980 was among the first wave of Chinese students allowed to study in the United States. He obtained a master's in international finance from Columbia University. When reformer Hu Yaobang was removed as Communist Party general secretary in 1987, Wang and several friends gathered one thousand signatures from Chinese students in the United States in an open letter to the Chinese government calling for continued reform. From this group, Wang and several friends created an organization named the China Business Association to encourage a market economy and a stock market in China. Wang and his compatriots returned to China at the end of 1988 to get started.

The budding stock market entrepreneurs not only had to persuade officials that they were serious, they also had to educate them about how capital markets worked. Wang and several others who were children of the Chinese elite arranged high-level meetings and enlisted allies. Wang enlisted Wang Qishan, then a young adviser to Chinese Premier Zhao Ziyang, and another young reformer then serving as a negotiator with the United States on GATT entry, Zhou Xiaochuan, whose father had been Jiang Zemin's boss at the machinery ministry. The stock market entrepreneurs in early 1989 received critical backing from the government when Wang Qishan arranged to establish the Stock Exchange Executive Council (SEEC) to build a regulatory structure for the rapidly proliferating stock trading that was cropping up informally all over the country.

The China Securities Regulatory Commission (CSRC) was established in October 1992. Gao Xiqing, one of Wang Boming's partners in the China Business Association in New York, was named head of the legal section and Wang himself was assigned to head the research department, a bow to his experience years earlier as a researcher at the New York Stock Exchange. But Wang found government work too bureaucratic. He also felt that he and his friends had fulfilled their initial goal. Now Wang wanted to make some money, so he turned the SEEC into a business.

He built an electronic government bond-trading system that was later shut down by the government, and started managing a $100 million fund for international investors while investing in and advising Chinese companies seeking to list on the stock markets. He also founded the *Securities Market Weekly,* which became the key information source on Chinese stocks. The magazine was dry and often technical and academic, but it was the only publication officially approved by the CSRC. It was an immediate success, becoming the top business magazine in China with a circulation of more than 1 million subscribers. But as companies continued to flood onto the Chinese stock markets and with more than 40 million people opening stock market accounts, Wang realized that there was a market for a more accessible and sophisticated magazine.

Wang and Shuli had toyed with a collaboration two years earlier, but Wang couldn't bring himself to ally with Shuli. She was always making impossible demands. He knew now that she hadn't changed and that she would make his life miserable. But he also knew Shuli was the best and most driven editor in China. For this new magazine, he would simply have to take whatever she dished out. The market was ready for a magazine with guts and integrity and Shuli was the person to produce it. Wang also knew that the Chinese officials who had helped establish the CSRC, Wang Qishan and Zhou Xiaochuan, now held top posts in the banking and finance bureaucracy and would appreciate a true media watchdog to protect investors. For her part, Shuli figured she would use Wang's deep pockets to create a publication with the integrity and aggressive drive to police the Chinese financial markets.

Before agreeing to work with Wang, however, Shuli laid out strict conditions. She demanded an editorial budget that included $200,000 a year for reporter salaries, so she could pay reporters enough to keep them honest. Wang didn't flinch. Then Shuli dropped the other shoe: "I will be in charge of all editorial decisions. You cannot interfere. We need to have a Chinese wall between editorial and advertising."

Wang accepted Shuli's terms and she set out to hire a staff that she could train to become real reporters. She brought in a few colleagues she trusted from the *China Business Times,* but she also searched for young people who hadn't worked as editors or reporters long enough to become corrupt or steeped in the self-censorship that reporters were expected to exercise. Once word spread that Shuli was starting a new magazine, to be called *Caijing* (shorthand for "finance and economics"), e-mails poured in from journalists across China eager to work for her.

Angry Phone Calls

The Asian financial crisis of 1997–98 showed China's leaders how crony capitalism could undermine a country's financial system and erase decades of growth and progress. In its April 1998 inaugural issue, *Caijing* carried a detailed exposé about a listed company named Qiongminyuan, a stock market high-flyer that had been suspended from trading for filing false financial statements. As usual, the CSRC had forbidden Chinese reporters to write about the company's troubles on the grounds that such scandals could dampen investor enthusiasm and tank the Chinese stock market. The government depended on the stock market to funnel the country's abundant personal savings into refinancing and revitalizing state-owned companies. Wang Boming had to send emissaries over to the CSRC for a week to apologize for the story. But his new magazine was an instant hit and many staffers in the CSRC welcomed its aggressive editorial stance.

Shuli and her reporters continued to expose stock market problems and solicited experts to write economic policy analysis that questioned some government policies. The result wasn't surprising: Wang Boming began receiving angry phone calls. Sometimes it seemed as if everyone he knew was angry at him and his magazine. Regulators complained when *Caijing* broke reporting prohibitions. Listed company executives screamed that *Caijing* was killing their stock price. Investment bankers fretted about *Caijing* digging out unflattering information about companies they were seeking to list. For someone who prides himself on being everyone's friend, the phone calls were painful for Wang. He would listen politely to the caller and then explain that he only owned the magazine, he couldn't interfere in editorial decisions. The angry callers were confounded. You own it, but you can't say what gets published? Wang was too embarrassed—and too frightened of her terrible temper—to tell Shuli to soften or kill stories critical of his friends. Nevertheless, it hurt him when advertisers withdrew from the magazine because of critical stories.

China's business community soon learned to both fear and respect Shuli. She doesn't play golf and she doesn't spend much time socializing. But if she doesn't share leisure pastimes with business executives, she does share their goal of reforming China. She speaks fast and walks fast, but neither her mouth nor her feet can keep up with her mind. There is no time for small talk. Her many friends are accustomed to getting a call from Shuli telling them what they must do for her, and the demands are made with such certainty and absence of guile that no one dares question her. She simply assumes the whole world works for her, but only for its betterment. While many government officials and financial executives have moved to modern glass-and-steel high-rise apartments on the eastern side of Beijing, Shuli still lives in a 1950s Soviet-style cement building with dark and dilapidated stairwells. Her furniture is sparse and basic, but the walls are filled with Chinese- and English-language books on history, finance, and politics.

Shuli's employees have great respect for her, but she runs them ragged. "She doesn't have management talent. She doesn't like running an organization. She is a reporter. She always wants to break stories," says one *Caijing* journalist. "She sets high standards and sometimes she can torture her subordinates. She is always pushing, pushing, pushing. She will never stop until you complain. Then she will back off a bit. We tell our new journalists that if you don't complain when she pushes you too far, it is your problem."

Shuli realized early that the Communist Party officials who scrutinized publications knew little about economics and nothing about finance. When Wang assigned a former Xinhua editor to review each issue of *Caijing* before it was published, Shuli made sure to include a political story the editor would want to argue about. That gave him something to do while she slipped controversial business stories right past him.

She thrives on controversy. In October 2000, *Caijing* sent tremors through China's entire financial industry with the publication of a package of stories on how the managers of China's new mutual funds were working together to manipulate the market. The core of the reporting was a secret report by an official of the Shanghai Stock Exchange that the government had suppressed as too embarrassing. Shuli obtained the report and packaged the information with analysis and explanation to put the scandal in perspective. The major Chinese securities houses fought back, taking out joint advertisements condemning *Caijing* in the stock market newspapers published by the Xinhua news agency.

A year later, in August 2001, *Caijing* again roiled the financial industry with a detailed exposé of Yinguangxia, a company with a rocketing stock price that was the darling of stock market investors. The company CEO came to Wang Boming before the article was printed, offering to buy advertising to ward off publication and then offering to buy the magazine. This was a company that had been lauded and visited by President Jiang Zemin and other leaders. Wang summoned Shuli and quizzed her about the story. She convinced him that she had iron-clad evidence that the company's financial statements were fake. Still worried about political repercussions, Wang Boming telephoned his old friend Wang Qishan, then head of the State Council Office for Restructuring the Economic System. His response: "Is the company real or fake? If it is fake, print the story."

Caijing reported that Yinguangxia had been filing false financial statements. The stock dropped from 34 to 7. An investigation by the CSRC reported that the company's financial reports were inflated way beyond what *Caijing* had reported. The company sued *Caijing* and lost twice.

Caijing spawned many imitations, the best of them launched by editors who worked for Shuli and then went off on their own. More often than not, their efforts are thwarted by publishers who believe that exposés and aggressive news reporting only bring trouble. There are some bright spots, but *Caijing* is still one of only a few publications in China that doesn't trade favorable articles for advertising or other payments.

Caijing pushed beyond its economic roots when China was hit by the sometimes fatal respiratory disease SARS in the spring of 2003. As people started dying in Guangdong province, the Chinese government ordered the media not to probe the issue and carry the official government line that SARS was an isolated and small problem. Rumors spread quickly, and Chinese citizens panicked that they were in the midst of an epidemic. *Caijing* jumped onto the story. Shuli went to the countryside in western China to interview officials and trace the pattern of the disease outbreak. She sent reporters to Hong Kong and Hanoi to examine those SARS hot spots. She even commissioned articles from a Canadian reporter about the Toronto outbreak. The magazine profiled the U.S. Centers for Disease Control and Prevention in Atlanta as a model for China to follow. *Caijing* even produced special weekly editions providing extensive SARS coverage.

"Shuli knew in this time of crisis it was time for a journalistic breakthrough," said a *Caijing* editor. "We knew we had an opportunity because the situation was so unclear. Today we can aggressively report on the stock markets, tomorrow we will be reporting on grassroots elections."

What This Means for You

When I was *The Wall Street Journal* bureau chief in China in the early 1990s, I was struck by how much Chinese reporters knew about what was really happening in the country and how little of it they could actually report. Hu Shuli is not alone as a journalist in China with high ideals, strong ethics, and a determination to find and tell the truth. I have watched many editors and reporters, and quite a few publications, bravely dig into stories that the government didn't want told. Perhaps the fate of journalists in China was best described by Cheng Yizhong, age thirty-nine, a principled and risk-taking editor of the *Southern Metropolis Daily* in Guangzhou. In the summer of 2004, he was arrested by local Communist Party officials on trumped-up charges of corruption involving newspaper expense accounts. The real reason was that local officials wanted to shut down the paper's aggressive reporting. They were especially irked by an exposé about the death of a recent college graduate in police custody. The report triggered nationwide outrage and led Beijing to change rules regarding police detention. Cheng was released without trial after five months in jail, the result of a campaign by retired officials, attorneys, and journalists. On his release, Cheng described journalism in China: "Freedom means knowing how big your cage is."

Both Liu Changle and Hu Shuli have a keen sense of the size of their cages. They know what the government wants, and what the country needs to be able to progress. Shuli's cage is the stock market and economic policy. Liu's cage is bringing international news into China and projecting China's image to the world. But both of them always have their political noses in the air, sniffing out opportunities to expand the size of their cages.

Unfortunately, Liu and Shuli are the exception, not the norm, in China's journalism establishment. Many reporters are corrupt, corpulent, and lazy. They are handcuffed so tightly when it comes to political, government, and social news that they focus on business news. But all too often business news becomes simply a way to make money for themselves by allying with Chinese entrepreneurs to inflate stocks or helping Chinese companies attack foreign and domestic competitors. The nationalism that swept China after Tiananmen continues to spill over into the commercial sector. So whether they are helping Chinese companies, or simply building a good rant against a foreign entity, Chinese reporters are generally free to attack foreign companies. The print media is now generally split between the commercial press and the party propaganda press. They both have business and financial pages. Advertisers want readers who have purchasing power. So the party press is losing out and turning to paid propaganda. Editors and journalists take money to print stories for businesses.

The commercial press often is worse. Private businesspeople have been allowed to take over the advertising and circulation portions of publications while the editorial side usually remains under at least nominal government control. As long as these publications don't stir up trouble with reports on politics or social issues, they have a free hand to do what makes money. Many have emulated Murdoch-style reporting of celebrity gossip and scandal, replete with secret tapings and electronic eavesdropping. These nascent Chinese media moguls also use their news columns to reward friends and attack competitors in the business world. The Chinese government doesn't speak of "press freedom" or "press reform," only "press commercialization." One insight into the leadership's attitude came during the 1989 demonstration when Jiang Zemin, then Communist Party secretary of Shanghai, explained his closure of a pioneering paper, The World Economic Herald. Jiang said that press freedom doesn't exist anywhere in the world. "The amount of money you have determines how much freedom you enjoy," Jiang said.

As a foreign company in China, you will live in a free-fire zone. Northwest Airlines has experienced this several times. In the most notorious incident, the airline faced indignant and overblown headlines, along with calls for a boycott of the airline, when a Chinese passenger claimed to have suffered a racist insult from a flight attendant when requesting a second meal. Toshiba was pilloried across China for weeks for failing to recall laptops that could have had a minor disc-drive flaw. Park rangers in Wuhan called in television cameras and smashed with sledge hammers an $85,000 Mercedes owned by their government wildlife park. They claimed that the car was a lemon and Mercedes had failed to fix its many problems. The Chinese media nationwide gnashed its teeth over the car company's irresponsibility. Nobody questioned what a government wildlife park was doing buying an $85,000 car. When Wal-Mart opened in Shenzhen, it was roasted in the press for everything from noisy air conditioners to selling audiovisual systems with "Made in the U.S." labels that had been assembled in China.

As a foreign company in China, your best defense is a good offense. The flip side of Nationalist indignation is that Chinese reporters are also quite compliant if you cultivate them.

Two key business lessons can be drawn from observing the saga of Murdoch and Liu Changle. One is that the most talented businesspeople in China are often the great human observers. Analyzing the human elements of a business situation is where the Chinese are brilliant. Just as lawyers in the West can help you navigate a path to success by finding legal loopholes and arguments, Chinese businesspeople navigate their way to success by working many people, from many angles, simultaneously. The best can nudge one group this way, nudge another that way, and nudge another to stay out of the way, all at the same time. Liu Changle is a virtuoso nudger.

We can also learn from the way Murdoch has handled his partnership with Liu. He didn't put all his eggs in one basket, and he kept developing his own government relations. This has allowed Murdoch to continue to create his own Chinese entertainment channels, and to develop a sense of personal trust with Chinese leaders. His partnership with Liu is strong because Murdoch has gotten out of the way. He has basically ceded control of Phoenix to Liu, and thereby allowed Liu to pursue his own agenda of news and public affairs. They gradually have moved into the usual formula for success in a joint venture in China: peaceful coexistence between the partners.

The Little Red Book of Business

- Avoid the "slobbering CEO syndrome." Don't fall for China's brilliant use of its huge size and two-thousand-year tradition of manipulative political pageantry to intimidate foreigners into accepting unwise deals.

- If your boss wants to do a quick deal in China, lose his or her visa.

- Make your business a fact of life in China. Then it will be hard to unseat you. This often entails taking big risks.

- You don't win in China by getting only to the top guy. You win by enlisting supporters at all levels.

- The most talented businesspeople in China are great human observers who can analyze the people elements of a business situation. Lawyers in the West find loopholes and use legal reasoning; the Chinese find people who can nudge their interests this way or that way.

- In business relationships, the Chinese seek stability and trust more than intimacy. They want to feel comfortable that you will offer no surprises that will hurt them, but they don't need to be your best friend.

- Reforms in China are achieved by networks of like-minded people who protect each other politically and push the envelope when opportunities arise.

- Don't cede government relations to your partner. Your Chinese partner has connections, but he also has his own agenda, issues, and baggage.

- Information is a tool that serves the interests of those in power in China. The truth is always shaded to preserve privilege and maintain harmony.

- The Chinese media is struggling between shaping the way people think and informing them sufficiently to compete in the global economy.

- Objective news is making progress when it serves the interests of the state, but don't expect a free press in China in your lifetime.

- Government propaganda is a key form of control, so the government is stuck in a pattern. It doesn't matter so much what they are saying because any message serves as a defense against other ideas popping up.

- Foreign companies live in a media free-fire zone. Chinese reporters, severely restrained in reporting on domestic politics and social issues, can attack foreign companies, something the government allows and often encourages.

- Treat reporters in China with respect, but be very wary. Most Chinese journalists have little or no professional training. Objectivity isn't part of their playbook. For many, being a reporter is just a stepping-stone to a business career.

- Educate key reporters about your business, maintain regular ties, and show them a good time. It is all about personal relationships. It is hard for Chinese journalists to attack friends, easy to attack faceless foreign companies.

- Your company public relations department can learn from the Communist Party. Keep low-key propaganda campaigns going. This doesn't mean always generating headlines. It means regularly putting out your own spin.

7

The Best-Laid Plans

Government planning and manipulation of foreign companies fueled China's construction of the world's largest telecom system. But this saga shows how entrepreneurship and the market can beat the planners.

THE GIANT BALLOONS shaped like babies and emblazoned with the words "Little Smart" did their job: thousands of customers flocked to the department store counters and street kiosks over which the balloons hovered in the remote northwestern China city of Lanzhou.

Curiosity drove the crowds. Was there yet another product that promised to make their child smarter? A new computer learning system? Another medicinal tonic to help students concentrate?

No, but it was almost as good. The inflatable Little Smart babies were signaling a mobile phone deal too good to refuse. The denizens of this struggling industrial city of 3 million along the upper reaches of the Yellow River couldn't afford to install home phones, much less join the country's mobile phone craze. But with calling charges 80 percent cheaper than the country's two mobile operators, China Mobile and Unicom, Little Smart promised to connect the Chinese masses to one another. Eager customers jostled one another for places in the long lines, waiting to subscribe.

Their delight was short-lived. In August 2000, the second

month of Little Smart service in Lanzhou, the city's phone system went haywire. China Mobile subscribers nationwide couldn't call through to the Little Smart customers in Lanzhou. Then people calling from their home and office phones in Lanzhou suddenly couldn't get through to friends on the China Mobile system. Unicom mobile subscribers just laughed. They were accustomed to lost connections.

This Lanzhou phone fight was the first public eruption of a fierce behind-the-scenes bureaucratic battle involving China's government phone companies. The incident made headlines in the *People's Daily*, much to the consternation of China's "telecom czar," Wu Jichuan. China's telecom system wasn't ready for this. It needed a few more years under his discipline and guidance to bring to every remote village and towering skyscraper the robust state-of-the-art network China needed to become a global economic power and preserve the Communist Party's grip on power. Building China's telecom system, and keeping it under firm government control, had been Wu's mission in life since he became Communist Party secretary of China's telecom ministry six years earlier. Now, as chief of the Ministry of Information Industry (MII), Wu controlled it all: the phone system, the Internet, the cable TV backbone, the manufacture of computers and phones, and the development and use of software. The industry was moving so fast that Wu made up new regulations by the week and sometimes changed them by the day. Throughout the world, Wu's words were parsed by the technology press much as Alan Greenspan's are by the financial media

Not bad for a peasant kid from Hunan.

But Wu was enraged that the Lanzhou phone fight showed everybody that the telecom world was no longer following his orders. Chinese technology companies were busily listing on domestic and overseas stock markets, raising billions of dollars that limited Wu's tinkering. Dozens of the world's biggest telephone companies were throwing piles of cash at Unicom to exploit cracks in the regulatory wall Wu had built to keep foreign telecom operators out of China. China's ferocious entrepreneurial instincts and wads of international money were ripping apart his best-laid plans for orderly competition. The market was taking over, and dragging him along with it.

Wu felt trapped. He was supposed to think like a telecom tycoon and maximize profits. But he also had a government mission to bring universal and affordable phone service to every corner of China.

Damned market. It can mess up even the best-laid plans.

Overview

With its traditional habit of setting grandiose socialist goals aimed at quickly surpassing the Western world, the Chinese government in the era of economic reform has become an awesome and awful planning machine. The last two decades of immense change in China has certainly been fueled by the ingenuity and relentless drive of the Chinese people, but they have often followed the path laid by Chinese planners. Almost all of China's senior leaders in the reform era are engineers, many trained in Moscow. They love to tinker and to plan. The Soviet-inspired five-year plans that once coordinated the socialist planned economy have now become a blueprint for China's global business ambitions. Since Deng made economic reform the party's core dogma in 1978, China every five years has laid out aggressive step-by-step plans to transform itself into a global business powerhouse. Some plans are aimed at building entire modern industrial and commercial sectors, such as steel, chemicals, silicon chips, and automobiles. Other plans are aimed at building infrastructure, including dozens of modern airports, a string of deep-water ports, and huge expansions of universities, railroads, bridges, and housing estates. The scale is mind-boggling. In the past fifteen years, China has invested $300 billion in building half a million miles of roads, including twenty thousand miles of expressways that crisscross the sprawling country.

Overseeing this expansion has been an elite group of Communist party bureaucrats whose mission is to build businesses and business infrastructure. Their goals are often so capitalistic they might properly be called "bizocrats." Among them, one-time telecom czar Wu Jichuan stands head and shoulders above the rest, the result of his enormous accomplishments. In ten years, beginning in 1993, Wu added more than 500 million telephones to the 30 million that existed in China when he took office. He propelled China's phone system from 1950s-era dial phones to a nationwide network of sleek, sophisticated mobile phones that even maids and construction workers can afford. China's telecom system is the world's most technologically advanced and has fueled the growth of a domestic telecommunications and electronics industry that employs millions of people and is setting its own global technology standards. Wu has been regulator, competitor, coordinator, and nursemaid for an industry that touches everybody.

Watching Wu Jichuan plan and build China's phone system revealed much about how the Chinese system works. As in many other industries, Wu used the lure of China's huge market to persuade foreigners to provide technology, capital, and training. He oversaw the greatest gold rush of China's reform era. But he also had to learn how to deal with markets, not least of which were the international stock markets that demanded high returns from Chinese listed companies and inspired ruthless competition among China's entrepreneurs and engineers.

This is the story of the struggle between planning and the market. Despite his enormous political power and intricate planning, Wu couldn't thwart a group of young Mainland Chinese who used the experience and knowledge they gained in U.S. universities and at Bell Labs to start UTStarcom and spread a technology across China that Wu had vetoed. UTStarcom's battle with Wu is a study in how to stay on the right side of the regulatory line by helping officials shift that line in your direction. A good product and value proposition for consumers can overcome the objections of even the most determined planners in China. UTStarcom drew its strategy right out of Mao's revolutionary playbook: "When the enemy advances, we retreat; when the enemy escapes, we harass; when he retreats, we pursue; and when he gets tired, we attack."

Bait and Switch

At age twenty-eight, Wu Jichuan became a junior engineer at the only telecom entity in China, the Ministry of Posts and Telecommunications (MPT), whose primary mission was to build and maintain sufficient telecommunications connections to enable the party to maintain close communications with local party leaders throughout the country. For nearly two decades, he worked his way up in the ministry's supplies and material bureaus, gaining a reputation for being decisive, well organized, and always curious to understand the changing technology. He was marked as a future leader in 1982 when his bosses assigned him to a coveted slot in the Communist Party's Central Party School. Two years later, he was appointed vice-minister of MPT, a huge promotion. More importantly, he was named as the ministry's party secretary, at the age of forty-seven, in 1984.

China's telephone system under Mao had been a vital national security tool. With Deng's economic reforms, Wu and his colleagues at the MPT were told to build a world-class telephone system while creating China's telecom technology and manufacturing expertise. China's telephone system would be aimed at spreading prosperity. Wu approached his assignment using the basic Chinese economic development model: bring in foreign capital, expertise, and technology, then block the foreigners from owning any key parts of the industry while building a domestic manufacturing base and supply chain. He would test all the new technologies and business models, then carefully choose what was best for China. The goal was Chinese ownership of the whole system, from equipment manufacturing to intellectual property.

To execute their ambitious plan, Chinese officials first sought help from AT&T, the American powerhouse and home of the famous Bell Labs. The Chinese offered AT&T the chance to establish the first joint-venture telecom switch manufacturing facility. A switch is equal to a telephone line, and China had plans to add tens of million of new phone lines in China. Surely AT&T would leap at the offer.

But AT&T was mired in negotiations to settle the lawsuit that resulted in the breakup of the company in 1984. AT&T executives also worried about passing advanced technology manufacturing processes to a country that was still under Cold War technology export restrictions. They offered a joint venture to make an earlier generation switch in China, but the Chinese balked. We want your most advanced technology or nothing, they said. China then approached Japan. But the Japanese, who had built their technological base by copying and refining products from the West, were wary, too. They knew China was studying their development model and Japanese companies didn't want to hand their technology over to China to be copied.

The solution came from Taiwan, where the government monopoly phone carrier had forced foreign companies to establish Taiwan manufacturing operations in order to sell switches and other telecom equipment on the island. China found its adviser in a smart, smooth MIT graduate named Robert Mao, who was then chief executive of an IT&T plant in Taiwan. Mao put together a deal in 1983 to create Shanghai Bell, a joint venture between IT&T of Belgium (later purchased by Alcatel), the Belgian government, and the MPT's equipment division, the Posts and Telecommunications Industry Corporation, which retained a controlling 60 percent share. As the plant was being built, the Chinese phone system was still primitive. Switching was done by hand in remote areas. Long-distance calls had to be booked in advance. Only top leaders had home phones. Shanghai, China's largest city, had only 100,000 phone subscribers.

The Shanghai Bell deal ignited the China telecom frenzy. Switches flew out the door at premium prices as fast as they could be made. Motorola, Nortel, Nokia, Ericsson, Siemens, and NEC all piled in to sell equipment. To its delight, China discovered that foreign countries had export financing programs that it could tap. Soon it became standard policy for China to import switches only if the supplier financed the sale with government export credit guarantees and low-interest, long-term loans. But the Tiananmen Massacre in 1989 made China an international pariah and effectively shut down that form of financing. Since China was very short on foreign exchange, Shanghai Bell's revenues soared because customers could pay in Chinese renminbi.

As Chinese companies, financed by the government, learned the basics, technology switch prices collapsed. The foreign producers sold mostly to big cities while new Chinese competitors sold to the surrounding rural areas. By 1994, the foreigners were trying to sell switches for $120 per line while Chinese companies sold them for between $45 and $60 per line. Worse, the foreigners were selling products that were overengineered and overpriced. Price pressures, coupled with local content requirements, persuaded most foreign companies to move telecom equipment manufacturing into China as partners with the new Chinese government companies.

Training Competitors

The partnerships were prompted by requirements that began with the first switch sales to China in the 1980s. As party secretary of the MPT in the 1980s, Wu Jichuan enforced very strict rules that required foreign companies to train the country's telecom engineers. The sale of all telecom equipment to China had to be accompanied by training. Early on, when the Chinese were buying a small number of switches, a standard was established that foreign companies had to provide a certain number of days of training for the dollar value of the contract. As switch volumes grew, the training requirement spun out of control. Ericsson once calculated that each management and technical employee of its Chinese partner would be spending a month overseas for training that included transportation, room and board, and spending money. Some groups of trainees were staying abroad for six months or more. The companies knew they were training their future competitors, but what choice did they have? The market was growing too fast, and had too much potential, to ignore. To miss out in China could jeopardize a company's global competitiveness.

As big vendors scrambled around China selling equipment, Wu and his MPT colleagues worried that they were creating a technological tangle with incompatible equipment. They also wanted to lay down the law on local manufacturing. In August 1989, the MPT convinced the State Council to issue a policy edict, known as Article 56, that in effect directed future Chinese purchases to Siemens AG of Germany, Alcatel NV of France, and NEC Corporation of Japan, all of which had set up joint-venture switch plants. The directive effectively banned AT&T from the Chinese phone switch market.

China neither forgives nor forgets. Chinese officials continually reminded AT&T executives that they had blown an opportunity. Worse, AT&T switches that had been installed in the central China city of Wuhan in the mid-1980s were full of technical glitches, the result of AT&T's underestimating how quickly call volume would build. Competitors quickly spread rumors that the Wuhan switches were full of "bugs," listening devices planted by American intelligence. The word went out: AT&T couldn't be trusted.

AT&T, realizing that China was a critical market, regrouped and humbly decided that sincerity and goodwill could overcome a dumb business decision. AT&T wasn't a company to do things in a small way. To build political goodwill, it launched an extensive senior management development program for Chinese officials. AT&T, working with the State Planning Commission, sent four dozen or so up-and-coming Chinese officials to the United States for a year of university training. Additionally, some seventy or so promising young telecom officials from across China were chosen for a program that combined university study with on-the-job training at Bell Labs and other AT&T facilities. The new training programs were beyond the required programs that accompanied all sales of telecom equipment in China. The stratagem succeeded and

AT&T emerged with a huge reservoir of goodwill among Chinese telecom executives and engineers.

AT&T also devoted enormous political resources to fixing the Article 56 ban. The company's intense lobbying was a major catalyst for the 1992 U.S.-China market access agreement in which China pledged to eliminate many of its import quotas and other market barriers over five years. The agreement effectively killed Article 56, but by then the market had moved on. Profit margins on switches for China's landline phone system were disappearing. Now the profits would be in building a mobile phone network for China. Again, technology standards tripped up AT&T. China chose the European mobile standard instead of the American standard.

The Bell Boys

While AT&T was struggling for a foothold in China, the company's storied research division, Bell Labs, was also scrambling to continue as the leader in myriad communications technologies. As R&D projects piled up, Bell Labs began bringing in engineers as "consultants" to work on specific projects. They were temporary workers who AT&T could hire and fire quickly as projects were begun or canceled.

Among the consultants was Chauncey Shey, a recent emigrant from Shanghai who had come to the United States in 1984 to study computer engineering. Shey had no desire to spend his life in research and engineering. He wanted to make money. One day he looked up from his desk at Bell Labs and realized that his most immediate money-making opportunity was surrounding him. Bell Labs needed an outside partner to recruit and screen other "consultant" engineers. Chauncey could do that, but he needed help. His search for someone who knew telecom technology but also had very high energy, entrepreneurial instincts, and excellent people skills led him to a telecom engineer from Beijing named Wu Ying.

The Chinese students who were flooding into the United States were incredibly diligent and driven, but Wu Ying was in a class by himself. When he had served as an assistant professor at Beijing Polytechnic University, he drove university security crazy, often remaining in his office long after the guards locked the building doors at 11:00 P.M. The guards were forever catching Wu Ying climbing out of the building windows at 1:00 A.M. or 2:00 A.M., heading home for a few hours of sleep before the next day's classes. Wu Ying's brains, diligence, and the fact that he spoke English won him a coveted spot at Stanford University. He opted instead for the New Jersey Institute of Technology, which offered him a teaching assistantship. He arrived in New Jersey in 1985 with thirty dollars in his pocket. He worked in a Chinese restaurant to earn spending money. After graduating in 1987, Wu Ying went to work at Bell Labs, as did his telecom engineer wife. They bought a house and a new car and began settling into life in America. But Wu Ying wasn't happy being just another research engineer in a big organization. While in school, he had worked part-time as the only employee of a startup company founded by a group of Bell Labs engineers. His job was to help design an automatic meter reading system for utilities, which could use a telephone line to automatically call in the reading. The product worked well, but it wasn't deployed because it would have eliminated union jobs. That didn't matter to Wu Ying. He had discovered that he loved being an entrepreneur.

Shey and Wu Ying formed their company, Starcom Products Inc., at the end of 1990 after a two-hour meeting and a handshake. At first, both Wu Ying and Shey continued to work full-time as consultants at Bell Labs. At night, working out of a bedroom in Shey's house, they interviewed and screened engineers. Business boomed. Wu Ying was a great judge of talent. Bell Labs loved the engineers from Starcom and clamored for more. Two-thirds of the engineers that Wu Ying sent over to Bell Labs were originally from China or India. Within a year, Wu Ying left Bell Labs to work full-time for Starcom, but he also started looking for new opportunities for the company. He especially wanted to get back into equipment engineering.

After a trip back to China, Wu Ying's wife told her husband about the myriad opportunities there. When Wu Ying traveled to China to see for himself, he decided on the spot to return permanently to China, leaving Chauncey Shey to handle the Bell Labs business. Before long, Wu Ying was running all over China, selling AT&T office telephone systems and Motorola trunking systems, all the while keeping an eye out for a big market opportunity. He settled on designing a unique billing system for the Chinese phone network that would allow Chinese consumers, who had debit cards but not credit cards, to charge phone calls to their debit cards.

In 1995, Wu Ying and Shey merged their company with Unitech Telecom Inc., a California company founded by Lu Hongliang, a Taiwanese who had grown up in Japan and later migrated to the United States. The new company, UTStarcom, gave Unitech much-needed expertise in the China market while Starcom benefited from Unitech's strong engineering and management resources. The new company trained its sights squarely on the China market.

The Man with the Plan

While the young Chinese telecom entrepreneurs were studying and starting their companies in the United States, Wu Jichuan was making himself one of the most powerful and feared bureaucrats in China. The party had promoted Wu in 1990 to deputy party secretary in Henan province. But Wu was a telecom engineer and sitting in the provinces while the telephone system was being built through policies he promulgated in the 1980s made him nervous. He wanted to be back in telecom running his own show. He maneuvered to have himself summoned back to Beijing in 1993 and appointed as chief of his old ministry, the Ministry of Posts and Telecommunications.

By the time UTStarcom was formed in California, Wu Jichuan was riding high in Beijing. In the 1991–95 government five-year plan, planners had set the ambitious goal of increasing the country's phone capacity from 10 million lines to 35.5 million lines. Instead, by the end of 1995, China's exchange capacity reached an incredible 85 million lines, the result of $30 billion being plowed into the phone system. With that kind of money being thrown around it was no wonder that the foreign telecom executives were falling all over themselves to cultivate Wu. China was the world's last great untapped market.

Wu was under extreme pressure to open China's telecom system to induce competition and expand foreign investment. But he convinced senior leaders that the telecom system was a national asset that required his ministry's complete control. Wu is a product of contemporary China, a patriot who believes in the system. His strongest backer was Premier Li Peng, who like Wu was a committed Nationalist who believed in the need for a government phone monopoly.

Foreign telecom executives found Wu charming, humorous, and absolutely impenetrable. He looked them right in the eye and displayed no emotion as they talked. He answered questions with Chinese parables or questions of his own.

When would the market be opened?

"You haven't eaten breakfast and you want to talk about lunch?"

Wu would usher foreign executives out of his office with smiles and jokes. When they got back to their offices and reviewed their notes they realized that he had told them nothing. He made them feel good with empty assurances.

Wu had all the attributes of a good CEO. Unlike most Chinese bureaucrats who keep all levers in their own hands, Wu trusted his subordinates and empowered them to run their own show once they had proven themselves. He also was a fierce bureaucratic infighter. He took no prisoners, and he only left his fingerprints on what looked good. Wu himself oversaw his department's studies of emerging telecom technologies, and he always had the final say on which technologies would be deployed. His strategy was simple but ambitious: build the world's largest and best telephone system, with other people's money, and create a new technology industry for China along the way. He knew competition eventually would come, but he wanted that competition to be very carefully managed. Wu's vision was for a national telecom system that consisted of several carriers, all under his leadership, each occupying its own niche.

While China's engineers and planners marveled at Wu's accomplishments, much of China hated the MPT. Wu kept calling rates and phone installation charges very high to help finance the telecom buildout. People waited months to get a phone installed. Many paid bribes of hundreds of dollars to move up on the waiting list. Only competition would shift the focus from engineering and infrastructure to customer satisfaction and financial results. Even Wu's trusted lieutenants began pushing for faster reform, urging that the system be opened to foreign investment. But Wu wouldn't budge and he had powerful supporters. In the State Council, he argued that national security would be compromised by multiple carriers managing international information connections.

Battling Bureaucrats

But Wu didn't control every telecom system in China. A new network was forming around a man who was once one of China's top five leaders, Hu Qili, a member of the party politburo standing committee who was purged for opposing martial law in Beijing during the 1989 Tiananmen demonstrations. Hu Qili was appointed electronics minister in 1993, and he devised the ambitious "Golden Bridge" initiative to wire China together with huge fiber optic pipes and satellite systems. The objective was to unify customs offices across China to stop corruption and to tie together the country's banks so the central bank could better control lending and build a credit reporting system for introducing national credit cards. Another, secret goal was to build a private network for the party's internal communications should the normal phone system go down. Constructing this system provided business for the telecom equipment companies that Hu Qili was cobbling together from the institutes and factories under his control.

But the Golden Bridge initiative was unable to provide Hu's companies with sufficient equipment orders. And Wu Jichuan was directing his procurement officials to buy equipment only from the companies formed under the MPT. He had no desire to help the electronics ministry become the country's main telecom equipment maker. But Wu's focus on engineering and equipment ignored consumers, whose complaints about lousy service were reaching high into the leadership. Wu's repeated requests for time to build the infrastructure got strong support from Premier Li Peng.

Hu Qili realized that his ministry had to diversify to build a reliable revenue stream for his telecom equipment companies, and that meant building his own telecom system to feed equipment orders into his factories. Otherwise Wu Jichuan, favoring his own suppliers, could put him out of business. For support, Hu turned to officials who oversaw his sector, persuading them of the importance of establishing a competing telephone network by cobbling together a new company on the base of fragmented networks operated by the army and the railway and power ministries. In December 1993, the State Council approved the creation of China United Telecommunications Corporation, or Unicom. Unicom's shareholders included the power and railway ministries, as well as an eclectic jumble of regional government agencies. The only problem was that Unicom didn't have any money. With Premier Li Peng and Wu Jichuan in strong opposition, the government was not going to open its spigots to fund the company. Unicom was on its own.

The Telecom Tycoon

Unicom assiduously avoided hiring any telecom ministry officials. At best, they would spy for Wu Jichuan. At worst, they would help him assert control over the company. Instead, Unicom recruited among bureaucrats at the electronics, power, and railway ministries. Zhao Weichen, a longtime colleague of then Vice-Premier Zhu Rongji, became Unicom's first chairman. Zhao was known as a creative problem solver, but also as an erratic manager.

Regional government officials were soon clamoring to meet with

Zhao, eager to establish Unicom branches to build and operate the Unicom phone system in their areas. At the same time foreign telecom executives were tripping over one another to secure a meeting with Zhao. This is what the telecom world had been waiting for: a second major carrier, the first step in Chinese telecom deregulation. This was the chance to get a China telecom equity play. The monopoly would be broken. The foreign telecom operators were giddy with excitement, as were legions of overseas China entrepreneurs from Taiwan, Hong Kong, and Singapore who smelled big money in the making.

But Unicom wasn't really a company. Rather, it was an unresolved ministerial dispute. Fortunately, Zhao had so many bosses that he really had none. Hu Qili and Vice-Premier Zou Jiahua would support him as long as he didn't make a mess of things. His shareholders were eager to make money from the telecom gold rush. They didn't care particularly how, as long as the profits came quickly. The first thing Zhao had to sort out was what kind of telecom company Unicom would be. When the railway ministry failed to throw its fixed-line network into Unicom, Zhao decided that Unicom would focus on building a mobile phone network. To do that, he had to wrest some radio spectrum out of Wu Jichuan's hands. It took an order from Vice-Premier Zou to overcome Wu's objections.

Zhao's second decision was that in order to be somebody, Unicom needed to act like somebody. Despite his empty pockets, Zhao began building an image for Unicom that would attract money. He appointed Henry Kissinger as an "honorary adviser." He gathered photos of himself conferring with Kissinger, former U.S. President George H. W. Bush, U.S. Senate Republican Leader Robert Dole, as well as many of the world's top telecom executives. The photos lined the walls of Unicom offices, reassuring other foreign telecom executives who wanted to be doing business with a powerful Chinese organization.

Everybody wanted to throw money at Zhao. But he knew that Wu Jichuan would cut his throat in the State Council if Unicom offered equity stakes in a Chinese telephone operating company to foreigners. How to get foreigners to finance this without ceding control? He needed to be creative and move fast before all those foreign telecom companies lost interest. He also told the local governments who were flooding to Beijing seeking a piece of the Unicom action that if they could find investors for their local Unicom network, he would cut them in as Unicom branch operators.

It didn't take long for Unicom officials to become arrogant and rapacious. The bureaucrats seconded to Unicom from the founding ministries all gave themselves the title of "vice-president." Not knowing who had real power, the foreign telecom companies scrambled to meet with any vice-president they could get on the phone. The foreigners were expected to kiss the feet of the Unicom bureaucrats. When foreign executives took them to lunch, the Unicom executives discussed the thickness of the abalone at length to hide the fact that they knew little about telecom and even less about Unicom's future direction. In fact, most of them cared mostly about not making mistakes that would jeopardize their political future.

Zhao had read about various leasing and build-operate-transfer schemes that China had been using to build toll roads and other infrastructure projects. He knew that Bell Canada was trying to hook up with local governments in Shandong province to build Unicom networks. Zhao persuaded Bell Canada executives to help him create what became known as the "Chinese-Chinese-Foreign" telecom investment structure. The "CCF" structure worked like this: foreign companies would form a joint venture with a Chinese company. That entity, now a Chinese legal person, would then form a joint venture with a local Unicom branch. Under this CCF joint venture, the foreign investor would provide the telecom equipment, build the network, and teach Unicom how to operate it. In return, the foreign entity would collect a share of the revenue. After twenty years, Unicom would own the network. Zhao thought it was a work of genius. Each contract also had a clause saying that if Chinese regulations changed, the foreign investment would transform into equity. Zhao knew that wouldn't happen, but of course he didn't say that to anyone.

The Bell Canada executives dubbed the plan "near equity" and sold it to the Bell Canada board. Bell Canada's CCF agreement with the Shandong city of Yantai was signed in Montréal during Premier Li Peng's state visit in October 1995. Vice-Premier Zou Jiahua, the godfather of Unicom, attended the signing ceremony. A photo of Zou Jiahua at the ceremony spread throughout the industry as proof that the CCF structure had the Chinese central government's approval.

Backed only by that photo, nearly every telecom operator in the world scrambled for "near equity" stakes in the China market. Lacking a lavish headquarters building, Unicom met with suitors at the old Negotiations Building in western Beijing, where Chinese bureaucrats had played foreign companies off against each other in the early stages of China's market opening. On any given day, Italians would fill one room, Canadians the next, Australians across the hall, Americans beside them, and groups of Taiwan and Hong Kong telecom-tycoon wannabes scattered throughout the building. It was a landmark China feeding frenzy. In its first year, Unicom signed thirty-eight letters of intent with foreign companies, and built initial mobile phone networks in Beijing, Tianjin, Shanghai, and Guangzhou.

Mobile Fever

As Unicom jury-rigged the outlines of a national mobile phone network, Wu Jichuan's local MPT branches across China were quickly moving ahead to build their own system. To do that, however, Wu needed more money. At the end of October 1997, China Telecom (Hong Kong) Ltd. listed simultaneously on the New York and Hong Kong stock exchanges, raising nearly $4 billion, ten times larger than any previous overseas listing of a Chinese company. Wu now not only controlled the world's fastest-growing phone network, but he also had wrenched huge piles of money from foreigners without ceding any real control to them. It was just in time. Wu's game of getting foreign governments to finance their company's telecom equipment sales to China, and raising money for domestic equipment purchases by maintaining high phone hookup and calling rates, was running out. Consumer complaints about high costs and poor service were continuing to flood into the State Council.

Prior to the listing, China's telecom expansion had been a free-for-all with provincial telecom authorities doing all kinds of deals to finance and build out their networks. While these local telecom bureaus fell under Wu's political structure, it was increasingly unclear who actually had legal control of local telecom assets. Wu used the listing to demonstrate clearly that all telecom assets were under his control. He strong-armed the Guangdong and Zhejiang province telecom bureaus into injecting their mobile phone assets into the new offshore company. That put telecom bureaus across China on notice that their independence was limited to creative ways of building, not owning, local telecom networks. Even as foreign investors celebrated what they saw as the first step in privatization of China's telecom networks, Wu had craftily reasserted his control over the country's fast-growing mobile networks.

The listing increased Wu's political power. He was the acknowledged master at using money from foreigners to modernize China without ceding control to them. It also earned him increased respect overseas. Wu was treated like a rock star when he went abroad to attend telecom conferences and visit foreign companies. Companies chartered private jets for him and he found himself surrounded by reporters when he attended public events. Wu genuinely liked being around other telecom guys. He enjoyed entertaining telecom CEOs visiting China and he was polite and modest when visiting foreign countries, eschewing the regal treatment that many Chinese officials demanded. He looked like your run-of-the-mill Chinese bureaucrat, with an artful comb-over, off-the-shelf local suit, and the oversize eyeglass frames common among old-line cadres. But

Wu's tinted glasses gave him a bit of a sinister look, which went well with the "Minister No" nickname foreign telecom executives used behind his back.

Still, Wu knew that technology and market forces were tearing away the edges of his empire day by day. Unicom's CCF structure was drawing so much foreign investment so fast that Wu had to tacitly endorse it. In April 1995, he told an international audience at a telecom conference that China was "experimenting" with legal structures that would offer foreigners a return on Chinese phone network operations without offering equity in the systems. Unicom gained more ground in its battle to become a legitimate second carrier in May 1997 when the State Council decreed that Unicom could operate fixed-line services in addition to the cellular and paging operations it already had under way. The decree tacitly acknowledged the fact that some CCF ventures were already building landline phone systems. The Internet further complicated matters. Wu was hearing about too many illegal phone activities fueled by new technologies, such as the two brothers who had downloaded IP phone software from the Internet and were offering an Internet-based long-distance phone service from their little electronics shop in the coastal city of Fuzhou.

To the Countryside

Meanwhile UTStarcom was searching for an appropriate technology for the China market. It found it in something called the personal handyphone system, or PHS, that had been tested, but rejected, by Japan and Thailand. The personal handyphone system was a mobile technology akin to having a cordless home phone with a range of several hundred yards. The equipment cost a fraction of that required by the mobile phone systems being deployed across China. UTStarcom engineers began improving the PHS technology as the company sought government approval of the PHS system. But Wu Jichuan wouldn't even consider allowing China to adopt an older technology that Japan had abandoned. Foreign vendors, who didn't want to lose equipment sales, helped fuel Wu's disdain, calling PHS "Japanese junk."

Short, sturdy, with a wreath of a beard resembling those on the monks in ancient Chinese paintings, Wu Ying was already well known and well liked in China telecom circles. People called him *da huzi,* or "big beard." At age thirty-six, he was also mature, patient, and persistent. Wu Ying was a master of networking, but Wu Jichuan refused to meet with him, even carefully avoiding Wu Ying at several telecom conferences when the entrepreneur tried to shake his hand and exchange pleasantries.

Wu Jichuan might not like UTStarcom technology, but the company's value proposition made perfect sense to telecom bureaus in the provinces. Wu Ying, UTStarcom's chief strategist, positioned the PHS service, which had been renamed "Little Smart," as an inexpensive mobile phone service for China's masses. He saw it as a market of 650 million phones. He figured that the top 20 percent of Chinese people could afford regular mobile phones, while the bottom 30 percent were simply focusing on getting basic necessities. It was the middle 50 percent that UTStarcom wanted. He made a compelling argument to local telecom officials: You can make back your investment on my system in three months, instead of the eighteen months or more it took for real mobile phone equipment.

Seismic Shift

In the first three months of 1998, the world changed for all the players. In March 1998, Wu Jichuan vanquished his bureaucratic rivals and was named minister of the newly formed Ministry of Information Industry (MII), with 34,000 people under him. The new ministry absorbed his old Ministry of Posts & Telecommunications, as well as the Ministry of Electronics Industry and big parts of the Ministry of Radio, Film, and Television. On paper, Wu was master of the bureaucratic universe. Floundering Unicom was now under his control. His pride and joy, China Telecom, spun off its fast-growing mobile networks into a new company called China Mobile (the name of China Telecom [Hong Kong] Ltd. was changed to China Mobile) that would compete, under Wu's careful management, with Unicom. China Telecom retained the fixed-line monopoly and was banned from the mobile market. Wu wanted to keep things orderly.

That set the stage for UTStarcom to attack. Wu Ying found a local phone official in the Hangzhou suburb of Yuhang who wanted to build his business. Like many local phone bureau bosses, the Yuhang official had a huge surplus of fixed lines. Attaching Little Smart technology to those fixed lines and offering them as cheap versions of mobile phones would allow the Yuhang phone system to obtain at least some revenue from otherwise idle lines. Wu Ying promoted the service as "an extension of fixed-line service" to get around the ban on China Telecom offering mobile phone service, but it really was mobile phone service at rates far below those charged by China Mobile and Unicom. Demand was gratifyingly strong. Wu Ying now knew that if UTStarcom moved fast, the company could make Little Smart a fact of life. Even Wu Jichuan couldn't rip up infrastructure that met his own goal of providing affordable, universal service to every hamlet in the country. Soon China Telecom officials all over China began deploying Little Smart as Wu Ying won them over with the financial and political value proposition of the system.

As consumers caught on and rushed to Little Smart, the debate over it became louder and louder. If Wu Jichuan had wanted to expend lots of effort in the State Council, he could have killed the system. Little Smart really irked him because it was the only telecom technology in China that he hadn't approved. He really couldn't argue with the value proposition, so every few months, he would make statements like "I don't like it" when asked about Little Smart. UTStarcom's contracts were constantly being delayed. But Wu Ying would get everybody in his company fired up again and business would resume. Wu Ying was in the right place at the right time with the right pitch. He always shifted the goal posts to stay just inside the legal boundaries. Many of the headquarters MII bureaucrats under Wu Jichuan hated Little Smart. But Wu Ying had recruited a very strong force behind him. Consumers in outlying cities were subscribing to Little Smart in droves. Wu Jichuan cut mobile phone rates, but Little Smart still could charge 80 percent less because it was classified as a "fixed-line extension," not mobile. When his colleagues at UTStarcom were ready to throw in the towel after yet another of Wu Jichuan's public putdowns, Wu Ying would tell them: "The only ally we have is the consumer. We can't lose confidence because we have them on our side."

Wu Jichuan knew Wu Ying was right, so he gave UTStarcom running room and turned his focus to bigger problems. The Chinese Internet was spinning out of control, growing like a bad rash as private Chinese entrepreneurs built thousands of websites with capital supplied by foreign investors. Even more worrisome, the CCF investment structure at Unicom was turning into a ticking time bomb.

"Irregular Structures"

Wu Jichuan's treatment of Unicom had been a masterpiece of bureaucratic passive aggression. The allure of CCF began fading among foreigners as 1997 wore on. The foreign telecom companies grew wise to Unicom's ploy of offering the same projects to multiple foreign companies and constantly squeezing them for market studies and business plans while giving nothing in return. Many of them also found that their "near equity" investment money was going to purchase cars, office blocks, and even a few restaurants for their Chinese partners. Some of the Chinese partners managed to evade paying the profit split due foreign investors by fiddling with the depreciation numbers and claiming they needed to keep the capital in the company. Unicom was not creating a clear identity nor gaining any measure of self-control. It existed only as a competitor to somebody else, a tribal alliance of bureaucratic interests in search of their piece of the telecom gold rush.

Wu Jichuan said and did little about Unicom for a year, giving Chairman Zhao Weichen enough rope to hang himself. At the same time, he sabotaged the company's growth by quietly dragging his feet on connecting Unicom to the Chinese phone system. When senior government leaders stepped in to force Wu to connect Unicom networks to the system, he acceded to their demands, but oh so slowly.

Throughout the 1990s, the two most headstrong and stubborn senior bureaucrats in Beijing were Wu Jichuan and Zhu Rongji, who had become premier at the same time that Wu became MII chief. Zhu wanted more competition in telecom. Wu didn't. They constantly butted heads. But they now saw eye-to-eye on the mess at Unicom. Foreign telecom executives were sending a flood of complaints to Zhu's office. He passed them on to Wu, telling him that it was the telecom minister's problem.

Salvation came in the form of Morgan Stanley investment bankers, who showed up in Unicom's offices just as the company was becoming desperate. Morgan Stanley had missed the China Telecom IPO, the biggest investment banking embarrassment in Asia in decades. Unicom would be the firm's revenge. Morgan Stanley told Unicom that if the CCF structures were unraveled, the company could raise more money in a global listing than it had ever imagined. This lucrative cleanup scenario wound its way to the top of the Chinese government. In August 1998, Zhu called the CCF structures "irregular" and ordered them cleaned up. By this time, there was a total of $1.4 billion invested in forty-six projects. Outraged investors in those projects formed a Unicom Investors Group to plead their case. In the end, investors had no choice but to accept the return of their initial investment along with a small amount of interest income. When Unicom in June 2000 listed simultaneously on the New York and Hong Kong stock exchanges, the stitched-together skeleton of a company raised $5.6 billion, the largest IPO in Chinese history.

Whack-a-Mole

Even as the sheer size of Wu Jichuan's empire as MII minister earned him the right to be called China's telecom czar, his real power had begun a precipitous decline. He began to resemble someone playing the amusement park game Whack-a-Mole, in which the player, armed with a rubber mallet, stands in front of a table with a few dozen holes trying to smash rubber moles as they suddenly and randomly emerge from and dive back into various holes.

The market was taking over. Foreign and local money was pouring into the communications sector, marrying up with entrepreneurs who were seeking future stock market listings, not permission from Wu's ministry. Wu began to think that investment bankers and venture capitalists were running the Chinese communications industry instead of engineers like himself. Politicians had their fingers in the pie, too. Wu knew that he had to give up trying to control every aspect of the domestic market, but he remained determined to prevent any form of foreign control in his sector. In April 1999, Wu threatened to resign when he learned that Zhu Rongji, who had just returned from a meeting in Washington with President Clinton, had been prepared to offer foreigners up to 50 percent ownership of China's telephone operating companies as part of China's accession to the World Trade Organization. Zhu's deal failed, but the United States published the details of his offer on the Internet.

Wu was so busy fighting his telecom turf battles that he failed to notice the growth of the Internet. Suddenly millions of Chinese people were surfing the global Internet, spending hours reading news, playing games, and even arranging dates on Yahoo-style portal sites. China's Internet was created by young Chinese entrepreneurs funded by Intel, IDG, Rupert Murdoch, Dow Jones, and a growing list of Silicon Valley venture capitalists who saw the Chinese Internet as the next global quick-money bonanza. In September 1999, Wu swung his rubber mallet at this group: foreign investment was forbidden in Chinese Internet companies and MII was determined to clean up any "irregularities."

His decree provoked an instant response. The major Chinese portals, poised for listing on the NASDAQ, pointed to the case of Chinadotcom, a Hong Kong company that wasn't even a player in China. Dressed up as a key China Internet player, it raised $84 million from clueless investors. If Wu's ban held, more offshore companies would follow suit, while the real Chinese Internet players would be left with empty pockets. Wu quietly backed down. He allowed the Chinese Internet companies to construct CCF-like structures in which the foreign investors would hold their shares in an offshore company. A series of contractual arrangements would give them virtual rights in the Chinese companies. Less than a year after Wu issued his Internet foreign ownership ban, China's three major portals—Sina, Netease, and Sohu—had raised some $200 million on NASDAQ.

Meanwhile, Wu Ying and UTStarcom were pushing ahead quickly, deploying Little Smart systems in smaller towns and cities across China. UTStarcom established its China headquarters in Hangzhou, the site of the first Little Smart network. But there were stronger reasons to settle in this city of 6 million people 120 miles south of Shanghai. Hangzhou, the capital of Zhejiang province, had thirty-five colleges and universities and some of the country's best software and engineering research institutes, all sources of employees for UTStarcom. The city and provincial governments also became strong allies.

Despite the tenuous legality of the company's main product, the Little Smart system, UTStarcom enjoyed a spectacular IPO on NASDAQ in March 2000, raising $180 million, the same amount as the company's 1999 revenues. The price tripled on opening day, stunning the global telecom community. Wu grabbed his rubber mallet again. He couldn't swing it right away, however, because his political patron, Li Peng, now chief of the National People's Congress, happened to visit Hangzhou at the end of the month. Zhejiang province and Hangzhou city officials brought him to the headquarters of UTStarcom, their pride and joy as Hangzhou strove to become a global telecom technology center. Local papers quoted Li Peng saying that the UTStarcom listing was a great achievement for China, and that as returned Chinese students, the company's founders were patriots making important contributions to China's development.

Two months later, Wu swung his mallet quietly by issuing an MII internal notice, announcing a requirement that China's telephone service providers temporarily halt new deployments of the UTStarcom system pending a technology review. When word of the review leaked, UTStarcom's stock dropped 50 percent, shaving $1.8 billion from the company's market cap within two weeks. The UTStarcom offices in the United States and China went into collective depression. They had figured that the NASDAQ listing would force Wu Jichuan to accept the company's phone technology in China. Wu Ying, as usual, turned the bad news into good news. He told his colleagues that Little Smart would be accepted because the value proposition could not be denied. He also pointed out the positive aspect of the MII review. Companies with competing PHS systems would stay out of China and leave the market to Little Smart.

Wu Ying and his colleagues educated the MII engineers conducting the review, showing them the improvements that UTStarcom engineers had made in the system. When PHS was first deployed in Japan and Thailand the range of the phones was only about 150 meters from the base station, and the system couldn't hand off between base stations. The signal was now able to cover large neighborhoods, and the calls could automatically switch from station to station. They also took the MII officials to the streets to talk to customers.

Behind the bravado, Wu Ying and his colleagues were deeply worried. Even Li Peng's positive comments hadn't forced Wu and MII to back off. By working through various supporters in the government, the UTStarcom founders were able to get through to President Jiang Zemin. They didn't meet with him personally, but were able to arrange for Jiang to be briefed about the company and its predicament. After the briefing, Jiang's office called Wu Jichuan and said that the government shouldn't be interfering so directly in an operating company. At the end of June, the MII concluded its review by saying that Little Smart systems and handsets could be used in China's smaller cities, towns, and villages.

That was enough for UTStarcom. Despite the midyear crisis, UTStarcom revenue in 2000 doubled to reach nearly $369 million. But the hammer fell again at the end of the year when an unidentified MII official announced the MII would be taking back the radio spectrum used by the Little Smart system for the use of "third-generation" broadband mobile phone connections. UTStarcom's customers hardly seemed to notice. Wu Ying shifted his government relations strategy to show how the deployment of inexpensive Little Smart mobile phone systems in remote western provinces was in perfect alliance with Zhu Rongji's campaign to build infrastructure in and attract investment to China's impoverished western regions. By the end of 2001, the company's revenue increased by another 70 percent to reach $627 million, and an MII vice-minister announced that the Little Smart spectrum wouldn't be taken back, but offered no clarity on the legality of Little Smart. By August 2002, Little Smart was available in more than three hundred cities and had 9 million subscribers. Wu Jichuan began to appreciate those numbers. These Little Smart subscribers were badly needed to dress up Wu's latest configuration of China Telecom, UTStarcom's main customer, which was preparing for a November 2002 listing in New York and Hong Kong that would raise $1.52 billion.

The Legacy

In March 2003, at the National People's Congress, Wu Jichuan retired. His last act was to throw in the towel in his fight with Wu Ying and UTStarcom. At the congress, Wu told reporters: "The government does not encourage its development, but it will not regulate Little Smart's progressive march into cities." Wu said MII wouldn't approve any other telecom technology access to the radio frequency that Little Smart used.

Wu Jichuan's retirement marked the end of an era. He was not a man of great vision, but his toughness, tenacity, and convictions had played a major role in the successful execution of the Chinese government's economic development model. In his tenure as "telecom czar," Wu had added more than 500 million phones to the Chinese system and fueled the creation of a formidable telecom industry from the leftovers of a rickety Soviet-designed research and production system. China's four telephone operating companies, which he had successfully fought to keep under his ministry's control, had annual revenues of $50 billion. He might have been ineffectual at managing the domestic market and domestic competitors, but he got high marks for holding foreign telecom operators at bay, giving China time to develop and refine its own domestic technology standards. He was a very good architect, but a poor referee.

The telecom and technology sector that Wu had created through the building of China's phone system was remarkable. Foreign and Chinese telecom companies had invested tens of billons of dollars in manufacturing facilities, employed hundreds of thousands of workers, and introduced the newest technology. Chinese technical schools and universities were graduating nearly half a million engineers annually. Wuhan, a university center in central China, had been transformed into "Optics Valley," the center of an industry of 120 companies churning out a half million kilometers of fiber optic cable a year and sophisticated optical networking equipment.

A New Era

UTStarcom's new $120 million headquarters looks much like a gigantic spaceship with a small river running through the middle. The five thousand or so employees based there can play a nine-hole pitch and putt course on the grounds outside. China has about 65 million mobile phone subscribers using the Little Smart technology.

UTStarcom got where it is by doing things differently. Its founders had cooperated with one another and focused on their individual strengths to build the company. That is almost unheard of in China, where management is a constant battle for personal power amid a culture that inspires corporate dictators, not cooperation. UTStarcom is laced with Western executives from Bell Labs and AT&T. The company slogan is "Western Innovation, Oriental Diligence," which is based on the belief that the Americans are very innovative and the Chinese are very disciplined and entrepreneurial. The company believes that innovation requires the willingness to fail. Wu Ying and other executives preach that a wrong decision is better than no decision, and try to make it okay to make wrong decisions by continually telling employees how the founders made a $100 million mistake in purchasing a Hong Kong beeper company, mistakenly believing they could make it into a wireless system.

UTStarcom's days as a NASDAQ darling ended when analysts began to question whether it can be more than a one-product, one-country company. UTStarcom designed and deployed several telecom products besides Little Smart, but the company has derived the vast majority of its revenue from the Little Smart wireless gear in China. Its biggest sales outside of China have been to Japanese companies owned by UTStarcom's largest shareholder, Softbank. Wu Ying believes that the company's future is in creating "innovative subversive technology, " products that improve on core technologies and fulfill a market need through high performance and reduced costs. He believes that China's large and varied market is the perfect place for such innovation. The company also claims to have the best of both worlds when it comes to engineering. The majority of UTStarcom's R&D force is in New Jersey, California, and Chicago, where engineers are more culturally attuned to experimenting and creative thinking. But the company also has a couple of thousand engineers in Shenzhen and Hangzhou, where the execution of product refinement is combined with intimate knowledge of every connector and transmitter in the Chinese phone system. There is also five-to-one cost savings with the Chinese engineers compared to the American engineers. In 2003, the company spent $150 million on R&D.

What This Means for You

The challenge facing Wu Ying and his generation of private entrepreneurs and government business bureaucrats is now as much cultural as it is political. China has built formidable state-owned technology companies by learning from foreigners and filling an endless supply of huge orders from government customers in a protected and vibrant market. But foreign companies still dominate the technology game. Many of the original telecom equipment joint ventures have evolved, with the foreign party buying majority shares or full ownership. The vast majority of China's technology exports are still coming from foreign-invested companies, the majority of them wholly foreign owned. As the foreign telecom suppliers saw their know-how and technology walk out the door to Chinese competitors, they got smart. They started holding back key components, and even designing products so that there was a key component that isolated the most valued technology. China built its telecom equipment industry through reverse engineering, which is often an uncomplicated matter of assembling configurations of components, many of which could be purchased from the original company's suppliers. The key is in the software and how it interfaces with the hardware. That is where the expertise is.

Chinese love to point out that they invented and created porcelain, silk, eyeglasses, paper, the printing press, the umbrella, watertight compartments in ships, and gunpowder. They were eating with sanitary chopsticks for one thousand years while Europeans were reaching into common bowls with dirty hands. But the crush of politically driven information and thought control, and Confucian traditions, have left China today a place where the people are capable of incremental innovation, but not innovative break-throughs. Breakthrough ideas come from the West. The Chinese are very good with hardware and gadgets, continually refining existing technology and products. Chinese people are very good at perfect execution. China has created fabulous pianists, violinists, and conductors, but very few original composers. Chinese people are taught to learn and emulate before they try to create.

Individually, Chinese engineers are very good, but working in groups is a challenge. It will take many years for the Chinese to learn to manage streams of work produced by many people to meet the milestones and processes necessary for technology development. It doesn't come naturally. R&D probably will follow the same path as manufacturing in China. The multinationals and Taiwan and Hong Kong companies trained thousands of Chinese factory managers as they built the country's export machine. Many of these Chinese managers have then gone off and created their own factories using the management techniques they learned from foreigners. The Chinese R&D talent pool is extremely deep. One academic study estimated there were nine thousand Chinese PhDs in Silicon Valley in the late 1990s. Foreign companies are setting up R&D facilities in China at an accelerating rate. There is little doubt that these multinational research centers will train thousands of Chinese researchers, who will then go off and form their own R&D operations and technology companies.

Currently, the incentives in China are for copying the products of others. In coming decades, the incentives will reward those who create new technologies and new products. There is little doubt that China will figure that out, too.

The Little Red Book of Business

- When Chinese see something that works, you don't have to talk them into expanding it. You need to get out of the way or get run over.

- China is taking off with the help of the Communist system, not in spite of it. Growth is fueled by the people's pent-up ambition and entrepreneurship. But government planning often provides necessary direction and focus.

- You can't ignore Beijing, but don't sit and wait for approvals. Do your politics at the same time as you develop your business. The best strategy is to avoid forcing a government decision.

- China is not one market, but a collection of many local markets, each with its own practices, traditions, and methods of local protectionism.

- It is often best to start your business at a provincial level where officials are more entrepreneurial and often resent control by Beijing. They can be very loyal and protect you.

- When introducing a new product in China, you need to combine a perfect sales pitch, a perfect political pitch, and unbelievable persistence.

- While China seeks the latest technology, it is often the most appropriate and affordable technology that wins in the market. Slimming down your price and focusing functionality for China is often the key to success.

- In China, you only need two companies to have a price war.

- Chinese state-owned companies are listing on overseas stock markets for the explicit purpose of getting money without ceding any control to foreigners.

- The most carefully constructed legal contracts will easily die when politics go against them.

- China doesn't forgive, and it never forgets. China has a long memory and seeks retribution when foreign companies defy its desires.

- China is limited to incremental innovation both by culture and politics. Rote education and a political system with information and thought control don't create an environment for breakthrough discoveries and inventions.

- The hundreds of research labs established by foreign companies in China could transform the above equation. As happened in manufacturing, Chinese researchers will adopt foreign management practices and research techniques to build their own world-class operations.

- Any tech company doing business in China should assume that its designs and products are being copied.

- Court protection of intellectual property in China is improving but remains unreliable and biased. China is building an electronics exporting powerhouse, but Chinese products will be blocked at foreign borders if they have pirated foreign technology.

- When forced to share your technology in China, isolate various technologies from each other so that your partner doesn't have the whole picture.

- Protect your technology crown jewels because China's tech sector is built on reverse engineering foreign products. One approach is to embed your most valued IPR assets in components built offshore.

8

Managing the Future

China is a nation always cramming for final exams, but it will take innovation, not prescribed solutions, to pass the global business test.

THE SKIT OPENS WITH MAO ZEDONG, dressed in his usual baggy Red Army uniform, gripping a book and talking with his trusted partner in revolution, Zhou Enlai. Their conversation reveals that Mao now knows that his revolution has turned into an entrepreneurial frenzy that is gripping the country.

Then Deng Xiaoping, the man responsible for this economic upheaval, comes onstage. Mao and Zhou look nervous as Deng inquires about their preparation for the big test. Zhou offers to arrange for a stand-in to take the test for Mao.

"No, no," Mao says. "We Communist Party members must be honest and aboveboard."

Deng agrees: "We need to grasp the future with two hands. One hand is for work, the other is for study."

"Yes," Mao says, "we must not only be good at destroying an old world, we must be very good at building up a new world. Comrades, we must establish socialism with Chinese characteristics."

While speaking, Mao reveals to the audience the title of the book he is holding: *Study Guide for the GMAT.* The GMAT, or Graduate Management Admission Test, is the entrance exam used by most of the world's business schools to screen MBA applicants.

A few moments later, a female Red Guard pirouettes across the stage to announce the GMAT scores. Mao, Zhou, and Deng have all passed with flying colors!

Mao grabs both of Zhou's hands, shaking them excitedly.

"Enlai, Enlai, we have scored another victory," he cries. "Now we will be MBA students together."

The crowd erupts into delighted laughter.

It is December 2003 and some five hundred Chinese in their thirties and forties, the men in somber business attire and the women in slinky evening gowns, are gathered in the ballroom of the glitzy Kerry Center Hotel in Beijing to celebrate the sixth anniversary of the government's approval of the Beijing International MBA School, known as BiMBA. BiMBA is a joint venture between a research institute affiliated with Beijing University, which is China's most prestigious school, and a coalition of twenty-six American business schools under the guidance of Fordham University.

The classmates and alumni greeting and snapping photographs of one another are China's new revolutionaries. Some are the top bosses of government enterprises. Others are private entrepreneurs, car dealers, property developers, or factory owners. There also are top executives responsible for the China operations of multinational corporations like General Electric, Siemens, Mitsubishi, Morgan Stanley, and Ericsson. All owe their current positions of wealth, power, and prestige at least partly to the education they received at BiMBA. Thus it isn't surprising that the crowd bursts into applause and cheers during a tribute to the man who put BiMBA together, Justin Lin. Justin is perhaps the most entrepreneurial, prolific, and well-liked scholar in China. As he steps onto the stage he flashes his trademark smile. But behind his oversize wire-rim glasses his eyes gleam with serene determination, the extent to which Justin displays emotion. As the tribute draws to a close, a photo is flashed on the huge screens flanking the stage. Justin is shown standing along a rocky stretch of seacoast. It is much like the place where, on May 17, 1979, Justin arrived in China, wading ashore after swimming to the Mainland from the nearby Taiwanese island of Quemoy.

Overview

For thousands of years Chinese society revered two things above all else: family and education. Everyone had a place in the family and, by extension, in the country. Filial piety was the main responsibility of children, which meant absolute obedience to parents. Parents, in turn, had the obligation to obtain for their children the best possible education.

For its part, education produced scholars, whose obligation was to serve the state. The country traditionally has been governed by bookworms. The path to status, success, and wealth was the memorization of poetry, history, literature, and Confucian philosophy, all of which was spouted back in an exhausting litany of tests that stretched over a lifetime. The brightest and most diligent rose—often only after decades of study—to high positions serving the emperor. This tradition has created a nation of people always cramming for final exams, not just in school, but also in their careers. The Chinese learn quickly by imitating, following role models, and absorbing prescribed solutions for every problem. The trouble is that in modern China, crashing its way onto the world scene as a rapidly growing economic powerhouse, there are no role models, no prescribed solutions, and no one to imitate.

The challenge confronting the Chinese today is learning to manage the large, complex organizations that will be necessary if the country is going to continue its ambitious climb to the top of the world's economic ladder. The country was built on two models. Before Mao's Communist revolution, business in China was traditionally a family affair that took advantage of the complex network of rights and obligations—and trust—within the family. The other model is the Soviet-style state-owned enterprise, the basis for China's rapid industrialization in the 1950s. That model failed, allowing Deng to unleash the capitalist hounds in 1978. As China now searches for a third way—global businesses with professional management and a mix of private and state ownership—managers in China face an overriding problem. The sudden transition from

Cultural Revolution in the 1960s and 1970s to the scramble for wealth in the 1980s and 1990s has left a deeply scarred society, one that is less Confucian, more confused. The country is not only experiencing an economic and social upheaval, but psychological, spiritual, and ideological upheavals, as well.

During Mao's era, China was essentially ruled by a bunch of bumpkins, the street-smart but ill-educated party cadres who had fought the civil war against the KMT. For the past two decades, China has been ruled by engineers. They have done a tremendous job of building airports, roads, railways, entire new cities, and telecommunications systems. China also has learned manufacturing. A survey in 2004 by the U.S. Manufacturing Performance Institute showed that Chinese factories have a 99 percent on-time delivery rate and 98 percent of manufacturers meet specs on the first try, both higher rates than in the United States. That proficiency, combined with China's comparatively low labor costs, has given the country a profitable base from which to continue building its economy. And, of course, the Chinese, economic creatures at heart, are always looking for ways to make money. Thus they have adapted quickly to a market economy that has raised huge amounts of capital, both for the state and for budding private enterprises.

But to reach the next step in its economic evolution, China must find ways to go beyond some of the lingering cultural, social, and psychological barriers that will soon impede that progress. The struggle now is to discover the management principles and techniques that will harness and focus the immense energy and intelligence of the Chinese to build efficient, innovative, and responsive companies capable of competing on their own with the best in the world. That means training managers to operate within organizations that are not dictatorships, to treat others as equals, to accept responsibility for mistakes, and to share information, all behaviors that have historically been almost absent in China.

Much of that groundwork will be done in China's universities, which have transformed themselves in the past decade from crumbling brick buildings where students were taught leaden coursework into vibrant but behaved centers of learning. Today they are beginning to produce some impressive research projects and startup companies and the pace at which they are forging ahead is accelerating. There are now some 4.2 million freshmen entering the university system annually, four times the number in the mid-1990s. But China also has thousands of self-made executives who consciously—or subconsciously, in some cases—graft the best of Western management techniques onto a Chinese corporate structure to create an efficient, effective hybrid company.

In my time in China I found there are some broad impediments preventing Chinese companies from competing on a global scale. Some are deeply rooted in the Chinese psyche and will be extremely difficult to overcome. Others are simply a matter of style. But taken together they give the foreign businessperson who wants to be part of the economic revolution in China some sense of the problems and possibilities inherent in the country. Some of China's most successful scholars and entrepreneurs are searching for the unique blend of Chinese and Western business concepts that might become the foundation for the country's next step onto the world economic scene.

The Scholar

No one but Justin Lin knows why he defected from Taiwan. Born in Taiwan in 1952, he was fifth in a family of seven. Justin was always at the top of his class. Yet in 1971, when he was admitted to Taiwan University, he demurred, choosing instead to attend Taiwan's military academy. His decision was a blessing for Taiwan's military. Taiwan's economy was booming and the military was having a hard time competing with private enterprise for the best and brightest, a worrisome trend in the face of Richard Nixon's rapprochement with Beijing. The KMT propaganda machine leapt at the opportunity to portray Justin as a model citizen, conveniently overlooking the fact that Justin's family could not afford Taiwan

University's steep tuition and that the military academy provided a free education.

Not surprisingly, Justin excelled at the military academy. He was commissioned an officer at graduation and everyone expected him eventually to rise to a high rank. He married and the couple had a child before Justin was assigned as a company commander on the disputed island of Quemoy, just two thousand yards from the Chinese Mainland. Then, on May 17, 1979, Justin waded into the swiftly moving tidal current separating Quemoy from the Chinese city of Xiamen and began swimming, leaving his wife, child, and a promising military career behind. He has never told anyone why he did it. Friends speculate that it was a combination of idealism, curiosity, and frustration of being a native Taiwanese on an island where all power was in the hands of KMT refugees who fled the Mainland in 1949. Whatever the reason, Justin does not discuss the subject of his defection.

The Communist party welcomed Justin, but not with totally open arms. When he told the authorities that he wanted to continue his studies, they agreed, but with the proviso that he attend Beijing University rather than the party's elite People's University. His political background was too questionable. For his part, Justin refused to allow the party to use him as a propaganda tool. He had had enough of that in Taiwan.

There was never any question that, left to his own devices, Justin Lin would make a mark. But chance always plays a role and Justin's big break came while he was studying for his master's degree in Marxist political economy at Beijing University. Theodore Schultz, a Nobel laureate in economics, came to the university for a series of lectures. Justin's fluent English, acquired during his childhood in Taiwan, made him a natural to serve as Schultz's translator. With Schultz's help, soon after he received his master's degree in 1982, Justin was bound for the University of Chicago and its prestigious doctoral program in economics. He was joined there by the wife and child he had left in Taiwan. After receiving his PhD, with a thesis on Chinese farm reforms, and doing a stint of postgraduate work at Yale University, Justin brought his family home to China in 1987, the first Chinese to return from America with a PhD in economics since the Communist revolution.

In China, Justin worked on designing further farm policy reforms at the Research Center for Rural Development under the State Council, which was then headed by Wang Qishan. But he also got involved in a major study aimed at integrating China's coastal economy into the global economy. It was a valuable experience that gave Justin an insider's view of how the Chinese government formulated policy. He professes no ideology of his own, neither Marxist economics nor the Chicago free-market school. Instead, he thinks and observes. "I never trust theories," he says. "I always try to understand the realities and from that look for areas of improvement."

In 1993, Justin was teaching part-time at Beijing University when its university president, Wu Shuqing, an orthodox but open-minded Marxist economist, was searching for ways to modernize economics research and education. Wu Shuqing sought Justin's advice and they forged a plan for an economics think tank that would be affiliated with Beijing University. It would, however, operate independently to isolate it from university politics and the influence of the university's party cadres. In August 1994, Justin and several other returned scholars opened the China Center for Economic Research (CCER) in vacant offices in the university's geography building.

The center's scholars each earned a regular professor's salary of $120 a month, all that Beijing University could afford. The rest was up to Justin. His first task was to arrange livable salaries if he hoped to lure top Chinese scholars back from American and European universities. The Ford Foundation, which had an office in Beijing, helped jump-start CCER by providing $10,000-a-year wage subsidies for two years for a half-dozen scholars. While modest, that amount was sufficient to lure back bright academics who could make ends meet by taking on additional research projects for the

World Bank, the Organization for Economic Cooperation and Development (OECD), and others.

CCER soon began to participate in the country's policy research debate, publishing research in newspapers and journals. Because economic policy discussions in China were becoming much more open than other kinds of policy debates, the CCER built a repository of confidence among Chinese leaders. CCER made an especially persuasive case in favor of China pressing for membership in the World Trade Organization. Individual researchers at CCER became influential in specific sectoral reforms. Zhou Qiren, a CCER researcher and UCLA PhD, became a leading proponent of competition within the telecom industry. Telecom czar Wu Jichuan began summoning Zhou for regular briefings after reading his essays in Chinese newspapers. Eventually CCER staffers were being invited regularly to participate in deliberations about China's five-year plans.

As the founder and leader of the CCER, Justin Lin gained a formidable reputation for his ability to navigate the treacherous political waters of economic reform as he churned out his own research papers and policy advice. While he doesn't talk about his defection from Taiwan to China, Justin clearly wants to highlight his accomplishments since arriving in China. His résumé, posted on the institute's website, is an exhaustive and exhausting twenty-five-page document that lists every lecture he has given, every paper he has written, every seminar he has attended, and all the books and book chapters he has written. But it was his skills as an entrepreneur and global networker that built the institution. Soon after forming CCER, Justin hit the road, recruiting ethnic Chinese professors and researchers from abroad and forming advisory boards and academic councils that blended together top Chinese policy makers, leading Chinese and American academics, and Hong Kong and Taiwan tycoons who were tapped for generous donations.

Many of the professors who returned to China to work at CCER had been caught up in the Cultural Revolution and sent to the farm fields as teenagers. They have a deep understanding of the country's political and economic problems. They returned only because Justin assured them that they could fulfill the traditional Chinese role of scholars, building the nation, while strictly adhering to the Western notion of honest scholarship. At CCER they were encouraged to innovate and do unbiased policy research. Had they returned to most any other Chinese university, they would have played at best a marginal role, their backgrounds considered to be tainted by the West. But over time CCER's high profile and the ideas its researchers brought to the leadership encouraged other schools to create their own programs. Before long, universities across China began establishing economic research centers modeled on CCER. Suddenly there was competition in the Chinese academic market. The old tradition of scholars advising the country's leaders began to revive itself.

BiMBA

Another tradition reviving itself was China's desire to learn business practices and management techniques from the West. There were two kinds of schools in ancient China. One trained students in Confucian philosophy and Chinese culture and history in preparation for the civil service exams. The other taught basic literacy and mathematics to artisans and merchants. Modern schools with liberal arts curriculum were introduced by Western missionaries in the 1800s. They established English-language high schools and universities in major cities as Chinese merchants sought to train their children for doing business with the West. When the Communist party took over in 1949, the twenty-four universities run by Christian missions were absorbed into a centralized national school system built with Soviet advice; they focused on literacy, political indoctrination, math, science, and technology, all necessities for building the industrial socialist state.

After Deng launched his market reforms, it became apparent to American and European university administrators that there was a lucrative market for Western education in China. Delegations of foreign university administrators began making the rounds in China, looking for opportunities and partners. Among them was Ron Anton, a Catholic priest and the dean of the business school at Loyola University in Maryland. In 1993, the deans of sixteen Jesuit business schools met to formulate an MBA program to take to China and appointed Anton to find a partner in China. Anton learned about Justin Lin's CCER from a Chinese colleague at Loyola who had done some research at CCER. It took Anton only two meetings with Justin to devise the framework for a program that would grant an American MBA to Chinese students in Beijing. Fordham University in New York led the consortium of twenty-six American Jesuit universities in the partnership with CCER. Each American school pledged to cover the cost to send one professor every fourth semester to BiMBA.

As Justin raised more money to expand CCER's offices and classrooms to accommodate BiMBA students, Chinese professors of business management returned from abroad to take up teaching posts at the now well-funded organization. Among them was John Yang, whose family personified the intellectual connection between China and the West. Both of his parents were Xinhua journalists who spoke English and were trained at Yanjing University, a Methodist school on the campus that now houses Beijing University. As Yang was finishing elementary school, the Cultural Revolution was just beginning. He wound up working alongside other children digging enormous caverns under Beijing as Mao prepared for a possible attack by Russia. But his English earned him a reprieve as a flood of Americans arrived in China in the wake of Richard Nixon's historic visit. As a tour guide for Americans, Yang learned about the world outside China and became determined to go abroad. He studied journalism and English at Beijing University and the Chinese Academy of Social Science and won admission in 1982 to Princeton University to work on a graduate degree in public administration. Although he won journalism internships at *The Wall Street Journal* and *The Washington Post* during the summers,

Yang decided journalism wasn't as interesting as human behavior. He went on to receive another master's degree—this one in sociology—from Columbia University and followed that by enrolling in Columbia's business school, where he obtained his PhD in management. His PhD thesis was a study of the management systems at more than one hundred Japanese companies.

In 1990, Yang took a post as assistant business professor at Fordham. He and his wife, Liu Hong, a lawyer, returned to China when she was sent there by an American law firm. During their two-year stint, Yang worked as a consultant to Chinese companies, getting a detailed insider's view of how some fifty Chinese companies were organized and managed. The couple returned to New York and Yang resumed his post at Fordham. As BiMBA opened its doors in 1998, Fordham sent Yang to the school as a management professor and coordinator for the U.S. schools.

Searching for Solutions

On a late December afternoon, I spent several hours with Yang in a dormitory room at Beijing University where he goes to think, write, and hide from the incessant demands of BiMBA students. As the late-afternoon sunlight reflected off the round, unlined face that makes him look fifteen years younger than his age of fifty, Yang beamed. He can't believe his good luck. Here he is, an expert in organizational behavior, immersed in trying to figure out what works and doesn't in Chinese business organizations. Yang and his colleagues believe that they are key players in building China's future, helping create managers and management techniques for Chinese companies.

When he arrived at BiMBA, Yang knew from his own experience that few of the Western professors sent to teach there would be prepared for the intensity of the experience. They may consider their American MBA students to be ambitious, smart, and energetic, but those students would be no match for Chinese MBA students, among the most aggressive and impatient in the world. No matter how hard the professors worked, they would be the butt of student complaints that they weren't working hard enough. Yang warned the Western professors to expect telephone calls and knocks on their doors at any time of the day or night from students wanting answers to questions.

Yang also knew that Western course work wouldn't be entirely appropriate in a Chinese classroom, but no one knew precisely how to change it. Tailoring an American MBA program to fit Chinese students would be an evolutionary process. One of the first lessons that came through clearly was that Chinese students didn't care how business was done in the West, they wanted to know how to do business in China. They considered the Harvard Business School case studies—the foundation for many Western MBA programs—to be irrelevant. Professors quickly began writing their own Chinese case studies or finding existing studies involving Chinese or at least Asian companies. They used any methods they could to get across key concepts. After U.S. jets bombed the Chinese embassy in Belgrade, some students burned dollar bills in protest. Lu Feng, an economics professor, used their example to explain that the greenback was in fact a liability of the U.S. government, so by burning the dollars they were actually helping the United States.

Courses with titles like Comparative Legal and Ethical Systems, Cross-cultural Negotiations, and China's Economic Development and Reform were created to insure that China's systems and interface with the West were included along with such practical skills as accounting, financial analysis, and administration in a Chinese environment.

Most of the MBA students had at least a modicum of real-world experience working in a Chinese company or the Chinese subsidiary of Western companies. The students who had worked in Chinese companies were thoroughly indoctrinated in Chinese management style, which accepts the boss as an overpowering figure who barks orders and issues withering criticism while focusing laserlike vision on the bottom line. The boss analyzes problems and dictates solutions. Employees merely execute orders. A decentralized decision-making process would suggest weakness and a lack of authority at the top. The students who had worked for Western companies, who had some exposure to the more benign and cooperative management philosophies of their Western bosses, were more receptive, but nevertheless confused by the collision of philosophies. Many students thought that a business education would provide them with formulas and tricks that could be used to get rich quickly. Applying real-world Chinese business experience to the academic study of management techniques took a great leap forward in 2000 when BiMBA launched an executive MBA program that attracted the bosses of companies with tens of thousands of employees. They were searching for more effective management techniques than those they employed by instinct.

Yang and his BiMBA colleagues still struggle to convey the idea that management is situational, that there is no magic formula that works for every company. They try to get their students to look at things from many different angles. One way to do this is to combine different business subjects in defining and discussing business problems. The professors want the students to learn that theirs isn't the only one way of explaining the failure or success of an organization. In one revealing exercise, Yang asked his students, "Who among you thinks he or she will become CEO of a company?" Only a few hands went up. Then he asked, "Who *wants* to be CEO?" All of the students raised their hands. However ambitious, even these hard-charging Chinese managers demonstrated that they don't believe they can control their own future.

"All of these issues are being reshaped in the business school environment," Yang says. "In China you are not passing on pure technical business school knowledge. The Chinese are engaging in a mental, spiritual, ideological, and psychological transformation of themselves."

Yang has spent much time thinking about cultural and behavioral issues and identifies two serious problems. One is that the Chinese have two identities: the individual person and the organization person. As a result, people often act one way but think another. The second is that Chinese don't separate the personal and professional, so power struggles and politics often dominate Chinese corporate behavior.

He illustrates his points by comparing China to Japan and the United States, the other two countries in which he has expertise in corporate organizational behavior. In Japan, Yang says, employees have only one identity, the organization man. Even the rituals of drinking and cavorting with prostitutes are considered company activities. Family life is separate and compartmentalized. In the United States, Yang says, companies are structured to make decisions based on merit and through predictable depersonalized systems that are designed to ensure cooperation among employees, regardless of their personal relationships.

In China, Yang says, surface harmony is at the core of the culture, so the organization person will perform the necessary rituals of obedience and conformity and accept orders and decisions from above. As individuals, however, they often disagree and go their own way. This results in the natural tendency to disobey orders, break rules, engage in graft, and violate company policies with which they disagree.

"Our job at the business school is to reduce the gap between the organization man and the individual identity," Yang says. "The situation is getting better, but it still isn't very good."

BiMBA is still struggling with how to depersonalize business in China. "Chinese work while they play, and play while they work," he explains. "In the mind of the Chinese, unless we become friends, I can't do business with you. I can't trust you. We need to combine the collective orientation and emotional bonds of the Chinese with the American win-win culture and professional relationships as we emphasize decoupling the professional and personal in the workplace."

Key Business and Management Issues

For nearly a decade, I have been discussing Chinese business and management issues with academics and executives across China. While people often look at things from different angles, and express their thoughts in distinctive ways, the conversations always seem to circle back to some core topics and issues. Here they are, summarized in my own words and packaged with my own opinions.

Stuffed Ducks Don't Quack

Chinese students are among the best in the world. But they learn under a system decried by Chinese themselves as *tianyashi jiaoyu*, or "stuffed duck–style education." It starts with memorizing and writing some five thousand Chinese characters in elementary school. Next, math, science, and history are all committed to memory and followed with prescribed solutions to problems. In college, Chinese students learn a lot about their specialty, but little else. Subjects are taught in isolation and rarely does anyone make a link between two subjects, like statistics and marketing. The scientific method so familiar in the West—observe, hypothesize, test—hasn't been part of the Chinese educational tradition. Chinese students haven't been taught to forge their own path or see problems from different perspectives. They are given role models and proven successes to emulate. Education in China even today prepares people to be led, not to lead. The result is a strong but often uninspired workforce. There are too few innovative business leaders and line managers capable of building the large organizations that will take China business global.

Ritalin Anyone?

Nobody waits in line in China unless somebody forces them to. At banks, on buses, everybody elbows to the front. And that's how business works. There are too many opportunities, people don't know which one is the right one, so there is a constant mad scramble to seize the next chance, and the next one after that. Chinese business is all about short attention spans. I suspect that if someone laced China's water supply with the attention-deficit drug Ritalin, the nation's GDP would drop by at least 25 percent. The focus is on getting rich now, fast. That makes some sense because the great privatization boom is well past its midpoint. But in their efforts to grab whatever they can, Chinese companies tend to diversify into anything and everything rather than paying attention to the core business. The consequences are often fatal. Some academics estimate the average life of a Chinese company to be five years or less.

It's Up to You, Boss!

Top-down management under a benevolent dictator has been the encoded social order in China for thousands of years, and by far the prevalent business management model in the country. Ancient China was ruled by the Confucian notion of the Five Relationships—ruler to minister, father to son, husband to wife, older brother to younger brother, and friend to friend—that were based on the principle that the superior and inferior in each relationship had both rights and obligations of benevolence, obedience, and proper behavior. Even today, the Chinese respond well to charismatic and visionary leaders who can tell them what to do to be successful and who will take care of them. In many cases, the boss is even a substitute for the law, handling any problem that arises, including disputes between employees or family problems. So far that approach has been reasonably successful, especially in a manufacturing economy. But once a company's reach extends beyond China's borders, or it needs creative talent in areas like research and development, the Chinese model falls short. Without professional management systems, few companies can survive beyond the lifespan of all-powerful founders.

The Curse of the Three Monks

Most Chinese know the parable of the three monks. One monk goes to the river and gets plenty of water by hanging buckets at each end of his shoulder pole. Two monks get less water because they hang one bucket between them as they carry opposite ends of the pole, each careful not to work harder than the other. When three monks get together, they don't get any water. Each wants to be boss while the other two carry the pole. The Chinese freely concede that while as individuals they are extremely capable, the more people involved in an endeavor the less effective each person is. To Westerners, China appears to be a collective society. They eat together, travel together, and have fun together. But always simmering just below that collective veneer is a dog-eat-dog competitive spirit that makes the Chinese among the world's most individualistic and selfish people. Alone, the Chinese are fierce and formidable businesspeople. But to have competition—or, more to the point, winning—at the core of the relations between Chinese people cripples the building of large organizations in which people share ideas and treat one another fairly. Cooperation doesn't come naturally to Chinese people, but the large corporate organizations that will be necessary to compete at the highest levels demand it. Overcoming the curse of the three monks is perhaps the single most important challenge confronting Chinese companies that want to be global competitors.

Whom Do You Trust?

The corollary of getting rich quick is "trust no one." China hit bottom during the Cultural Revolution and the Chinese psyche still carries the scars. A society that treasured education closed its schools. A society in which students were taught to revere teachers suddenly had student Red Guards beating and sometimes killing their teachers. A society based on filial piety had children denouncing parents at mass rallies. Then Mao died and Deng rose and said, "Go forward and get rich. Don't talk about the past." It isn't surprising that China's rush to get rich is accompanied by deep distrust of the system, and anyone outside the immediate family or circle of close friends. The result is a business environment steeped in dishonesty and in dire need of transparency and systems of dispute resolution that can be trusted to be fair. Only hints of such necessary changes are visible today. It is all about money, even to those who have accumulated significant wealth. There is no social security, no safety net. You must build assets for your family now, during the gold rush. The world is turned upside down and the rapid pace of change leaves people unsettled and afraid.

Paper-Tiger Tycoons

Deng declared "to get rich is glorious," but wealth in China is dangerous. The large state enterprises in China that are being transformed into multinational companies are not only struggling to build management systems, they are also trying to sort out ownership. The leaders of these organizations become famous as Chinese business tycoons, but many are paper-tiger tycoons with few legal assets. Nobody really knows who owns what because it is often too dangerous to delineate. Typically, when state companies list on stock markets, they float some 15 percent of the company, with the rest held by various state entities. What about the bosses who have built these multibillion-dollar enterprises? In a few cases, enlightened local governments have provided them with significant stakes in the business. But more often than not, company executives quietly open offshore accounts or siphon off shares at the time of listing. Without establishing incentives that are legal and transparent for significant wealth accumulation by top state-enterprise executives, it won't be easy for these companies to become global competitors. Everybody will be too preoccupied with taking care of themselves. The larger question that looms above this is just how much of the Chinese economy the government will allow private enterprise to control.

From Dumplings to Layer Cakes

The normal Chinese management structure looks like a Chinese dumpling. The boss is the meat in the middle, wrapped in a protective barrier of his dough homeboys. Hong Kong bosses surround themselves with Hong Kong managers, Taiwanese with Taiwanese, Singaporeans with Singaporeans, and so on. The pattern is repeated at many foreign multinationals in China, with a cabal of Americans or Germans or Swedes forming an exclusive management circle. It is a formula for disaster. Any professional corporate culture is smothered by the inevitable struggles over status and cultural differences and jockeying for position in the pecking order. Employees become demoralized as companies become divided between the rulers and the ruled, the insiders and outsiders. To succeed, companies in China will have to dump the dumplings and create a layer cake that pulls together a diverse mix of ethnic backgrounds and Chinese from various regions. Purposely layer your management from top to bottom with a mix of overseas Chinese, westerners, and mainlanders from various regions. That way companies can build a clear and effective corporate culture and focus on business instead of falling victim to the Chinese pecking order phobia.

Trial and Error

China isn't waiting for academics to figure out how to manage the way to the future. The country already has had a remarkable run on the world economic scene. When Deng launched his reforms in 1978, China had a primitive state-run command economy, no business culture, and no private businesses. Now, just over twenty-five years later, the country has built almost from scratch every industry and service you can think of, from steel to tourism to technology. And it's all the result of trial and error. People make up new management techniques and styles every day, blending East and West, weaving a market economy out of a web of state-owned industry overseen by an authoritarian political system. What follows is a look at three companies that are sorting out the management techniques that work best for them. Two are established successes that can provide guidance to others. The first is a husband-and-wife team that tried to blend the East and West, but ended up picking the best aspects of each and isolating them from each other. They also tapped the Chinese propensity for fierce individual competition by constructing a brutal up-or-out management system. The second is a company built by a marketing genius who also represents the gold standard of the Chinese "benevolent boss" who knows all, does all, and inspires all while keeping the government happy. Finally, we'll look into the future at the newest business model in China, the global joint venture of IBM's personal computer division and Chinese computer maker Lenovo, a partnership that, if successful, will become a model followed by many others.

Splitting the Difference

It was the most unlikely of matches. Zhang Xin holds a master's degree in development economics from Cambridge University and worked for a few years as an investment analyst, first for Goldman Sachs in New York, then for Travelers Group in Hong Kong. She is smart, aggressive, and assertive, given to occasional screaming tantrums.

Pan Shiyi, a graduate of a government petroleum institute, worked for a while in China's petroleum ministry before drifting into the property development business in Hainan and Shenzhen. He and several partners formed Beijing Vantone Company after seeing the forest of high-rise apartments that cover Hong Kong. Pan is quiet and introspective and had never been abroad.

Yet within a week of being introduced to each other by a mutual friend, Zhang and Pan were engaged. They celebrated their wedding just four months later and set out to conquer the world together. Their honeymoon was devoted to forming a real-estate development company called Beijing Redstone Industries, which was later renamed SOHO China Ltd. When Pan introduced his new wife and partner to associates he brought in from Beijing Vantone, they were shocked. With her educational background, her aggressive speech, and sophisticated airs, she was something of an alien. They were locals, the first generation of Chinese real-estate developers since 1949, and it wasn't a business that attracted many women. She had lived outside China for fifteen years and, like most Chinese who spent that much time abroad, she wouldn't understand how China worked. Soon enough, their worst fears were confirmed. Zhang immediately set about imposing Western management on the company.

Zhang quarreled with people in the company by day, and with her husband by day and night. Pan was an experienced manager with several large and successful projects behind him, but Zhang knew management theory and structures. Before he married Zhang, Pan would make his own decisions, set targets, and then issue straightforward simple instructions to the people working for him. Process meant nothing to him. With her Wall Street background Zhang was all about procedure. There were procedures for setting targets, procedures for training people to reach those targets, endless conference calls, and endless meetings. Zhang was convinced that her background could take their company to a world-class level of productivity and profits on the road to a Wall Street listing.

Soon Pan found himself sitting silently in meetings that Zhang would convene to consider a big decision. She didn't want to tell people what to do, she wanted them to find their own way to the right conclusion. Pan's partners and subordinates, initially cowed by Zhang, begin to warm to the idea that they might have a voice in making a decision. Pretty soon, they were happily arguing in front of Pan, something they wouldn't have dreamed of doing before Zhang showed up. The trouble was, they argued against Zhang's ideas. Instead of opening the way to logical discussions, Zhang found that she was inciting chaos. At first, she blamed Pan for not helping her get her ideas across. But as Zhang realized that the Chinese aren't trained to think and act independently, she backed off. She and Pan didn't really need to get everyone's opinion. They could guide the people and reward them well if they performed, but anything much beyond that just confused the situation.

Zhang also had some innovative ideas that worked extraordinarily well. Chinese banks were permitted to offer residential mortgages, but hadn't tried to market them, and most home buyers either weren't aware of or didn't understand mortgages. At the same time, the typical Beijing high-rise apartment was being sold with small windows, bare walls, no furniture, and no carpet. Buyers had to hire their own contractor to finish the barren concrete shell. Zhang's experience in Britain and the United States convinced her that there was a market for well-appointed luxury apartments, with big windows and wood floors that would be sold fully decorated according to her own trendsetting tastes. She and Pan believed that mortgage financing could not only draw customers, but could be used to help finance a development. They had a chance to test their ideas when she and Pan obtained an eighteen-acre lot in a prime location at the edge of Beijing's emerging central business district. They knocked down the failing state-owned rice liquor facility that stood on it and set about creating a new kind of residential development. Based on the Japanese concept of "small office, home office," or SOHO, the new development was called SOHO Newtown.

Zhang and Pan first convinced the China Construction Bank to set up a field office for mortgage applications in the development's sales office. Then they invited a second bank, ICBC, to do the same, prompting competition between the two lenders that speeded up the approval process. Once a model apartment had been set up and decorated to reflect Zhang's design ideas, the doors were opened for preconstruction sales. The first reaction was that the finished and decorated apartments would deprive customers of choosing their own designs. But that didn't last long. Wealthy buyers from other provinces, seeking a foothold in trendy Beijing, flocked to purchase the stylish, modern apartments as a symbol of their own progressive tastes. By the time Zhang and Pan had started their second SOHO development, other Beijing real-estate developers were copying their model.

It wasn't easy, but Zhang and Pan have worked out a curious hybrid management style that suits their own personalities and backgrounds. Zhang brings a distinctively Western view to the business while Pan's approach is deeply rooted in Chinese tradition. He thinks problems out by himself. Zhang talks them out, using

Pan as her sounding board. Pan is convinced that Asians are more emotional in their thinking and decision making while Westerners are more analytical and rational. They wake up each morning and immediately begin discussing business. If they have disagreements, their employees don't know it. They have learned to keep disagreements to themselves.

Zhang is responsible for every aspect of a project's design, from which architect to hire to the design of the cardboard boxes that hold the moon cakes in the sales office. She steadfastly refuses to become involved in intraoffice feuds and disputes, leaving it to the combatants to work it out for themselves. And she is convinced that a company doing business in China should never hire an MBA. She found that she had been trained for a very programmed and predictable environment. China is chaotic and complex, requiring a more dictatorial management structure that doesn't have room for democracy or discussion.

"The more meetings and discussions we had, the more wrong decisions we made," Zhang says. "If everybody agrees to a plan, it is very likely you're just following the market. You only get great ideas when they come from a visionary."

MBAs also have big egos that get in the way of getting things done. Life experience, Zhang maintains, is the best education to be had in China. Even with all her Western sophistication, Zhang freely admits that in meetings with Chinese government officials she doesn't know when to speak, what to say, or what tone to use.

Pan is responsible for establishing prices, obtaining government approvals, and managing the sales force. Pan says he has learned to appreciate the value of education and knowledge. The more knowledge one has, the better and more creative decisions can be made. Yet the management system he has devised is simple and brutal: up or out. Of the eighty-five salespeople, the poorest performing ten are let go at the end of each quarter. The incentive to perform well is promotion and more money. Salespeople can earn $40,000 after taxes. Their direct bosses, the four sales directors, earn $120,000.

They, too, are subject to Pan's rigorous weeding-out process. Each quarter, the sales director heading the worst-performing sales team is demoted to salesman. The top salesman among all the salesmen takes over the leadership of the lagging team.

Outside contractors aren't cut any slack, either. Pan always has at least two contractors working on projects and competing against each other. The loser doesn't get another contract. Even the office staff falls under Pan's merciless system. Pay includes bonuses that are determined by ratings. Employees rated A get big bonuses, while B-rated employees get much less. Anyone rated C gets the boot. "You have to set up a system in which people accept responsibility," Pan says.

Zhang and Pan were smart enough to realize early on that they couldn't blend their individual styles, so they split their responsibilities. Still, they remain one of China's most admired couples, the style mavens of China. Zhang spends lavishly on clothing, appearing one day in a faux leopard-skin coat, the next in an electric blue Mao suit. Pan favors traditional black Chinese jackets accented by stylish accessories that Zhang often selects for him. And while most Chinese entrepreneurs shun the popular media, Zhang and Pan cultivate the fashion and style magazines. It isn't a coincidence that the couple is usually featured on the cover of one or another magazine each month. And all the while, the apartments and homes they develop just keep on selling.

The Perfect Pitch

Zong Qinghou was a nobody in 1987. With his junior high education, he had risen about as high as could be expected, to head of sales at a school-run business in Hangzhou, marketing Popsicles and milk products to local grocers. Then Zong one day heard about a tonic invented by a local medical professor to increase the energy level and stimulate the appetite of children. Zong saw the opportunity of his lifetime.

China's notorious "one-child" policy was just beginning to take hold in 1987. Chinese parents had seen famine more than once in their lives, and they were terrified that if the crops failed one year, their only child might succumb to starvation or to other ills that resulted from malnutrition. In China, a fat child was a healthy child. Using a $17,000 grant from the Shangcheng district government that ran the school, Zong formed a company in partnership with the government and obtained rights to the tonic, naming the product Wahaha from the sound of a happy child laughing in a children's folk song. In October 1988, the first bottles of Wahaha oral tonic appeared on grocers' shelves with a beguiling message: "If you drink Wahaha you will enjoy your food." That was a promise worried parents couldn't pass up and the medicinal-looking vials of tonic began flying out of stores as fast as they arrived. Word of the tonic's amazing effects spread quickly and soon parents all over China were prowling their local stores, demanding that the proprietors obtain Wahaha tonic for them, too. Imitators began to spring up and the government presented Zong with a national award for scientific development.

As demand rose, Zong struggled to keep pace. If Wahaha couldn't satisfy customer demand, his competitors would. In 1991, when Wahaha itself had only one hundred employees, Zong and his government partner cobbled together $10 million and purchased the bankrupt Hangzhou state-owned canned food factory with two thousand workers. Within three months the plant was profitable, its entire capacity devoted to churning out Wahaha tonic. Still, demand climbed. Requests for the seemingly magic elixir poured in from all over China. Production wasn't the only bottle neck slowing sales. The rail lines and roads that served Hangzhou weren't good enough to permit efficient shipping to all parts of China.

The Chinese government was beginning construction of the massive Three Gorges Dam at the time. The dam would flood a corridor several hundred miles long through Hubei and Sichuan provinces, inundating cities and villages and forcing the relocation of more than one million people. But it would be years before the dam was complete. In the meantime, state-owned businesses in the flood zone were withering, their local government owners lacking the expertise to compete in the growing market economy. Zong traveled to the area to investigate a possible expansion. He found three bankrupt factories in the riverside town of Fuling where he could begin production almost immediately. There was ample labor available and Zong could tap government funds intended to help those who would be displaced by the Three Gorges Dam, although he promised to repay the money within three years. Suddenly Zong was being proclaimed by government newspapers as a model national entrepreneur. It wasn't long before other cities with bankrupt factories were offering to finance new production facilities for Zong.

Demand for Wahaha and its many imitators slowed when news reports revealed that young girls who had been dosed with stimulative tonics were reaching puberty early. Many of the products on the market were found to contain hormones. Wahaha was accused of putting hormones in its tonic, but was exonerated in a local court in 1996.

All the while Zong was establishing subsidiaries in more than a dozen cities, taking over the workforces and factories of failing state-owned companies. He also began offering other products under the Wahaha label, including sports drinks, teas, and fruit juices, which the Chinese prefer over the sweet soft drinks so popular in the West. Zong consciously avoided the larger cities where Taiwanese companies, Coca-Cola, and Pepsi dominated the market for such beverages. Instead, he would surround the cities, offering his products in locales that the big guys didn't seem to care about. But Zong knew that he needed foreign expertise and capital to get big enough to compete with the global players.

He found a company that needed him as much as he needed it: Groupe Danone of France. Small joint ventures in biscuits and yoghurt in Shanghai, and a disastrous investment in two beer factories, had taught the French they couldn't do more than touch the edges of China's consumer market without strong local partners. In 1996, Danone offered to buy a controlling stake in Wahaha for $45 million. Zong could certainly use that kind of capital, but he didn't like the idea of turning control over to Danone. He knew what had happened to Haomen beer after Danone purchased it. Since demand for Haomen beer was strong, the new French bosses jacked up prices. Consumers immediately fled to cheaper brands, which, along with shenanigans by Danone's local partner, destroyed Haomen. Danone was insistent about having 51 percent. Zong finally negotiated a deal with Danone in which he created five subsidiaries in which Danone could have a 51 percent share, but he denied the French any stake in the mother company.

With Danone's payment in hand, Zong decided to add seven production lines to the two he already had. Danone told him to add only two more. He ignored the warning and the seven lines were soon operating at capacity. After that, he banned Danone employees from the Hangzhou office. The closest Danone executive is an accountant in Shanghai who is periodically allowed to examine the books in Hangzhou, one hundred eighty kilometers away.

Wahaha continued to diversify. In 1998, the company launched Feichang cola, which translates as "Extreme cola," but is called in English "Future cola," in a red-and-white can very similar to Coke. The beverage is a direct competitor to Coca-Cola and Pepsi Cola, but Zong continues to believe that by the time those companies begin trying to penetrate China's rural areas, Wahaha will be too deeply entrenched for the westerners to make much progress. In 2002, he launched Wahaha children's clothing stores. A studio in Paris designed the fashionable but inexpensive clothes.

Today Wahaha has seventy subsidiaries, twenty-nine of which are joint ventures with Danone. As a result, the Danone joint ventures account for about 30 percent of Wahaha's overall operations in China. Wahaha's ownership is much clearer than most state-owned companies in China. Zong and his employees hold 55 percent and the Hangzhou government holds 45 percent of the mother company. Wahaha and its subsidiaries now have more than ten thousand employees, 825 with college degrees, fifty-three with master's degrees, and eight with doctorates. Unlike most entrepreneurs in China who depend on family and people from their own hometowns, Zong recruits from the best universities throughout China, surrounding himself with aggressive young executives.

Zong is a brilliant hands-on entrepreneur, utterly familiar with every facet of his operations and constantly searching for ways to cut costs. When plastic beverage bottle prices began to climb, he set up his own bottle factory to save money. He also has his own shipping box factory. He gets a production report from each factory every day, faxed to him at his office or the hotels he favors during his extensive travels. When he travels to industry conferences and exhibitions overseas, a dozen of his engineers accompany him, but he's the one climbing under the equipment to poke its innards. They return home lugging suitcases full of beverages collected from local supermarkets to taste and study.

Zong is a tough manager. It doesn't take much to get fired or demoted at Wahaha. When some defective product was shipped from a Wahaha factory, the company's director of quality control suddenly found himself working as the factory's quality control manager. New employees are sent to a nearby PLA base for a dose of basic military training in marching, running, and shooting guns to instill discipline.

Pay can be very good, but a large proportion is in the form of bonuses that are based on company performance. On average, plant directors make about $35,000 a year. Corporate executives are paid between $60,000 and $120,000. Office workers are paid an average of about $6,000. Every year, the best performing three thousand employees get company-paid one-week vacations.

Wahaha's distribution network caters to the Chinese predilections to be an entrepreneur, to engage in graft, and to refuse to pay bills without a battle. To overcome the corruption and payment problems, Zong requires each distributor to give him a cash deposit equal to several months of expected business volume. He pays interest on that deposit at a rate slightly higher than bank rates. The resulting national distribution network is rivaled only by the one built by Procter & Gamble over fifteen years. Wahaha's network includes thirty-five Wahaha sales offices, twenty-five hundred sales team employees, some fifteen thousand wholesalers and distributors, and several million retailers. The sales teams are responsible for maintaining constant contact with retailers lest the wholesalers miss a market shift or try to feed Wahaha bad information.

In addition to his management talents, Zong has perfect pitch, both in sales and politics. He has very strong instincts for what Chinese consumers want, honed by many hours of wandering through markets, talking to people and watching what they buy. He also knows how to do well by doing good for the government. The company's expansive display room is a virtual shrine to the party, filled with photos of Zong with senior Chinese leaders, most of whom have visited Wahaha headquarters. A poster shows that 80 percent of the company's management are Communist party members, and each subsidiary has its own party cell. A photo from the party's eighty-first anniversary shows Zong and several dozen other Wahaha managers standing in formation with their fists raised in tribute in front of a Chinese flag. In each plant, large bulletin boards at the entrance display the latest party slogans along with individual portraits of the plant's top managers that note the date on which they joined the party. Such close ties pay big dividends. In the mid-1990s, three young girls died in Anhui province after drinking a Wahaha tonic that apparently had been poisoned. Zong rushed to Beijing and persuaded the Communist party's Propaganda Department to ban news of the incident. When the editor of one newspaper violated the order, the party demoted him.

Zong is always attentive to the needs of government, both local and national. While his famous foray into the Three Gorges Dam area to provide jobs to the displaced is well known, he also makes many smaller gestures of civic concern, which also serve his marketing purposes. For the safety of children walking or bicycling to school, he donated fifty thousand yellow baseball caps sporting the Wahaha logo to kids in Henan. The company's motto sums it up: To Run a Company Is to Serve the People.

He also employs nationalism when it serves his purposes. When

U.S. planes bombed the Chinese embassy in Belgrade in 1999, Zong saw a marketing opportunity. He created a commercial in which a cruise missile flies over the Chinese landscape and hits a gigantic can of Future cola. When the explosion clears, the Future cola can is undamaged. An announcer says: "Future cola, the Chinese people's own cola." China's government-owned national broadcaster CCTV makes sure that Future cola and other Wahaha products are visible on the set during the annual Chinese New Year's Eve broadcast watched by nearly everyone in China.

Zong claims that he is training his executives to run the company without him, but right now Zong *is* the company. It would be hard to conceive of Wahaha without his forceful personality constantly driving it forward. "He's kind of an emperor," says one company executive. "It's simple to work here because Boss Zong makes all the decisions."

The specter of Boss Zong's ultimate demise keeps Danone executives awake at night. While partnering with Wahaha has helped the French company make deep inroads into the China market, Wahaha will have to undergo a significant culture and management transformation to survive beyond the founder.

At age fifty-eight, Zong says that he still has many years of building the company ahead of him. Sitting with me in the executive lounge of the China World Hotel in Beijing discussing his business, Zong looks unworried but weary. He is in Beijing to visit nearby factories and receive a patriotism award from the People's Liberation Army. His hair is swirled around in a creative comb-over popular among middle-aged men in China. He is energetic and quick to laugh, but dark bags under his eyes belie the grinding pace he keeps. Three retainers in their early twenties sit nearby, their luggage piled beside them as they wait for the discussion to end so that Zong can catch a late-night flight to visit more Wahaha factories. Wearing a wrinkled Hugo Boss shirt and chain-smoking Davidoff cigarettes in the nonsmoking lounge, Zong reflects on the management lessons he has learned in the two decades of building his business.

His management philosophy is simple. "Care for your employees with strictness and love," he says. "Use the carrot and the stick. Allow them to constantly improve their living standards. Show them they have a career path. But if somebody makes a mistake, give them a good hard punishment."

He helps the government, but doesn't become directly involved in politics. "As an entrepreneur in China, you need to understand politics, but you cannot participate in politics," Zong says. "If you don't understand politics in China, then you can't do well in business. If the government doesn't support you, you can hardly move one step. Your company has to help solve the country's problems."

He adds that with China's fast-growth economy and the Chinese consumer's seemingly insatiable appetite for new products, the boss of the company must keep his or her finger directly on the pulse of the market. He admits that obesity among children has become a big problem as the result of more sedentary lifestyles, fast food, and the sugary drinks that Wahaha and its competitors sell. But he has a solution for that, too. The next product he plans to introduce is a weight-loss tonic.

What This Means for You

While foreign companies in China won't be able to—and don't want to—completely replicate the business and management models of successful Chinese companies, there are many lessons to be gleaned from them.

In a relatively short time in its history, China has gone from a country ruled by bookworms to one ruled by bumpkins and then by engineers. The bookworms are coming back, but this time they are focused on innovative business management techniques and building a new future for China, not rote lessons in Confucian philosophy. And they aren't only in the universities. The next generation of Chinese leaders—those now serving as provincial government and party leaders—are highly educated. More than two-thirds of these people have advanced degrees, and more than two dozen of them have PhDs. Right now there are twenty provincial leaders who have been educated in the West.

China has been rebuilding itself with profits from low-cost manufacturing labor, and building large domestic companies through easy access to government money, protected markets, and government procurement. Those companies will now have to become internationally competitive and that will require modern and effective Chinese management systems.

It won't be easy. All the education in the world can't overcome thousands of years of ingrained behavior. When I was doing venture capital in China, I was constantly amazed at the educational achievements and raw ambition of the Chinese entrepreneurs I worked with, but what surprised me most was what I came to call the Mao Zedong management model. The entrepreneurs whose companies I came to know all had advanced U.S. degrees, most of them MBAs, and some had many years of working at IBM, HP, and other multinationals. Once they became the boss of their own company in China, however, many of them reverted to replicating the system in which they grew up. They became dictators—outwardly all-knowing, but insecure inside—who hired yes-men and relatives. As their ever-expanding egos grew, they often pursued businesses based on whim rather than planning and market research.

For foreign companies building an effective Chinese executive corps, the single most effective technique is well-planned mentoring. China's fast-growth atmosphere, and the competition for talent, has resulted in many Chinese rising to top management positions very quickly. While outwardly confident, many are terrified by their responsibilities. They can be helped through serious mentoring programs involving real projects in which they learn how to make decisions by doing research, talking to experts, and gathering different opinions rather than relying on their gut. Such training must be continuous. Foreign companies have found that without periodic reinforcement, Chinese managers will revert to their old habits.

The best laboratory in which to study a blended Chinese and

Western management model was formed in December 2004 when IBM agreed to merge its personal computer business into Lenovo, China's leading PC maker. The combined company has ten thousand people from IBM and nine thousand from Lenovo. It is managed by former IBM executives from New York. IBM owns just 19 percent of the new global Lenovo. Chinese government entities have a 46 percent stake and the rest is owned by Lenovo and its shareholders.

To succeed, IBM and Lenovo will have to combine two very different business cultures and ways of thinking—Big Blue meets Big Red—and compete in a business with slim margins and fierce competition, while patching together complicated supply chains and sales networks. Lenovo will retain the IBM brand for five years, the treasured ThinkPad brand forever. When IBM and Lenovo were negotiating, the Chinese government nodded its approval but didn't participate in the talks, a significant break from the past. The Chinese government sees the merger as China's boldest commercial step yet. IBM sees the deal as its ticket into China as a domestic player.

Lenovo is about the best state company the country has to embark on such an experiment. It was founded in 1984 by Liu Chuanzhi, a military radar specialist, and ten other scientists at the Chinese Academy of Science. Liu is a natural leader, but he had no business experience. The company took off when it joined forces with a Hong Kong entrepreneur who helped the scientists establish a sales and distribution network for imported PCs in China. Within six years, the company, then known as Legend, was making its own brand PCs. Liu listed the company in Hong Kong in 1994, and offered generous share options to lure top university graduates and aggressive young Chinese executives from multinationals. He mentored the best of them and gave them increasing responsibility. He also brought in McKinsey consultants who almost lived in the company for several years, building Western-style management and logistics systems and recommending that Lenovo follow IBM and diversify into software services.

Still, the company is far from world class. It is beset by the same debilitating politics of all Chinese companies. Its strong suit is distribution, not research and development. Most of Lenovo's technology is licensed from others. The company failed in earlier efforts to expand into overseas markets and into services. At home, it was losing market share to Dell, which in recent years has built huge manufacturing operations in China. Lenovo's stock price had dropped 34 percent in the year before the deal. IBM's PC operations were in similarly dire straits. In the three and one-half years before forging the Lenovo merger, the IBM PC division suffered losses of about $1 billion.

IBM CEO Sam Palmisano said the goal was to build a truly international Chinese corporation. IBM has always been smart in China. The company wired the country with IBM mainframes before the Chinese even knew how to use them. The financial markets and much other key infrastructure were built on the back of IBM technology. When the merger was announced, IBM had 4,200 employees in China, nearly a thousand of them software engineers and some 150 scientists doing research tied into IBM's global operations.

So far both companies have done a few things right. As part of the deal, the sixty-year-old Liu retired, an almost unprecedented move by a Chinese company founder. The key to success will be the relationship between the CEO of the combined company, IBM executive Stephen M. Ward Jr., and Yang Yuanqing, a China-educated computer engineer and protégé of Liu who is chairman of the combined company. Yang summed up the deal in simple terms: "I need them and they need me."

Through the merger, IBM and Lenovo aligned the company with the Chinese government's goals and strategies. "We don't have any special deal with the Chinese government or any other government really," Palmisano explained after the deal was signed. "It's a much more subtle, more sophisticated approach. It is that if you become ingrained in their agenda and become truly local and help them advance, then your opportunities are enlarged."

These two organizations seem as compatible in their own corporate ways as Jack Wadsworth and Wang Qishan were a decade ago when they put together the joint-venture CICC investment bank for Morgan Stanley and China Construction Bank. While Lenovo didn't get a monopoly like CICC did, Lenovo has significant Chinese government support because its success will be a matter of national prestige and a further step in China's integration into and conquest of global commerce. Just as Jack Wadsworth was the quintessential American executive, and Wang Qishan the prototype of success in China for his generation, Lenovo is still very much a Chinese company, and there is nothing more American in the corporate world than IBM. The cultural integration of these companies will be an adventure—and the main key to success or failure.

Let's hope they learn from the lessons of those who came before them.

The Little Red Book of Business

- What are the four most important—and troubling—words in a Chinese company? "Up to you, boss!"

- Chinese entrepreneurs tend to diversify into anything and everything rather than paying attention to the core business. The consequences are often fatal.

- Education is China's greatest strength and greatest weakness. The Chinese are great memorizers, mathematicians, and scientists who run tedious routines. But the rote education system leaves many weak on powers of analysis and leadership.

- Layer your management. Your top managers will surround themselves with their own kind, be they Hong Kong Chinese, Taiwanese, Shanghainese, or Beijingers. For your corporate culture to dominate, instead of the ethnic culture or Chinese pecking order rivalries, place foreigners and Chinese from various places at all levels in the management structure.

- Management is situation, requiring flexibility and creative decisions. But Chinese managers are looking for techniques and formulas to follow.

- Deep scars from the Cultural Revolution and the upheaval of a sudden shift to getting rich has created an atmosphere in which nobody trusts anybody. In China business, the expectation is to be cheated.

- Long-term mentoring is the single most effective technique for foreign companies to build an effective Chinese executive corps. Mentoring should involve real projects where people make decisions and can learn how to make them in the future.

- An entrepreneur in China must understand politics but cannot directly participate in politics. Your company also has to help solve the country's problems.

- The Chinese have two identities: the individual and the organization person, which results in people acting one way but thinking another.

- The Chinese don't separate the personal and professional, so power struggles and politics often dominate Chinese corporate behavior.

- The traditional path to status and wealth has been through passing an exhausting litany of tests. This tradition has created a nation of people always cramming for final exams, not just in school, but also in their careers.

- The Chinese appear to the West to be a collective society. They eat together, travel together, and have fun together. But always simmering just below that collective veneer is a dog-eat-dog competitive spirit that makes the Chinese among the world's most individualistic and selfish people.

- Chinese respond well to charismatic and visionary leaders who will take care of them and who can tell them what to do to be successful.

- China's greatest management challenges are to create organizations that are not dictatorships, to treat others as equals, to accept responsibility for mistakes, and to share information, all behaviors that have been almost absent.

- China's rush to get rich is accompanied by deep distrust of the system, and anyone outside one's immediate family or circle of close friends. This has created a business environment that is steeped in dishonesty and in dire need of transparency and fair dispute resolution systems.

- If you ever get depressed by Chinese ill-treatment of foreigners, or foreigners' ill-treatment of Chinese, take solace in the knowledge that the Chinese are treating one another even worse.

Acknowledgments

THIS BOOK WAS A FAMILY ENDEAVOR. My wife, Cathy, daughter, Sally, and son, Grady, uprooted and moved across the world while offering me constant encouragement and selfless support during this book's long journey from conception to completion. They have my love and deep gratitude.

While I take responsibility for every word printed herein, this book contains wisdom and knowledge gleaned from so many people that to acknowledge everyone would create a volume larger than the book. The same goes for the people to whom I am indebted for generous assistance and support. Leading both of those lists are my editors, Fred Hills of Simon & Schuster, and Doug Sease, formerly of *The Wall Street Journal*. Fred and Doug are the best in the business, and they have been astute, patient, and inspired guides for a sometimes frustrated and often frustrating author. My agent, Amanda Urban, who took a chance on a first-time author and has since patiently taught me the book business, has no peer in the publishing world. Peter Kann and Karen Elliott House of Dow Jones made this book possible by providing me with abundant opportunities in China journalism and business over the years, and now through Wall Street Journal Books as copublisher. I will always be thankful to Miles Young, Matthew Anderson, T. B. Song, and Scott Kronick of Ogilvy who engaged me as Ogilvy's China adviser and thereby helped keep food on my table throughout the research and writing. I also owe great thanks to my dedicated and diligent China research assistant, Anne Xu, who made invaluable contributions every day.

This book was a two-year project during which I interviewed more than three hundred people—Chinese, Americans, Europeans, Japanese, and other nationalities; people from every occupation:

academics, schoolteachers, businesspeople, politicians, government officials, police and military officials, attorneys, judges, accountants, engineers, sociologists, psychiatrists, demographers, historians, journalists, a criminal or two, and more than a few Chinese peasants and laborers. My goal has been to write a book that teaches newcomers about doing business in China while also articulating and affirming the essential truths and core business behaviors that seasoned China businesspeople know by instinct but often can't put into words.

There is no substitute for time and experience in understanding China and doing business in the country. So in my nearly two decades as a journalist and business entrepreneur in Greater China, I have collected China knowledge from others like an archeologist collects pottery shards to perhaps one day assemble into a masterpiece. Bits and pieces of knowledge from the several hundred China books I have read and collected. Layer upon layer of business anecdotes and lessons related by people I have encountered. Thousands upon thousands of slivers of information and experience. All of these I have now endeavored to assemble into a structure worthy of those I have learned from.

China, all of Asia really, is a place where people constantly cycle in and out. Over the years, I have become friends with and learned from many thousands of people. What follows is a partial list of those people, the work colleagues, business partners, business competitors, friends, bosses, employees, news sources, and China experts who have taught me about China and helped further my China journalism and business career. These are the people who also helped make this book possible, and I thank you all from the bottom of my heart.

Steve Adler, Christopher Alberti, Barbara Alighiero Animali, Craig Allen, John Aloise, Jacob Alpren, An Lin, Andrew Andreasen, Ron Anton, Husayn Anwar, James Areddy, Leo Austin, Greg Bach, Mark Baldwin, Howard Balloch, Alisa Barba, Denny Barnes, Charlene Barshefsky, Peter Batey, Richard Baum, Clark Baurer, Mark

Bayuk, Jasper Becker, Brian Bedard, Christopher Beede, Ernst Behrens, Bei Yunli, Dirk Bennett, Paula Bennett, Katie Benson, Michael Bergmeijer, Jan Berris, Chris Billing, Daniel Blanchard, Julia Chang Bloch, Kenny Bloom, Thomas Lee Boam, Hyam Bolande, Pieter Bottelier, Norman Bottorff, William Bowles, Ray Bracy, Kevan Bradshaw, Sabina Brady, Laurence Brahm, Marcus Brauchli, William Brekke, Willie Brent, Faith Brewitt, Rodney Briggs, Myron Brilliant, Dan Brody, David Brooks, Patrick Brown, Tobias Brown, Andrew Browne, Michael Browning, John Bruns, Neil Budde, Sandy Burton, John Bussey, Michael Byrnes, Cai Jinqing, Cai Jinyong, Tim and Nancy Callahan, David Cantalupo, Cao Haili, Philip Carmichael, Steven Carroll, Robert Cassidy, Payson Cha, Gerald Chan, Ronnie Chan, Nayan Chanda, Gareth Chang, George Chang, Humphrey Chang, Iris Chang, Leslie Chang, Phyliss Chang, Howard Chao, John Cheh, Caroline Chen, Dawn Chen, Jackson Chen, James Chen, Jay Chen, John Shouzong Chen, Johnny Chen, Chen Kaiyan, Kathy Chen, Chen Li, Shelby Chen, Chen Xiaoyue, Chen Xuzheng, Chen Zhili, Chen Zhiya, Meiwei Cheng, Cheng Wenhao, Cheng Zhongxiao, Josh Cherin, Tai Ming Cheung, Antonio Chiang, Mary Chiang, Frank Ching, Mike Chinoy, Helen Chiu, Steve Chiu, Frederic Cho, Richard Chong, Johnny Chou, Henry Chow, Jon Christianson, Wah Chu, Reginald Chua, Shenan Chuang, Doug Clark, Duncan Clark, Neil Clegg, Mark Clifford, Tim Clissold, Jerry Cohen, Don Cohn, Matt Comyns, Paul and Stacey Condrell, Byron Constable, Rob and Maggie Cox, Patrick Cranley, Peter Crowhurst, Cui Shuwen, Charley and Robin Cummings, Dai Yunlou, Jamie Davis, Smitty Davis, Wilbur Davis, Jason Dean, Ted Dean, Rob Delaney, Robert Delfs, Chris DeMarino, Fritz Demopolous, Kenneth DeWoskin, Clinton Dines, Ding Xinghao, Dermot Doherty, Dou Changlu, Bruce Dover, Walt Doyle, Jane and Steve Drake, Nick Driver, Myles and Chris Druckman, Du Feng, Suman Dubey, Paul and Becky Dulac, Serge Dumont, Matt Durnin, Roger Dutton, Gal Dymant, Graham Earnshaw, Dorinda Elliot, Matthew Estes, Seth Faison, Fan Gang, Fang Fenglei, Fang Xinghai, Maggie Farley, Feng Bo,

Feng Tao, Elaine Feng, Joseph Fewsmith, Robert Flint, Jaime Florcruz, John Foarde, Don Forest, Matthew Forney, Mario Francescotti, James Friedlich, John Frisbie, Fu Jun, John Fugh, Stu Fulton, David Fung, Michael Furst, Allan Gabor, Gao Aiguo, Sheldon Gao, Gao Xiqing, Gao Xiuqin, Gao Yunfei, Diana Garrett, Geng Weimin, Jeanne-Marie Gescher, Frank Gibney, Bates Gill, Jim Glowacki, Thomas Gold, Stephen Goldmann, Carl Goldstein, Gong Jun, Gong Xueping, Thomas Gorman, James Gradoville, Peter Grady, John Gruetzner, Gu Yaoming, Guan Dongsheng, Guo Feizhou, Guo Qiyuan, Sam Guo, Guo Wenjun, Tom Gurnee, Gordon Gustavsson, David Hager, Jonathan Hakim, Paul Hallett, Scott Hallford, Stephanie Hallford, Han Xiaoxi, Jonathan Hannam, Peter Hannam, Harry Harding, James Harding, James Harkness, Su Cheng Harris-Simpson, John Hart, Steve Harvey, Eric Harwit, Myrick Hatch, Frank Hawke, Bill Hawkes, Mark Hayden, He Wei, He Weiwen, He Yafei, Harmut Heine, Dave Hess, Peter Hessler, Earl Hicks, Murray Hiebert, Andrew Higgins, Masaharu Hishida, Bob Hitt, Kevin Hobgood-Brown, David Hoffman, John Hoffmann, David John Hofmann, Arthur Holcombe, John Holden, David Holley, Frederick Hong, Hong Huang, Rupert Hoogewerf, Patrick Horgan, Lucy Hornby, Jamie Horsley, Fraser Howie, Nicholas Howson, Clark Hoyt, Kenneth Hsu, Hu Hong, Jay Hu, Hu Shuli, Hu Yanfei, Min-Hwa Hu Kupfer, Annie Huang, Huang Bing, Charles and Angela Huang, Huang Chenglian, George Huang, John S. Huang, Martha Huang, Huang Qifan, Yukon Huang, Huangfu Yingjie, Peter Humphrey, Mike and Jean Hupka, Graham Hutchings, Charles Hutzler, Adi Ignatius, David Jacobson, Jim Jarrett, Peter Jen, Jia Shumei, Jiao Yang, Jin Binghua, Jin Ligang, Jing Shuping, Candace Johnson, Ian Johnson, Tom Jones, Joseph Kahn, John Kamm, Ginny Kamsky, Charley Kan, Bob Kapp, Joan Kaufman, David Ben Kay, Lincoln Kaye, William Kazer, Ivor Kelly, Willem van Kemenade, Donald Keyser, Bob King, Tom Kirkwood, Henry Kissinger, Miguel Ko, Arthur Kobler, Kathy Koenen, Helena Kolenda, Victor Koo, Charles Krabek, Barry Kramer, Jurgen Kremb, Bill Kreuger, Nick Kristof, Arthur Kroeber, William

Krueger, Nina Kubik-Cheng, Anthony Kuhn, Greg Kulander, Elaine Kurtenbach, John Kuzmik, Phelim Kyne, James Kynge, Elaine La Roche, Willy Wo-Lap Lam, David Lampton, Ian Lancaster, Thomas Lane, Frank Langfitt, John Langlois, Michael Laris, Leon Larkin, Michael Laske, Richard Latham, Susan Lawrence, Handel Lee, Karby Leggett, Padraig Lehane, Urban Lehner, Deborah Lehr, Lei Li, Lee Lescaze, Bowen Leung, Julia Leung, Natalie Leung, Burton Levin, Eric Levin, Henry Levine, James Lewis, Robert Lewis, Charlotte Li, Cheng Li, Li Chunjia, Li Daoyu, David K. P. Li, Eric Li, Li Guoqing, Li Hong, Li Liangying, Li Peiying, Li Qingyuan, Li Xiaolin, Li Xiguang, Li Yifei, Li Yuanyuan, Liang Congjie, Kenneth Lieberthal, James Lilley, Benjamin Kang Lim, Edwin Lim, Michael Lim, Chris Lin, Jennifer Lin, Justin Lin, Martin Lin, Shirley Lin, Larry Lipsher, Roberta Lipson, Liu Changle, Charley Liu, Liu He, Liu Hong, Shaun Liu, Liu Shuang, Liu Shujie, Tommy Liu, Tony Liu, Liu Zhaochen, David Livdahl, Yolanda Lo, Wes Lohec, Luisa Lombardi, Long Yongtu, Diane Long, Peter Lovelock, Lu Feng, Lu Shumin, Sara Lubman, Stanley Lubman, Tara Lucas, Robert Ludan, Danny Lui, Christina Lund, Kristie LuStout, Nandani Lynton, Jack Ma, Ma Lei, Mary Ma, Ma Yong, Andrew Mac-Arthur, Kevin MacDonald, Consuelo Mack, Davin MacKenzie, Rebecca MacKinnon, Meg Maggio, Mary Kay Magistad, David Mahon, James Mahoney, Grace Mak, Justin Mallen, Jan Malm, Ainsley Mann, Jim Mann, Mao Bo, Daniel Mao, Geoffrey Mao, Richard Margolis, Douglas Markel, Allan Marsen, Charlie Martin, Frank Martin, Joseph Massey, David Matas, Conor McCabe, William McCahill, Iain McDaniel, Michael McDermott, Hormuz Mehta, William Melton, Sheila Melvin, Fraser Mendel, David Michael, Matei Mihalca, James Miles, Dan Mintz, Paul Mitchell, Paul Mooney, James Moriarty, Lauren Moriarty, Jim Morrison, Rex Moser, Wangli Moser, Matthew Mouw, Kin Moy, Steve Mufson, Karen Mullis, James Mulvenon, Christopher Mumford, Jim Munson, Christian Murck, David Murphy, David J. Murphy, Tim Murray, Andrew Nathan, Eric Ng, Dede Nickerson, Jesse Ning, Henk Nordholt, James Oberstar, Bill O'Brien, Joe O'Neill, Mike

Oksenberg, Dele Olojede, Joseph O'Mara, Mark O'Neill, Gordon Orr, Ricky Ow, Cynthia Owens, Robert Oxnam, Douglas Paal, Armand Pacher, Derek Palushuk, Philip Pan, Pan Shiyi, Richard Pascoe, Robin Pascoe, Norm Pearlstein, Peng Yan, Tony Perkins, Jack Perkowski, Blair Pickerell, Thomas Pixley, Ted Plafker, Nicholas Platt, Don Polishuk, John Pomfret, Donald Pongrace, Matt Pottinger, Pat Powers, Mitchell Presnick, John Prestbo, Michael Primont, Russell Probert, Lucian Pye, Qian Liying, Sam Qian, Helen Qin, Qiu Huakun, Qiu Lixia, Qiu Xiaoyi, Andrew Quinn, Joseph and Cathy Ragg, Paul Rasch, Ekkehard Rathgeber, Alan Reid, William Reinsch, Ren Qian, Ren Xinrong, Hugo Restall, Jon Reynolds, David Richter, Michael Ricks, Dagmar Riehle, Sidney Rittenberg, Adam Robarts, Dexter Roberts, Matt Roberts, Bruce Robertson, Barbara Robinson, Michael Robinson, Jim Rohwer, Chito Romana, David Rosenberg, Elisabeth Rosenthal, Claudia Rosette, Lester Ross, Robert Ross, J. Stapleton Roy, Rui Chenggang, Ann Rutledge, Michael Sacharski, Ahmed Sahib, Anthony Saich, Catherine Sampson, Lee Sands, Caroline Sapriel, James Sasser, Chuck and Ouida Savage, AnnaLee Saxenian, Orville Schell, Peter Scheuer, Stephen Schlaikjer, Rudy Schlais, David Schlesinger, Sabine Schmitt, Stuart Schonberger, David Schweisberg, Scott Seligman, Henny Sender, David Shambaugh, Shan Weijian, Shao Lei, Don Shapiro, Peter Shay, She Duanzhi, Greg Shea, Hank Sheller, Shen Dingli, Eugenie Shen, Shen Guofang, Sheng Chongqing, Chauncey Shey, Shi Jian, Shi Lei, Steven Shi, Shim Jae Hoon, Hugo Shong, John and Susan Shuck, Frank Siegel, Patrick Siewert, Elyse Silverberg, Denis Fred Simon, Brad Simpson, Whitney Small, Craig Smith, Laurie Smith, Rick Smith, Song Jianyang, Song Xingshuang, Dan Southerland, David Spindler, Don St. Pierre, Peter Stein, Tim Steinert, Anne Stevenson-Yang, Tom Stilmock, Robert Stone, Ian Stones, Nadia Stoyle, Caroline Straathof, Tim Stratford, Joe Studwell, Su Jie, Wei-chou Su, Robert Suettinger, John Sullivan, Chang Sun, Lena Sun, Sun Lina, Nora Sun, Sun Peng, Sun Qi, Sun Zemin, Sun Zhenyu, Karen Sutter, Michael Swaine, Christopher Szymanski, Kelly Tai, Reginald Tai, Winnie Tam, Johnson Tan, Tan

Lu, Tang Chaoying, Tang Maoying, Rone Tempest, Dian Terry, Carsten and Kirsten Thøgersen, Len Thomas, Marty Thomas, Edward Tian, Loretta Tofani, Jeff Tonkel, Tong Qiting, Steven Toronto, Thomas Trueb, Micah Truman, K. S. Tsang, Alan Tsoi, Daniel Tu, Alan Turley, Mary Lee Turner, Mia Turner, Patrick Tyler, Roger Uren, Vesna Vick, Ezra Vogel, Richard Vuylsteke, Jack Wadsworth, Barry Wain, Gregory Wajnowski, Tony Walker, Carl Walter, Angela Wang, Wang Boming, Wang Chaoyong, Wang Chunlei, David Wang, Wang Deming, Wang Hong, Jesse Wang, Wang Jisi, Wang Likuang, Luna Wang, Patrick Wang, Wang Ran, Rick Wang, Wang Ruoxiao, Wang Shuang, Wang Shuo, Wang Wenlian, Wang Xiaojing, Wang Xiufen, Wang Xuegong, Wang Yan, Wang Yixun, Wang Yongsun, Wang Zhidong, Ray Warhola, William Warwick, Jeremie Waterman, John Watkins, Craig Watts, Lisa Weaver, George Wehrfritz, Wei Chun, Andrew Whitaker, Kathy Wilhelm, Max Wilhelm, Endymion Wilkinson, Ted Willard, Adam Williams, Emory Williams, Ken Witty, David Wolf, Ira Wolf, Peter Wonacott, Jan Wong, Walter Wong, Kim Woodard, Charles Wu, Wu Hongtao, Wu Ying, Chris Wurzel, Joerg Wuttke, Xiong Lei, Xu Haoyan, Xu Lei, Xu Meihong, Xu Weiwei, Xu Yaping, Xu Yihe, Xu Yuping, John Yam, Yan Jin, Richard Yan, Yang Fan, Yang Huaiding, Yang Ji, John Yang, Yang Ke, Nick Yang, Yang Qi, Serena Yang, Victor Yang, Yang Yang, Yang Zhi, Mary Yao, Stephen Yao, Pam Yatsko, Don Ye, Kippy Ye, Randy Yeh, Ying Yeh, Mona Yi, Yin Jizuo, Diane Ying, Harrison Young, Shirley Young, Steve Young, Yu Fei, George Yu, Yu Jiafu, Yu Jian, Peggy Yu, Yu Ping, Yu Yuanming, Yuan Haiying, Victor Yuan, Yuan Wei, Tony Zaloom, Zhai Zhihai, Charles Zhang, Zhang Fan, Ken Zhang, Zhang Ligang, Zhang Lin, Zhang Lu, Zhang Mingming, Zhang Qu, Tracy Zhang, Zhang Xin, Zhang Xindong, Zhang Yan, Zhang Yifei, Zhao Quan, Zheng Bijian, Christine Zheng, Cindy Zheng, Zhou Hanmin, Zhou Mingwei, Zhou Qiren, Zhou Yunfan, Zhou Yupeng, Zhou Zhewei, Zhou Zhixiong, Zhu Baoxian, Zhu Jiang, Zhu Jingyu, Zhu Xiaoming, Zhu Yonglei, Zhuang Nanbin, Geoffrey Ziebart, David Zing, Zong Qinghou, and Eric and Tori Zwisler.

Index

About the Author

JAMES McGREGOR has spent nearly two decades as a journalist and business executive in Greater China. He developed a deep interest in Asia during a tour of duty in Vietnam. At age thirty-three, he quit his job as a reporter covering the U.S. Congress, sold everything he owned, and moved to Taiwan with his wife, Cathy. Within a few months, he became *The Asian Wall Street Journal*'s Taiwan bureau chief, chronicling the island's rocketing economic success and its rough-and-tumble transition to democracy. Appointed *The Wall Street Journal*'s China bureau chief following the 1989 Tiananmen Massacre, McGregor moved to Beijing and spent the next four years traveling to every corner of China. McGregor's ability to navigate the bizarre world of Chinese business won him the appointment in 1994 to build Dow Jones's business operations in China. Over seven years, he built a portfolio of businesses that employed some 150 Chinese professionals with offices in Beijing, Shanghai, Shenzhen, and Hong Kong. McGregor left Dow Jones in 2000 to become a partner and the China managing director for GIV Venture Partners, a $140 million venture capital fund specializing in technology investments in China and India. For a decade, McGregor has served as a governor of the American Chamber of Commerce in China. In 1996, he was elected chairman of that organization. McGregor is a member of the National Committee on U.S.-China Relations, a member of the International Council of the Asia Society, and he serves on a variety of China-related business and philanthropic advisory boards. McGregor is currently an investor in businesses in China as well as a China investment and business adviser for many others. He also serves as Senior China Advisor for Ogilvy Public Relations Worldwide.

McGregor can be reached at info@onebillioncustomers.com.